THE CARNIVAL CAMPAIGN

How the
ROLLICKING 1840 CAMPAIGN
of
"TIPPECANOE AND TYLER TOO"
Changed
PRESIDENTIAL ELECTIONS
Forever

RONALD G. SHAFER

CHICAGO
REVIEW
PRESS

Library of Congress Cataloging-in-Publication Data
Names: Shafer, Ronald G., author.
Title: The carnival campaign : how the rollicking 1840 campaign of
    "Tippecanoe and Tyler too" changed presidential elections forever / Ronald
    G. Shafer.
Description: Chicago, Illinois : Chicago Review Press Incorporated, 2016. |
    Includes bibliographical references and index.
Identifiers: LCCN 2016019215| ISBN 9781613735404 (hardback) | ISBN
    9781613735435 (epub edition) | ISBN 9781613735428 (kindle edition)
Subjects: LCSH: Presidents—United States—Election—1840. | Harrison,
    William Henry, 1773–1841. | United States—Politics and
    government—1837–1841.
Classification: LCC E390 .S53 2016 | DDC 324.973/58—dc23
LC record available at https://lccn.loc.gov/2016019215

Typesetting: Nord Compo

Printed in the United States of America
5 4 3 2 1

To my wife, Mary Rogers, and our children, Kathryn Shafer Rivers, Daniel Rogers, and Kaitlin Rogers. And to our granddaughters, Kaylie Ryan Rivers and Veronica Rogers Nunley.

CONTENTS

INTRODUCTION

The most remarkable political contest ever known was that of 1840.

—Author A. B. Norton, 1888

Tippecanoe and Tyler Too. Just about everybody has heard of that famous political slogan. But what does it mean?

The catchy phrase refers to the Whig Party's 1840 presidential ticket of William Henry "Old Tippecanoe" Harrison and John Tyler. It became their battle cry in their campaign against Democratic president Martin Van Buren. But the significance of that campaign goes far beyond the memorable phrase.

The 1840 campaign, many historians agree, was the mother of modern presidential contests. For the first time, a political party launched a full-on grassroots campaign, generating massive rallies across the country. The gatherings were part three-ring circus and part old-time revival meeting, complete with marching bands, floats, and political preaching. There was even a traveling Bear—not an animal, but a speech-making blacksmith by that name. Many of the parades featured the world's tallest man, standing at more than seven and a half feet. All of this was put to music with hundreds of campaign songs. Nothing like it had ever been seen before. It was the beginning of presidential campaigning as entertainment.

Harrison became the first presidential candidate to campaign for himself and give his own speeches to support his election. And surrogate speakers in unprecedented numbers took to the hustings in state after state. To the shock of many people, women began playing an active role in presidential politics. Big campaign donations emerged as an influential factor. The debate over small government versus government intervention began. The Whigs, meantime, mounted the first image advertising campaign for a presidential candidate, establishing forever a basic tactic of political campaigns. It is called lying.

The chief target of Whig ridicule was the sitting president, known as the Little Magician. But both sides engaged in plenty of mudslinging. Personal attacks were so vicious that one might have thought the candidates should be in the jailhouse instead of the White House. The rollicking run of Tippecanoe and Tyler Too changed presidential campaigns forever.

It all began in the winter of 1839 in Harrisburg, Pennsylvania.

1

A COMPROMISE CANDIDATE

*[The Whig nominee's] imbecility and incapacity
is universally acknowledged by every candid
man who is personally acquainted with him.*

—*Ohio Statesman*, an anti-Whig newspaper

Suppose they held a presidential convention and none of the candidates showed up. That was the situation on the morning of Wednesday, December 4, 1839, as delegates to the Whig Party's first-ever presidential convention crowded into the newly rebuilt, redbrick Zion Lutheran Church in Harrisburg, Pennsylvania.

None of the three men seeking the Whig nomination for the 1840 election was even in town. Not one of them planned to attend the convention to give an acceptance speech if nominated. Nor could they direct their candidacy from home, because the telegraph and the telephone hadn't been invented yet. At the time it was unthinkable for a presidential candidate to campaign openly or give speeches for himself. It had never been done. The office sought the man, not the other way around.

The great Kentucky statesman Henry Clay was the top betting choice going into the convention. The sixty-two-year-old senator was the man who had said earlier in 1839, "I had rather be right than be president." He was lying through the snuff in his nose. Senator Clay would do almost anything to become president.

Trailing behind were two military heroes. One was fifty-three-year-old General Winfield "Old Fuss and Feathers" Scott. The pompous, six-foot-four-inch Scott recently had won renewed renown by helping to settle a dispute with Canada on the Maine border.

William Henry Harrison. *Library of Congress*

The other candidate was General William Henry Harrison. He was famed as "Old Tippecanoe" after winning an 1811 battle against Native Americans near the Tippecanoe River in the Indiana Territory. The problem was that at the age of nearly sixty-seven, Harrison would be the oldest man ever to run for president. Also, he had been out of politics for most of the past twenty-five years and now lived on a remote farm in Ohio.

The choice in Harrisburg was in the hands of 254 Whig delegates, all of them white males. Most arrived by train at the state capital's brand-new rail station. One delegate, John Johnston, a military officer who had served under Harrison, rode his horse from Piqua, Ohio, a distance of more than 450 miles. In cities and rural areas alike, people traveled by horseback, stagecoach, and horse-drawn carriage, as well as by train and steamboat.

The delegates came from twenty-two of the twenty-six states, stretching as far south as Georgia and as far west as Louisiana in a growing America of seventeen million people, including about two-and-a-half million slaves. (The total was slightly less than the modern population of New York State.) Politicians and lawyers dominated the state delegations, but they represented a wildly diverse mix.

The Whig Party was formed in 1834 to counter President Andrew Jackson of the Democratic Party. "Whig" had been the name adopted by colonists who opposed King George III during the Revolutionary War. The current Whig Party united foes of "King Andrew." Its members ranged from rural farmers to urban bankers, from abolitionists to slaveholders, and from industrial titans to shopkeepers and laborers. The Whigs—sometimes called Republicans—favored some federal action, such as building roads across connecting states. The Democrats flatly opposed federal intervention. In this respect, the Democratic Party was more like modern-day Republicans, and the Whigs/Republicans were closer to modern Democrats.

As the convention convened, the weather was unseasonably warm following recent snows. The delegates and party officials noisily began taking seats in the cavernous church sanctuary as the morning sunlight streamed through stained-glass windows. A gentleman's business dress of the day was a cutaway suit coat, a vest, and tight trousers. A large scarf-like cravat was tied around the removable high collar of a white linen shirt. Men usually were clean-shaven, but with longish hair that flowed into lengthy sideburns.

The convention began promptly at noon, and delegates chose former Virginia governor James Barbour to preside. For the first time at a presidential convention, newspaper reporters were invited to take seats on the convention floor.

The Whigs were desperate to find an electable nominee to break the Democratic Party's twelve-year grip on the White House, where President Martin Van Buren now resided. It was a time of turmoil both at home and abroad. In America, slavery was an increasingly divisive issue. The independent republic of Texas was clamoring to become a state, but it faced opposition in the north because it would be a slave state. US troops were still battling Seminole Indians in the Florida territory. Under President Jackson, more than fifteen thousand Cherokees had been sent west from Georgia, the Carolinas, and Tennessee to land that would become Oklahoma. During the forced march, more than four thousand Native Americans died along the Trail of Tears.

Tensions were rising with Great Britain, where young Queen Victoria was about to wed her cousin Prince Albert of Germany. British sailors were boarding and searching American vessels in Africa. Meanwhile, Spain was demanding the return of the runaway slaves who revolted, killed the captain, and took over the Spanish schooner *Amistad* near Cuba. After the United States took the slaves into custody off the coast of New England, American abolitionists went to court to try to get the slaves freed and returned to Africa. The case was pending in the US Supreme Court, where the slaves were being represented by former president John Quincy Adams, now a seventy-two-year-old Massachusetts congressman. Much of Europe was in an economic nosedive, and the fallout had spread to the States, where the economy was down and unemployment was way up. Voters were in a mood for change, if only the Whigs could find the right nominee.

Balloting at the convention was by secret vote, with the totals tallied by a Grand Committee. Sure enough, Clay led his two rivals on the first ballot and a second one. But at 103 votes, he was still short of the 138 needed for nomination.

Behind the scenes, some Whig leaders began buttonholing delegates in smoke-filled hotel rooms, lobbies, and bars. Clay couldn't win a national election, they suggested, because he had too many political enemies. In addition, as a slaveholder himself his outspoken backing of slave states would cost him too many votes in the North. Maybe it was time to consider an alternative candidate for the good of the party.

But which one? In his meetings with delegates, forty-two-year-old Thurlow Weed, New York's Whig party boss who controlled the state's large delegation, urged other states to get behind the Empire State's choice. That was General Scott, who lived in New York City.

Weed, a newspaper publisher from Albany, was known as the Jolly Drummer because of his convivial and persuasive personality. The tall, dark-haired New Yorker's negotiating style was to filter in and out of hotel lobbies and drinking establishments cajoling delegates with what one New York reporter described as "all the energy and cunning of Satan when he tempted Eve to sin."

Meantime, meeting with delegates in his hotel room, Thaddeus Stevens, Pennsylvania's most powerful politician, lobbied for General Harrison. In contrast to the smooth-talking Weed, Stevens was a rude and crude bachelor from Gettysburg with the personality of a grouchy bear. The forty-seven-year-old lawyer walked with a limp caused by a clubfoot he had since birth. A childhood disease also led to the loss of his hair. He wore a bad chestnut-colored wig to cover his bald head.

Stevens, believing that he had been promised a cabinet post in a Harrison administration, argued to delegates that General Harrison had more political appeal than either Scott or Clay. As a military hero, Harrison was a twofer. Besides being the "Hero of Tippecanoe," he also was famous as the "Hero of the Thames." He had commanded American troops in the War of 1812 in a key victory over the British and their Native American allies at the Thames River near what would become Ontario, Canada. During the battle, the great Shawnee chief Tecumseh was killed.

What's more, even though Harrison had been one of four regional Whig presidential candidates in 1836, his political views were so obscure that he was less open to attack than Clay. Harrison had retired from the military twenty-six years earlier. After a few stints in Congress, he now lived on his farm in North Bend, Ohio, near Cincinnati, where he was the Hamilton County clerk of the court.

William Henry Harrison was a genial, religious, well-educated man with a passion for Roman history. Standing about five foot nine, he combed his graying brown hair forward over his forehead like the Roman emperor Caesar. Frankly, some party members considered him something of an intellectual lightweight. Harrison had "a lively and active, but shallow mind," according to former president Adams; he was "not without talents, but self sufficient, vain and indiscreet." The general's supporters argued that he was a smart and proven leader.

As their backers feverishly sought to sway delegates on their behalf, the three missing-in-action candidates could only sit and wait at home with no say in their fate. On Friday morning, December 6, the third ballot began. When the results were announced, Clay still led, but his total had dropped to ninety-five votes compared with ninety-one for Harrison. On a fourth ballot, the numbers were unchanged. Scott, in third place, still had enough votes to keep the convention in deadlock.

With a fifth ballot scheduled for 9:00 PM, Pennsylvania's Thad Stevens decided to act. Stevens had an ace up his sleeve—or, more precisely, in his pocket. It was a letter that General Scott had written to New York Whig congressman Francis Granger expressing sympathy for antislavery abolitionists. Stevens, who got the letter from Granger, limped over to the headquarters of the Virginia delegation.

The decidedly proslavery delegation was mulling over Scott as its backup choice to Clay. After his arrival, Stevens casually dropped the Scott letter on the floor, where alarmed Virginia delegates discovered it. They promptly turned to Harrison as their alternative. The news set off a stampede to Harrison by pro-Scott delegates, who considered abolitionists too radical.

The key now was Thurlow Weed, Scott's major supporter. Weed was a conservative but practical politician who only wanted to win. He dropped Scott like a lit stick of dynamite and moved the New York delegation behind Harrison.

The Grand Committee announced the final tally at about 10:30 PM: Harrison 148 votes, Clay 90, and Scott 16. It was done. William Henry Harrison, the oldest presidential candidate to date, was the Whigs' nominee for 1840. His was the first presidential nomination brokered behind the scenes in smoke-filled rooms.

The antislavery newspaper the *Emancipator* hailed Clay's defeat. "Praise God!" the newspaper said. "We have faith to believe that no slave-holder will ever again be permitted to fill the Presidential office in this Republic." The paper's celebration would prove to be premature.

The next morning at the convention, the Whigs, for the sake of party unity, scrambled to find a Clay supporter from the South to be the vice presidential nominee—but nobody wanted the honor. Vice president was considered a meaningless post with little chance for advancement. Finally, without consulting their presidential nominee, delegates unanimously chose former Virginia senator John Tyler as Harrison's running mate.

The forty-nine-year-old Tyler reportedly cried when Clay failed to land the presidential nomination (he later denied this, saying, in effect, that there was no crying in politics). Tall and thin-faced, Tyler was an unlikely choice, because he was a Johnny-come-lately to Whiggery after only recently bolting from the Democratic Party. He was an ardent advocate of states' rights and was a slave-holder in Williamsburg, Virginia.

The Whig ticket would face many contentious issues in the coming campaign. So to keep the slate clear for their presidential nominee, the Whigs purposely avoided adopting a party platform. There was no stirring acceptance speech by the party's presidential choice. Instead, Ohio judge Jacob Burnet, Harrison's convention campaign manager, presented the case for his friend of forty years. Burnet's stated goal was "to throw a ray of light on the almost forgotten life of one of the most useful, virtuous and patriotic citizens our country has ever produced."

John Tyler. *Library of Congress*

Mainly, Burnet seemed intent on dispelling rumblings about the aging Harrison's mental faculties. The general had a "penetrating mind—far, very far above mediocrity," the judge declared. "Let me assure you and this assembly, and the American people, that his mind is as vigorous, as active, and as discriminating as it was in the meridian of his days."

Burnet closed his remarks by urging the Whig party to close ranks behind Harrison. "Union for the sake of Union!" he declared. His speech so impressed Whig party leaders that they had it published in English, German, and Welsh for distribution to voters.

Despite Burnet's call for unity, Henry Clay was still on the minds of many of the delegates. Several paid tribute to the Kentucky senator. An aging old friend stood to deliver the most dramatic tribute: "I envy Kentucky," he said of Clay in a trembling voice, "for when he dies, she shall have his ashes."

The tribute underscored the main worry of Whig leaders: whether disappointed Clay backers would rally behind Harrison. On the convention's final day, a speaker rose to read a letter that Clay had written to be presented should he not be nominated. In the letter, Clay urged support for the nominee whomever he might be. Delegates roared their approval of the noble gesture. The convention was adjourned.

Clay was the first of the contenders to learn about the outcome. In Washington, DC, on the evening after the convention ended, he began drinking heavily at Brown's Indian Queen Hotel, where a big sign outside with a colored image of Pocahontas beckoned travelers. Clay eventually crossed Pennsylvania Avenue to his boardinghouse to await word. He was sitting in a chair in the lobby when two friends brought him the bad news from delegates who had just arrived at the train station.

In contrast to his magnanimous letter to the convention, the tall, thin Clay angrily jumped up from his chair, his dark eyes flashing. He began cursing and stomping around the room on his spindly legs. He had been betrayed, he shouted. "My friends are not worth the powder and shot it would take to kill them." He shook his fist and yelled that he was the most unfortunate man in the history of political parties, but his rant would get him nowhere.

General Scott, waiting anxiously at his home in New York City, was the next to get the word. The general was deeply disappointed to be beat out by a man whom he believed to be his inferior. But he took the news with a stoic military demeanor.

In faraway North Bend, Ohio, William Henry Harrison didn't know that he had been nominated as a candidate for president of the United States until a week later. That's when the local *Cincinnati Gazette* ran a brief article noting the nomination, but the paper had no details. Travelers along the National Road had brought word of the nomination to the state capital in Columbus. The local postmaster there scribbled the news on the outside of a paper he used to wrap letters going to Cincinnati.

Finally, an official letter from the Whig Party arrived at Harrison's farm in North Bend. The candidate responded on December 19. In his letter, he indicated surprise at the great honor (though he had privately been lobbying for the nod for months), and accepted the nomination with gratitude. He made just a single promise: if elected he would serve only one term. He also asserted that he would rarely use the presidential veto, but would instead leave most decisions to Congress as the representative of the people.

Harrison didn't bother saying anything about issues, claiming that because of his long public service everybody already knew his views—which they didn't. In a later letter, Harrison went even further. He suggested what would be a dream campaign for any presidential candidate: never having to discuss anything you had talked about before. Voters could simply look at his past record and statements. What intelligent person could ask for more?

Privately, Whigs knew that Harrison wasn't in Henry Clay's league as a statesman or an intellectual, but he was the best available candidate. Whig leaders declared that despite differences, the party had come out of the Harrisburg convention united. One Clay supporter reluctantly agreed: "We are now in the field, and Huzzah for Old Tippecanoe."

The party turned to the task of campaigning against President Martin Van Buren, who was certain to be nominated for a second term at the Democratic convention in May. But before the Harrison campaign could even get started, it ran into a crisis.

2

THE FIRST IMAGE CAMPAIGN

*Passion and prejudice, properly aroused and
directed, would do about as well as principle and
reason [in a presidential contest].*

—Whig campaign adviser Thomas Elder

One evening in early January 1840, twenty-two-year-old newspaper editor Richard Smith Elliott knocked on the massive wooden front door of a two-and-a-half-story blue limestone mansion overlooking the Susquehanna River in Harrisburg, Pennsylvania. He was greeted by seventy-three-year-old Thomas Elder, the city's leading banker and a former state attorney general.

Elder was an influential wheel in the Pennsylvania political machinery headed by his old friend Thaddeus Stevens, a machine that would help shape the Harrison campaign. New York's Thurlow Weed also was a major national strategist. In Ohio, Harrison had his own campaign committee, led by his old military comrade Colonel Charles Todd.

Elder had invited Elliott over to discuss a serious political problem that had erupted thanks to the newspapers of the day, which were openly partisan. Their editors often played major roles in political campaigns. As the editor of the pro-Whig *Harrisburg Intelligencer*, Elliott was a key cog in the Harrison campaign. He boasted that his political approach was to never defend or explain anything, but persistently to assail the other party.

The young newspaperman had been a Harrison fan since growing up in Lewistown, Pennsylvania. His father was a farmer and also editor of the local paper, the *Gazette*. While his father was planting corn one day, young Richard wrote up an editorial calling for William Henry Harrison to run for president. Elliott's dad, having served in the War of 1812, admired the general, and he published the editorial. It would be impossible to prove that his editorial in the *Gazette* led to Harrison's nomination in 1840, Elliott later joked, "but I am sure no one can prove that it did not effect [*sic*] it."

Elder led the younger Elliott down a long hallway to one of the mansion's numerous rooms, perhaps the spacious parlor or Elder's office for his banking business. The house was one of Harrisburg's most historic and prestigious homes. John Harris Jr., the son of the man for whom Harrisburg is named, built the initial house in 1766. John Harris Sr., an English trader, had obtained land grants in the frontier area of Pennsylvania and had begun a successful ferry operation.

In 1785, John Jr. developed a town on the land and named it after his late father. He also became one of the community's wealthiest men after helping start the Harrisburg Bank and a bridge company. Thomas Elder, an attorney and the bank's second president, bought the house in 1835 from one of Harris's sons.

Elder and Elliott sat down in front of one of the house's many fireplaces to warm themselves from the winter chill. Elder pulled out a bottle of excellent Madeira wine and poured two glasses. Then he got to the issue at hand.

On December 11, 1839, a writer for the *Baltimore Republican* —a Democratic newspaper, despite its name—published an article depicting Harrison as a feeble old man ready to be put out to pasture. "Give him a barrel of hard cider and settle a pension of two thousand a year on him, and take my word for it, he will sit the remainder of his days in his log cabin," the paper said.

Other Democratic papers jumped on the issue of Harrison's advanced age. Some called him Old Granny Harrison, while the Whigs were dubbed Grannycrats. The *New York Herald*, harshly referring to the old general as a woman, said, "Mrs. Harrison of Ohio is undoubtedly a very excellent matron for her time, but if we must take a woman president, let's have youth and beauty, and not age and imbecility."

The *New York Evening Post*'s Washington correspondent mocked that Harrison's poverty had awakened the sympathy of the capital's ladies, who were moved to solicit clothing for the "war-worn hero." So "if you have any old shoes, old boots, old hats, or old stockings, send them on and they will be forwarded to the 'hero of the North Bend.'"

This was not exactly the image the Whigs were planning to project. They were preparing to portray General Harrison as the George Washington of the West, a dashing military hero leading his charges into battle on a white horse. The campaign was readying a poster based on a portrait of the general as a young man. The portrait was initially painted in 1800 showing a twenty-seven-year-old Harrison in civilian clothes. In 1814, the noted artist Rembrandt Peale had painted a military uniform over the civvies, transforming Harrison into a youthful-looking general. It was this persona the campaign would seek to promote.

The soldier-for-president strategy wasn't new. It had worked for General Andrew Jackson, hero of the Battle of New Orleans. So why shouldn't it work for Harrison? Indeed, since the beginning of the Republic, said the cynical John Quincy Adams, more often than not "the direct and infallible path to the Presidency is military service coupled with demagogue policy." And in the absence of military service, he said, "demagogue policy is the first and most indispensable element of success."

Now the Whigs had to counter the image of Harrison as a pitiable old man drinking alcoholic cider in a log cabin, and they had to do it fast. As they sipped their wine, Elder and Elliott agreed that the attacks on Harrison were intolerable. They discussed how the Whig newspapers already were full of righteous indignation over the slurs against the old general.

The Whig paper in Galena, Illinois, complained that eastern officeholders' pimps sneered at Harrison as the Log Cabin Candidate. Other Whig papers wailed that it was monstrous that vile Democratic papers were so contemptuous of a general who had never lost a battle and who was the hero of Tippecanoe, a scholar, and a Christian gentleman living quietly on his farm in Ohio.

The two men noted that the angry responses went far beyond Harrison himself. The Whig papers saw the Baltimore article as an attack on America's heritage. Few people still lived in log cabins, but many of their pioneer parents and grandparents had. Log cabins were a symbol of American settlers. Whigs quoted from French writer Alexis de Tocqueville's book on his tour of America: "As soon as a pioneer arrives upon the point which is to serve him as a retreat, he fells a few trees and builds a log house." In addition, the hard cider made from fermented apples was a drink of the common man.

A log cabin was the birthplace of many of America's greatest leaders, declared a letter published in Cincinnati, Ohio. "Why ye graceless and soul-less witlings, did you not know that these log cabins have been the nurseries of the real intellectual giants of the land?" he wrote. "Go to the halls of Congress and ask the most prominent and eloquent debaters there if they know anything of log cabins, and the majority of them will tell you that they were born in one."

In an editorial in his *Albany Evening Journal*, Whig leader Thurlow Weed (who was born in a log cabin) wrote, "The log cabin is a symbol of nothing that Van Burenism knows, or feels, or can appreciate. It tells of virtues that dwell in obscurity, of the hopes of the humble, of the privations of the poor, of toil and danger, of perseverance and patient endurance, of hospitality and charity and frugality. It is the emblem of rights that the vain and insolent aristocracy of federal office-holders have lost sight of, or crushed and trampled on."

An insult to Harrison was an insult to millions of Americans across the country. Those who considered "the Log Cabin Candidate" to be a term of reproach exposed themselves as pampered officeholders "who sneer at the idea of making a poor man president," said the *New York Daily Whig*.

Major General William Henry Harrison. *Library of Congress*

The attacks gave the Whigs a giant opening to steal away traditional Democratic voters. Democrats had claimed to be the party of the working man and the poor, while painting the Whigs as the party of rich bankers and business owners. "Listen to the fawning minions of power casting sneers at the venerable hero of Tippecanoe on account of his poverty!" wrote a Whig editor in North Carolina.

The Democrats, said George Prentice, editor of the *Louisville Journal*, were making a big mistake with their smear. "Do they not know that a log cabin is all the better for being daubed with mud?"

Back in his Harrisburg mansion, Thomas Elder—"a shrewd old gentleman"—had an idea. Rather than trying to rebut the log cabin insult, why not embrace it? Build a log cabin or something, he suggested. Get voters involved at the grass roots. Take the campaign "down to the people" and stir the passions and indignation of average voters. Use Harrison to reverse the image of the Whigs as the party of the rich and the Democrats as the party of the poor.

Elder's idea played into the voter demographics of the day. More Americans than ever before would be eligible to vote in 1840. Initially, only white, male property owners could vote in elections, which resulted in a string of Eastern Establishment presidents, mainly from Virginia. In the early 1820s most states began eliminating property requirements and allowed all white males to vote if they paid taxes or had served in the militia. By 1840 the vote was open to just about all white males, adding thousands of middle- and lower-income voters to the rolls. These new voters were up for grabs.

As Elder and Elliott continued to talk, the banker came up with the idea of making the log cabin a symbol of the Harrison campaign. Elliott whipped out a pencil and a pad of paper. He roughly sketched a one-room log cabin with a chimney of sticks and mud. A raccoon skin was tacked onto the building. Outside stood a woodpile with an ax stuck in it. Next to the cabin was a barrel of hard cider.

As he left the mansion, Elliott promised to work further on the project. After returning home, he improved on his sketch, much to the amusement of his family, who knew of his lack of artistic skills. The next day he hired a local man who painted carriages to work up a final, secret version. The result was not merely a painting; it was a four-sided transparency, a glass-paneled box with images painted on the panels that were illuminated by lit candles within.

Elliott decided to unveil his proposed campaign image at a January 20, 1840, state meeting of Whigs at the county courthouse in Harrisburg to ratify the nominations of Harrison and Tyler. As soon as the confab opened, Elliott obtained approval to present his final product. A committee was appointed to arrange the presentation.

A short time later, a state senator from Philadelphia began speaking. Suddenly, the audience started to murmur. Something was going on behind the speaker. The senator looked over his shoulder to see a man walking into the room carrying over his head the glowing, four-sided transparency.

A drawing of a one-room log cabin was on one side of the transparency. The Battle of the Thames was pictured on the second side, and the American flag adorned the third. On the fourth side was the motto DEMOCRACY, REFORM AND ONE PRESIDENTIAL TERM.

Wild cheers erupted from the audience. Or as one Harrisburg newspaper put it, "the air became vocal with the huzzahs of the multitude."

Without missing a beat, the state senator quickly picked up on the theme. He began praising Harrison as a plain and unpretentious man who represented the common citizen. He and other speakers went on for three hours, describing Old Tippecanoe as the candidate of the poor man. By the time they finished, the crowd was in a frenzy.

Whig papers quickly spread the news about the log cabin transparency. Within weeks, the theme raced across the county. Cries rose for the Log Cabin and Hard Cider Candidate. Poor farmers praised the Farmer of North Bend as one of their own. Pro-Harrison songs popped up everywhere:

> They say that he lived in a cabin
> and lived on old hard cider, too;
> Well, what if he did? I'm certain
> He's the hero of Tippecanoe
> He's the hero of Tippecanoe!

Some songwriters envisioned the log cabin theme carrying Harrison all the way to the presidency:

> By whom, tell me whom, will the battle next be won?
> By whom, tell me whom, will the battle next be won?
> The spoilsmen and leg treasurers will soon begin to run!
> And the Log Cabin Candidate will march to Washington.

1840 log cabin woodcut. *Library of Congress*

Indeed, the *Jeffersonian Republican* newspaper in Stroudsburg, Pennsylvania, looked forward to the next presidential inauguration day: "The people are of the opinion that General Harrison has lived in a log cabin long enough, and they intend on the 4th of March 1841 to give him free rent of the great white house in Washington city."

Over a bottle of expensive Madeira, a wealthy banker and a young newspaper editor had succeeded in conceiving the first presidential campaign that would be based on an image: William Henry Harrison as the poor man's champion, a great military hero now living as a simple farmer in a log cabin and sipping hard cider.

When Harrison first heard of the Baltimore newspaper's sneering characterization of him, he had laughed. Indeed, he joked to his friends that such insults by the opposition would ensure his election. But the candidate personally played no role in the creation of his own campaign image.

The Harrison campaign strategists, excited by the favorable public response, couldn't wait to capitalize on their success. They decided to take the show on the road.

3

HELLO, COLUMBUS

We marched through the streets of Columbus,
And bravely we tramped the mud through.
To show the silk-stocking gentry,
How we'd stick to Old Tippecanoe.

—Harrison campaign song

Heavy rains in Columbus, Ohio, on Saturday, February 22, 1840, transformed the city's dirt streets into channels of oozing brown mud. But the steady downpour failed to dampen the spirits of celebrating crowds who had gathered in the state capital, ballooning the city's normal population of six thousand people to nearly thirty thousand men, women, and children.

The celebrants had swarmed into central Ohio from more than two-dozen counties for the two-day Whig state convention, which started on Friday afternoon and promised a parade of delegates on Saturday morning. A speakers' platform had been erected on the public square near the city center at the corner of Broad and High Streets, two wide, dirt roads. A second platform for itinerant speakers was put up a block away.

Heading south on High Street, wooden tenement houses gave way just after Broad Street to the five-story National Hotel on the right and the old statehouse with its church-like steeple on the left. A giant banner stretched across High Street proclaimed, HARRISON AND TYLER—THE PILLARS OF REFORM.

At the national Whig convention in Harrisburg, Whig leaders had urged state parties to hold their own conventions on George Washington's birthday, February 22. One goal was to build grassroots enthusiasm before the Democrats met for their

19

national convention in May. Another goal now was to see if the new Harrison log cabin campaign theme had caught on. Ohio, as Harrison's home state, was the biggest test.

Excitement was in the air among Whigs in Marysville, Ohio, thirty miles northwest of Columbus, as Union County delegates wrapped up their preparations for the big parade. Men chopped down some local buckeye trees, cut the wood into logs, and constructed a one-room log cabin atop a large wagon with four wheels.

Early on the morning of February 21, the cabin was ready to roll, pulled by four horses for the trip to Columbus. As the conveyance reached the outskirts of Columbus, a group of men inside the structure began singing "The Log Cabin Song," which a local man, Otaway Curry, had written especially for the occasion. The song praised General Harrison for protecting the homes of pioneers from Indian attacks: "*It was Harrison that fought for cabins long ago.*"

Official delegates and thousands of spectators flocked into Columbus from all directions as the sun shone down. They came on horseback, in horse-drawn wagons and carriages, and on foot. More than one thousand men walked in a procession from Ross, Pike, and Jackson Counties. Another seven hundred men arrived aboard twenty-seven canal boats that docked downtown on the Scioto River. "On they came, carriages, horsemen, music, banners and nags . . . until you would have thought that none had been left at home," the *Dayton Journal* reported.

The image and the passion hoped for by Whig strategists clearly had taken root. In the spirit of the campaign, many of the celebrants arrived dressed in the buckskin clothes of pioneers, right up to the coonskin caps. Some people waved miniature log cabins. The newspapers picked up on the theme: that this crowd represented the average man, not rich bankers.

"Yes, they are bank men," wrote an enthusiastic reporter for the pro-Whig *Ohio State Journal*—meaning that they came from the banks of the Ohio River, from the banks of Lake Erie, the banks of the Scioto River, the banks of the Miami, the Muskingum, and the Maumee Rivers. "And they have the evidence of their occupations with them, MUD. They are farmers. Their occupation is the noblest, for it is the natural employment of man."

All of the city's hotels and boardinghouses were filled by 10:00 AM. Residents opened their doors to provide strangers with places to sleep, ranging from mattresses to beds of straw or plain wooden floors. Downtown streets overflowed with humanity. Local taverns were jammed. No matter: the Whigs thoughtfully provided barrels of free hard cider on nearly every street corner.

In the evening, as storm clouds rolled in, large crowds gathered in the public square and beyond to listen to speakers, trade tales, or sing songs. Many sat around a huge bonfire as military veterans told glorious war stories about serving under Old Tip. Every now and then, a loud and long shout echoed across the city: "Whoo-oo-oo-o-ra-aa-ah for old Tippeca-noe!"

The town clock struck midnight. Suddenly, the skies opened and the rain fell. People ran to their sleeping quarters, retiring amidst excitement for the big procession the next day.

Saturday dawned to the sound of a band playing military music. Despite a driving rain, promptly at 10:00 AM groups of delegates began taking their places in the great procession for the march through city streets to the center of town. The parade stretched more than a mile.

Cheering crowds lined the muddy streets. Hundreds of flags and banners waved up and down the parade route. Some read, THE PEOPLE ARE COMING. And come they did, with at least sixteen bands playing at full volume. Leading the way were scores of marching volunteer militia infantry soldiers from three counties in full military dress, a tribute to General Harrison's war heroics. (Once again, the old general himself was not in attendance, abiding by the old you-can't-campaign-for-yourself custom.)

Right behind the militia came a big canoe on wheels, pulled by eight white horses. But it wasn't just a canoe. Rising from the front was a forty-foot- high buckeye tree with a full-length portrait of the Hero of Tippecanoe in his prime. Another rolling canoe made from large sycamore trees was seventy feet long and held fifty people. The assembled crowd roared huzzahs. Others waved from windows in the tenement houses. Cries of Tip and Ty echoed across the city.

Then the onlookers fell silent out of respect. Riding by on a white horse came a silver-haired, eighty-year-old Revolutionary War veteran. He was the last remaining bodyguard for General George Washington himself. Behind him pranced a riderless white horse symbolizing Washington's mount. On the steed's back was the great general's actual saddle, which had been sent over from his niece in Marietta, Ohio. Behind the two horses more aging veterans of the Revolutionary War trudged through the ankle-deep mud.

The crowd roared with patriotic cheers at the next sight. It was the Crawford County delegation carrying a ten-foot-high buckeye pole, atop of which perched a majestic symbol of liberty: a live bald eagle.

Continuing the military theme was a replica of an actual fort such as one that General Harrison had defended. This fort, carried on wheels, was forty feet long, had twelve cannons, and carried forty men. It took six horses to pull it. The onlookers shouted their approval. The delegation from Cincinnati, two hundred people strong, waved flags and banners in honor of their North Bend neighbor.

Log cabins on wheels were a central theme. The largest was fifty feet wide and was drawn by twenty horses. Onlookers whooped and hollered at another log cabin on wheels carrying the "Mad River Trappers." They sat on top of the cabin, ate corn bread and bacon and drank hard cider, and sang bawdy songs while live raccoons ran around the cabin's roof.

Next came a mock steamboat on wheels drawn by five horses. Men on board turned a crank to make the paddle revolve and steam rise in puffs from pipes. From Cuyahoga County next to Lake Erie came eighty men sitting on a full-sized boat on wheels with Harrison's portrait on the masthead. Another group lugged a huge banner with a life-sized drawing of the FARMER OF NORTH BEND at his plow as he stopped to sip a cup of hard cider.

Finally, the onlookers themselves joined the back of the parade to its finish at the speaking stand for the convention's official business. With the rain still streaming down, delegates selected Congressman Thomas "Wagon Boy" Corwin as the party's gubernatorial candidate. The convention pledged its support for

Harrison and Tyler. Speakers roused the crowd by defending the old general against his attackers.

The convention finally adjourned at 4:00 PM amid the sounds of thirty thousand people erupting like thunder in the rainstorm. They shouted, "Huzzah, Huzzah. Harrison and Reform."

No political rally like this had ever taken place in America. "I am this evening half crazed with the unceasing shouts and huzzahs of the people for Old Tippecanoe; and the moment I am writing, the sidewalks and streets are literally crowded with living forms," wrote the reporter for the *Ohio State Journal*. "It is indeed almost impossible to crowd through this great mass of people, even to reach the end of the single square."

Journalists covering the event were at a loss for words to tell readers what they had witnessed. One wrote that he watched the great gathering so that he could write a description of it, "but we cannot describe it." The anti-Whig *Ohio Statesman* had no trouble describing the gathering as a rowdy party by a bunch of baboons drunk on hard cider. There was no discussion of serious issues, the paper complained; instead, "songs and drinking and carousing and appeals to men's worst passions are introduced into the political meeting instead of argument and appeals to their senses."

John G. Miller, the editor of the pro-Whig *Ohio Confederate* and an eyewitness to the event, countered that the charges of drunkenness were overblown. Instead, he argued, the people were intoxicated with the spirit of the Great Convention. The campaign had "touched a cord [*sic*] which vibrates from the rivers to the ends of the land."

The first trial run of the log cabin theme was a smashing success. The question now was whether the campaign could maintain the momentum. Several delegates from Cleveland provided one answer. They had rolled a ten-foot-high paper ball to Columbus with pro-Harrison sayings pasted all over the sphere. It was an orb of campaign propaganda that could be rolled from town to town to keep the Harrison buzz alive. In the process, a new phrase entered the American lexicon: keep the ball rolling.

The ball kept rolling in more ways than one. When energized delegates from nearby Zanesville, Ohio, returned home, some of

Rolling Harrison ball. *Roger Butterfield's* The American Past, *New York Historical Association Library, Cooperstown, NY*

them began searching for a new campaign song to capture the spirit of the Columbus rally. A local jeweler, twenty-seven-year-old Alexander Coffman Ross, came up with lyrics to set to the tune of a minstrel ditty called "Little Pigs." His new song began:

> *What has caused the great commotion, motion, motion,*
> *Our country through?*
> *It is the ball a-rolling on*
> *For Tippecanoe and Tyler Too.*
> *For Tippecanoe and Tyler Too.*

Tippecanoe and Tyler Too would soon become the first—and the most famous—slogan of any presidential campaign. For Harrison campaign planners, the Columbus convention exceeded their wildest dreams. Somehow they had tapped into the pioneer spirit of the American people.

The Ohio gathering had successfully established the image of Harrison as a gallant old war hero living like the common man in a humble log cabin. There was just one problem: much of the image was simply untrue.

4

OLD TIP: HERO OR COWARD?

*[General Harrison is] the hero of defeat and
failure.*

—*Washington Globe*, an anti-Whig newspaper

Stunned by the Whigs' triumph in generating log cabin fever,
Democrats launched a counteroffensive. In early April, Ohio congressman Alexander Duncan took to the floor of the House of
Representatives to denounce the humble Harrison image as a fraud, a
falsehood, and downright humbuggery. The Democrats also assigned
a young Michigan lawmaker to attack the general's military record.

Partisan newspapers promoted the arguments of each side.
But what was a voter to believe? There were no nonpartisan fact
checkers to sort out the truth. If there had been, they would have
found plenty of dubious claims on both sides.

For starters, William Henry Harrison—portrayed by the Whigs
as the champion of the poor—grew up in a magnificent Southern
mansion. He was born February 9, 1773, not in a log cabin but in
a Georgian two-and-a-half-story brick house with six white columns rising two stories above the front porch. It was the Harrison
family home at Berkeley Plantation, which sprawled over fourteen hundred acres on the James River in Charles City County,
Virginia, between Richmond and Williamsburg.

William Henry was the youngest of seven children born to
Benjamin Harrison V and his wife, Elizabeth Bassett Harrison, a
niece of Martha Washington's sister. The senior Harrison helped
lead the American rebellion against the British. He was one of the
signers of the Declaration of Independence in 1776. After that, he
was known simply as "the Signer."

The 250-pound Harrison joked that if the signers were hung for treason, he would not dangle in agony as long as his skinnier compatriots would. There were no hangings, but in 1781 British troops led by General Benedict Arnold—that traitor!—trashed Berkeley Plantation. They burned family portraits on the lawn and shot cows for target practice. William Henry was eight years old at the time.

After America won the Revolution, Ben Harrison became a three-time governor of Virginia. At Berkeley, young Billy Harrison was schooled at home with his two older brothers and four sisters. He learned to swim, ride horses, and shoot guns.

Benjamin Harrison ran the plantation with more than one hundred slaves. Tobacco was the cash crop. The slaves lived in quarters outside the house. The kitchen, where slaves prepared the meals, was connected to the main house by an underground tunnel. Inside the house, Billy Harrison grew up listening to political conversations by visitors who included such Virginia movers and shakers as George Washington, Thomas Jefferson, Patrick Henry, and James Madison. Jefferson even offered remodeling tips, suggesting that the senior Harrison take down the house's aristocratic crown molding and put up simple plaster walls.

In fact, the Whigs' entire ticket sprouted from the Virginia aristocracy. John Tyler grew up right down the road in Charles City County at the slave-holding Greenway Plantation. Tyler's father, also named John, had been Thomas Jefferson's roommate at the College of William and Mary in Williamsburg. The senior Tyler later became a governor of Virginia and a judge.

William Henry Harrison and young John Tyler weren't childhood friends, because Harrison was seventeen years older. But the families knew each other well. Indeed, Benjamin Harrison and John Tyler Sr. were often political rivals. What wasn't widely known in 1840 was that Harrison and Tyler were cousins.

John Tyler the son also became a Virginia governor and a US senator. He lived on his own slave-holding estate on the James River in Williamsburg. The Whig ticket was geographically balanced because Harrison had long since settled in Ohio.

At a time when few Americans could afford to send their children to college, William Henry was shipped off to Hampden Sidney College in southern Virginia to study the classics at age fourteen. There he developed an intense interest in Roman history. He moved on to study medicine in Richmond, where—much to his father's dismay—he briefly joined a Quaker abolitionist humane society. He then was sent to Philadelphia to study medicine under the famous physician Dr. Benjamin Rush. His guardian was Robert Morris, another signer of the Declaration of Independence.

In 1791, at age eighteen, Harrison's life took a drastic turn. His father died suddenly; his mother would pass away two years later. Berkeley Plantation passed to his oldest brother. William Henry inherited some property, but he would have to make a living on his own.

Harrison was an ambitious young man. He began building a career using connections that no common man could dream of: the Founding Father friends of his late dad.

Harrison had no interest in studying medicine; that had been his father's idea. He wanted to join the army and fight Indians. One of his father's old friends, President George Washington, authorized an army officer commission for the eighteen-year-old Harrison. Carrying volumes of Roman philosopher Cicero in his backpack, Harrison set off walking three hundred miles to Fort Washington next to Cincinnati, which was then a village of twenty-five to thirty cabins.

At Fort Washington he served under the command of General "Mad Anthony" Wayne, fighting Native Americans as far north as the Maumee River on Ohio's northern border. His coolness under fire impressed Wayne, who eventually promoted the young soldier to captain. Harrison took part in negotiating a treaty with Native Americans at Greenville, Ohio, near the Indiana Territory border.

While serving at Fort Washington, Harrison wooed dark-eyed Anna Symmes, the daughter of the area's richest landowner, John Cleves Symmes. Though the father at first disapproved of the union, the couple was married in 1795 in Symmes's house by a justice of the peace. Harrison was twenty-two years old and Anna was twenty. Her father left town rather than attend the wedding. Eventually Symmes came around and for $450 sold Harrison a small house on property at the north bend of the Ohio River. Asked by his father-in-law how he would support his new wife, Harrison responded, "By my sword and my own right arm, Sir."

Anna Symmes Harrison. *Library of Congress*

Harrison, however, had already begun lobbying friends for a more lucrative occupation. In 1798, another Founding Father friend, President John Adams, appointed Harrison secretary and then governor of the Indiana Territory. The job paid $2,000 a year, while a laborer at the time was lucky to earn $200 a year. Harrison also briefly represented the territory in the US House of Representatives in Philadelphia.

The Indiana Territory stretched far beyond Indiana. It also included the future states of Illinois and Wisconsin as well as parts of Michigan and Minnesota. Native Americans and white settlers frequently clashed in these vast woodlands. Harrison settled in the territorial capital of Vincennes, located on the western border of modern Indiana, across the Wabash River from Illinois. It was a former French trading village of about seven hundred people. After selling some of his inherited property, the future log cabin candidate bought three hundred acres of land along the Wabash to build one of the biggest mansions in the West.

He called the two-and-a-half-story, twenty-two-room mansion Grouseland because there was a preponderance of grouse, a ground-dwelling game bird. It was the first brick house in the territory, built with more than two thousand bricks. Harrison imported lumber from Cypress and glass windows from England. A cantilevered staircase curved up from the central hallway. The mansion was finished in 1804, just as the Harrisons welcomed their fifth child. The home cost an estimated $20,000.

Harrison's new abode with four two-story white columns could have been called Berkeley Plantation West, because it resembled Harrison's old Virginia home. To help run it, he brought in from Virginia several slaves whom he had inherited from his mother. Slavery was illegal in the territory. Harrison tried to get the law changed. After that effort failed, as governor he got a law written allowing "indentured servants," who supposedly could work for their eventual freedom.

Still another family friend and Founding Father, President Thomas Jefferson, reappointed Harrison as governor of the territory. Jefferson was into real estate. In 1803 he made the Louisiana

Purchase, which covered 828,000 square miles of land in the West, encompassing fifteen future states from Louisiana to Minnesota. The United States paid France about $15 million, or less than three cents an acre.

Jefferson added the new purchase to the Indiana Territory, and he and Harrison began corresponding. The president urged the young governor to buy land for the United States from Native Americans tribes. "The system is to live in perpetual peace with the Indians, to cultivate an affectionate attachment from them," Jefferson wrote Harrison in one letter. The goal, the president said, was to promote "a disposition to exchange lands, which they have to spare, and we want for necessities."

Harrison did as he was instructed. He bought Indian land on the cheap, sometimes with a few well-placed bribes. Over twelve years, Harrison negotiated at least a dozen treaties with tribes and bought more than sixty million acres of land.

All was going well until Harrison's encounter with Shawnee chief Tecumseh. The Shawnees didn't control any of the land the United States was buying up. But Tecumseh believed the Great Spirit didn't want any Native Americans to give up their property. "These lands are ours," he said. "No one has a right to remove us because we were the first owners."

One August afternoon in 1810, Tecumseh, who was in his early forties, paddled up the Wabash to Vincennes with about four hundred warriors in eighty canoes to argue his case; he took about half of them to a council at Harrison's house. Harrison had set up chairs on the veranda, but Tecumseh insisted on sitting outside on the ground under a clump of walnut trees. To Native Americans, the ground was their mother, he said, and he was happy to sit on his mother's bosom.

The talks between Harrison and Tecumseh grew increasingly tense. Finally, the Shawnee chief jumped up in anger, called Harrison a liar, and reached for his tomahawk. Harrison calmly drew his sword. He said Tecumseh was a bad man and asked him to leave. Tecumseh did, but that wasn't the end of it.

Chief Tecumseh and Governor Harrison. *Indiana Historical Society (0483): Bass Photo Co. Collection, Indiana Historical Society*

Tecumseh and his one-eyed half brother, a religious leader called the Prophet, began assembling Native Americans from many tribes in a village called Prophetstown at the Tippecanoe River near Lafayette, Indiana. After Indian raids on local settlers, Harrison obtained federal permission to close down the place, peaceably if possible.

In the fall of 1811, knowing that Tecumseh was away recruiting more tribes and the Prophet was in charge, Harrison took about a thousand men on a 150-mile march from Vincennes to Prophetstown. Most of the men were federal soldiers, but some were volunteers from the Kentucky militia. The governor led the way, riding his horse, wearing a buckskin shirt with fringes on the sleeves and a beaver cap with an ostrich feather sticking up on top.

On the evening of November 6, Harrison decided to camp for the night on a ridge overlooking the village. Just before dawn, about five hundred Native Americans with rifles attacked the camp, which was lit by bonfires. Harrison was already up, and he jumped on a ready horse and directed the defense. Though his troops eventually routed the attackers, sixty-two of Harrison's men were killed and more than a hundred were wounded. One of those who died, Thomas Randolph, asked with his dying breath for Harrison to take care of his daughter. The next day, Harrison's remaining troops destroyed the now-abandoned village.

Despite a two-to-one advantage in manpower, Harrison's forces suffered more losses than the Native Americans. Yet as word of the battle spread, he gained fame as the "Hero of Tippecanoe."

America suspected that Great Britain was stirring up the Indians as tensions rose between the two nations. England began seizing US sailors on the high seas and forcing them into the British Navy. Finally, President James Madison declared war in the summer of 1812. His plan to invade the British territory of Canada started off badly with the loss of a US town, Detroit, at the Canadian border. So Madison, another old family friend, named Harrison general and commander of the Northwest forces.

Harrison immediately resigned as governor of the Indiana Territory and moved his family to one of the finer neighborhoods in Cincinnati. As a general, Harrison earned about $200 a month, plus a supply of rations valued at about $500 monthly.

In the spring of 1813, Harrison headed to Fort Meigs in northern Ohio. His main mission was to hold the fort, which housed the artillery for the next military campaign. Soon after his arrival, the British and their Native American allies attacked the fort, sustaining the assault for a dozen days in late April and early May. Despite the siege, Harrison's troops held control, but there was no way to go on the offensive unless the Americans could cut off the British supply lines over the Great Lakes.

Harrison conferred with twenty-seven-year-old Commodore Oliver Hazard Perry. In September 1813, Perry launched a sea attack against the Royal British Navy on Lake Erie. His fleet waved a fighting flag with the words DON'T GIVE UP THE SHIP. Perry was quite a quotable fellow. When he won the Battle of Lake Erie, he wrote to Harrison on the back of an envelope, "We have met the enemy and they are ours."

Perry's ships carried Harrison and his troops across Lake Erie, where the general then recaptured Detroit. He pursued the British forces and their allies—though he apparently took his sweet time in doing so. The two sides finally faced off on October 5, 1813, near the Thames River in Canada. Harrison, with a force of about three thousand men, contemplated his strategy. Ahead alongside the Thames were about one thousand British troops with artillery. To their right, Tecumseh had gathered about five hundred Native Americans behind a swamp.

Harrison at first planned a traditional infantry charge until he saw the British troops widely separated in open lines. He called up a mounted rifle group from Kentucky led by Colonel Richard Mentor Johnson, who had left a seat in Congress to fight in the war. They decided to mount an unorthodox surprise attack on horseback.

The tactic was not anything he had ever seen or heard of, Harrison said later. "But I was fully convinced that it would work. The American backwoodsmen ride better in the woods than any other people. . . . I was persuaded that the enemy would be quite unprepared for the shock and that they could not resist it."

At Harrison's order, one group of Kentuckians galloped through the woods to launch a surprise assault that quickly sent the British troops running. A second group led by Colonel Johnson rode over the swamp ground to take on Tecumseh. Each cavalryman carried a rifle, a knife, and a hatchet.

In the bloody battle, gunshots hit Colonel Johnson five times, but he kept fighting aboard his white horse. When his horse was shot from under him, Johnson continued to fight on foot. Suddenly, a tall Native American came charging toward him, waving a tomahawk. Johnson shot him dead. The man may have been Tecumseh. In any event, the Shawnee leader perished in the battle; with him gone, the Native Americans soon surrendered.

The Battle of the Thames was the biggest American win in the war so far. Taking a leave, Harrison began a victory march to Washington, DC, to begin planning a spring offensive. Throngs lined the streets to cheer him in New York, Philadelphia, Wilmington, and Washington. In New York, public buildings were lit up like Christmas trees. In Philadelphia, crowds paraded in the streets as bands played military marches. "The people were then hurrahing for the Hero of the Thames," the *Niles' Register* reported. "Such demonstrations of joy have been exhibited in almost every town and village we have heard from." But in May 1814, with the war far from over, Harrison abruptly resigned at age forty-one.

Now, in a presidential campaign nearly three decades later, the cheers for General Harrison were about to turn to jeers by Democrats. On February 14, 1840, thirty-five-year-old Michigan representative Isaac Crary interrupted debate on the Cumberland Road (later US Route 40). In an opening jab, Crary declared that he wanted to talk about Harrison "not as he is in his old age, with mental infirmities fast thickening upon him." He wanted to set the record straight on the old general's military record.

The Battle of Tippecanoe, he asserted, was in reality a defeat. Harrison's troops had suffered huge losses because he had failed to protect his camp from the surprise Indian attack. "Anyone who will put himself to the trouble of reading the official account of the battle of Tippecanoe will see that General Harrison performed no great act of generalship on that occasion," Crary crowed.

Democrats also raised the charge of what might be called Horsegate. They contended that during the surprise attack Harrison had another officer ride his usual white horse for fear that the Native Americans would target him. The charge wasn't true. The attackers did kill an officer who was riding his own white horse, and they may have thought he was Harrison. But Harrison's favorite horse was a spirited gray mare that was kept saddled in case of an attack. When the attack came, Harrison's servant couldn't find the mare, so Harrison jumped on the first available horse. In the battle, Harrison said, Indians shot the horse he was riding in the head and another bullet whizzed by his own head, "very nearly terminating my Earthly career."

Moving on to the War of 1812 in his speech, Congressman Crary declared that the real Hero of the Thames was Richard Mentor Johnson, or as he was known, "Old Dick." Johnson was now Van Buren's vice president. By contrast, Democrats charged that during the fighting Harrison was two miles away picking huckleberries. The critics said in battles with Native Americans, Harrison usually hid out in the woods. They noted that the general never was wounded in battle. Harrison was a coward, declared Democratic newspapers. Then, rather than finish the fight against the British, he resigned his post to try to capitalize on his fame.

The attacks on Harrison's military service outraged the Whigs. Old soldiers who had served with him vouched for his courage. Though like General Washington he had never been wounded, Old Tip had plenty of near misses. A bullet zipped through the brim of his hat at Tippecanoe. At the Battle of the Thames, enemy bullets flicked the tree leaves above his head. As for hiding out in the woods, Harrison himself noted that the safest place in a battle with Indians would be *out* of the woods.

In the House debate, a Whig lawmaker read from a speech made in the Ohio legislature by one of Harrison's former soldiers after a Democratic attack in that body against the general. "I know, sir, that cannon balls, and bombshells, flew thick around him in these battles. . . . Horses were shot down under him," the old soldier said. "I speak what I know, and what my eyes have seen. General Harrison is not a coward; and those who call him a coward know nothing of him. He was a brave, prudent, and fearless general."

A survivor of the Battle of Tippecanoe later recounted that during the fight rumors flew that Harrison had been killed. The troops seemed panic stricken. Then Harrison rode up and, with bullets flying, calmly called out orders. The soldiers gave him three cheers and won the battle.

"I can safely say that I never in my life saw a braver man in battle, one more collected, prompt and full of resources, than General William Henry Harrison," declared one of Harrison's military aides, John O'Fallon.

General Harrison's commanding style was to build rapport with his troops, his soldiers said. He would talk to each man personally, rather than give general orders. If rations were limited, he and his staff shared in the cutbacks. During combat duty, he carried all of his belongings in a single valise. He wrapped a single blanket over his saddle, and usually slept in accommodations no better than those of his troops.

Harrison resigned in the middle of the War of 1812, his backers contended, only because US war secretary John Armstrong reassigned the general to a meaningless outpost. The two men had clashed over military strategies. Harrison expected President Madison to refuse his resignation, and he probably would have, but Armstrong accepted the resignation before Madison saw it. Armstrong then replaced Harrison with General Andrew Jackson of Tennessee, who soon gained fame by winning the Battle of New Orleans on January 8, 1815.

Harrison's victory at the Thames arguably was more important than Jackson's more famous win. The Thames battle ended the British threat from Canada; the Battle of New Orleans came after America and Britain had reached a peace agreement in December, but the word didn't reach New Orleans until after the battle there. Nevertheless, the Battle of New Orleans would eventually propel Jackson into the White House as a war hero.

President Madison meantime appointed Harrison to a commission that negotiated peace treaties with Native American tribes in an effort to keep them from hooking up with the British. In Greenville, Ohio, Harrison smoked a peace pipe with chiefs of several tribes before all agreed on a treaty under which the tribes would no longer fight for the British and the US forgave those who had previously fought for them. In 1816, Ohio voters elected Harrison to fill out a vacancy in the US House of Representatives in Washington, DC.

The day after Congressman Crary's attack, the Whigs sent forty-five-year-old Ohio congressman Tom Corwin to respond. Corwin was known as the comedian of Congress. After defending Harrison's record, Corwin launched into a critique of Crary's own military credentials. Crary had been a brigadier general in the Michigan militia, but with the nation at peace, this was a ceremonial post.

Corwin conjured up a picture of Crary in the most dangerous assignment of a militia general during peacetime: marching in a parade. Riding a bushy-tailed horse, General Crary leads troops armed with umbrellas, hoes, axe handles, and other "deadly implements of war," Corwin declared. In the heat of the encounter, Crary brandishes his sword and fearlessly slices watermelons for his troops. Then all drink whiskey from the sliced melons as ancient soldiers had drunk wine from the skulls of vanquished foes.

By now, a crowd had gathered around the House floor, as senators came over to see what all the noise was about. Spectators and House members roared with laughter. The next day Whig congressman John Quincy Adams spoke sarcastically of "the late General Crary." The Michigan lawmaker's political career was over.

General Harrison may not be among America's greatest military leaders, but the facts show that he served honorably and with valor. So the image of Harrison as a military hero on a white horse was valid. As for the log cabin and hard cider, that was a horse of a different color.

5

HOME SWEET LOG CABIN HOME

He is a rich man and lives in a magnificent frame house surrounded by a princely estate.

—Ohio Democratic congressman Alexander Duncan

Describing the home of William Henry Harrison on the north bend of the Ohio River as a log cabin was like comparing the White House to a summer cottage on the Potomac.

The Harrison house stood in North Bend, Ohio, fourteen miles west of Cincinnati near the Indiana and Kentucky borders. It had been a two-story, four-room log cabin when Harrison bought it from his father-in-law forty years earlier. That would not be enough to house the couple's ten children—eleven counting the daughter of Thomas Randolph, the man who died at Tippecanoe beseeching Harrison to take care of his child—so as their family grew the Harrisons tore down most of the original cabin and built a wood-frame house covered with white clapboard.

By 1840 the house, which sat atop a high terrace with a majestic view of the Ohio River, stretched over twenty-two rooms. It was known locally as the Big House. All that remained of the original cabin was one wall that was left exposed inside a large closet in one of the bedrooms of the larger house.

The front of the house was so wide that there were three front doors. The house opened to a main building with two rooms, one on each side of a wide central hall. At the ends were two wings, each a story and a half high. The interior of the house was finished in rich mahogany and cherry. Each room had an open fireplace. Fine oil paintings hung on the walls.

William Henry Harrison estate in North Bend, Ohio. *Emmet Collection, Miriam and Ira D. Wallach Division of Art, Prints and Photographs, New York Public Library, Astor, Lenox and Tilden Foundations*

Outside the house, large locust and catalpa trees grew along one side of the long stone driveway. Surrounding the front of the house was "a beautifully kept velvety lawn of six acres." Lilac bushes, flowering shrubs, grape arbors, and a row of bright hollyhocks adorned the walkways. On the east side of the house, grassy knolls led down to a rocky stream called Indian Creek.

Thanks to the Whigs' image campaign, many voters believed that Harrison really did live in a log cabin. There were no photographers to show them otherwise. And visiting reporters who wrote for friendly Whig newspapers neglected to mention the size of the domicile.

Plenty of visitors flocked to the North Bend house. Upon leaving Vincennes, Harrison had told his troops that the latch to his door would always be open. Many of his former troops from various commands took him up on the invitation by dropping in at North Bend. So did other travelers, many of them strangers. Harrison always invited them in. The Harrisons entertained so many guests for meals that they served more than 365 hams each year.

Some visitors from the East assumed that Harrison was a bumbling backwoodsman until they met him. When one Boston man stopped by the farm on a trip to Ohio, he was surprised to find the old general to be a man of some intellect.

"There is a degree of gravity in his manner, yet it does not amount to formality," the visitor told the *Boston Atlas*. Harrison "converses readily and pleasantly upon all subjects," yet without affectation. "He does not hesitate for dates, names or facts as some persons of his age do. You must see him and hear him to get the full measure of his electrical powers." The Boston man went away believing that Harrison's judgment and abilities were the equal of each of America's first six presidents, except perhaps the sixth one, the highly intellectual John Quincy Adams.

Another guest in the summer of 1840 was James Brooks, the editor of the pro-Whig *New York Express*. He traveled to the public boat landing in Cincinnati to meet Harrison for the fourteen-mile steamboat ride to North Bend. The presidential candidate arrived dressed in buckskin clothing with saddlebags slung over one arm and a tin pail in the other hand. Brooks was struck by "the simplicity of his manners."

The reporter planned to stay at North Bend for just a day, but Harrison persuaded him to remain a week. Like the Boston visitor, Brooks was won over. "Seldom, if ever, have I passed any time of my life more agreeably," he wrote.

At the Harrison home, visitors often gathered in the big kitchen around a huge open fireplace and a large brick oven with kettles hanging above. Mounted over another fireplace was a yellow brass telescope that Commodore Perry had used to spot the British fleet in the Battle of Lake Erie; he presented it to Harrison as a gift from one old friend to another.

Supper usually was served before six o'clock. The meals consisted of ham, chicken, or other fresh meat from the farm along with homemade cornbread and butter. In the summer, as guests dined, a maid waved a rolled-up newspaper over the table to shoo away flies. There was homemade pie for dessert.

After supper, Harrison usually led his guests to a sitting room. He brought out a decanter of whiskey for those who wished to imbibe. The general was an urbane and well-mannered man. Politicians marveled at his ability to always say the right thing. He entertained his guests by telling military stories, expounding on the growing expansion of the West or boasting about his prized Durham bull. He could recite entire theatrical scenes and was an accomplished mimic. He rarely talked politics.

About nine o'clock Harrison typically headed off to bed. Guests were put up in a carpeted guest room that had a four-poster bed and a table with a book about the signers of the Declaration of Independence. Harrison also had a large library stocked with books on Roman history, military wars such as the Battle of Tippecanoe, and biographies, including at least one about him. He also read Shakespeare, but never novels.

Harrison was an early riser. Shortly after dawn, the newspaperman Brooks found the general at his desk reading stacks of letters and newspapers without the aid of glasses. The general tried to read everything written about him, even if he didn't like it. Guests were served a big breakfast, including their choice of hard- or soft-boiled eggs. It was said that Harrison was prouder of his homemade smoked bacon than any military medal.

The old general did some of his own farming. But the image of Harrison as the small farmer of North Bend plowing his land was as bogus as the log cabin. His "farm" covered more than twenty-eight hundred acres—or four and a half square miles—of fields, woods, and waterways. The main crops were wheat and hay, plus corn that grew as high as fourteen feet. Cattle grazed on the front lawn. The estate also boasted sheep, hogs, and chickens, as well as numerous vegetable gardens.

Slavery was outlawed in Ohio, but to help run the estate the general had a large staff of African American servants, many of whom he had brought from Virginia as slaves years ago. They included Gabe, a cook who specialized in roast pork, Rose, who waited on the family table, plus Aunt Lue and Aunt Pigeon, who performed various household duties.

A vivacious Frenchwoman oversaw the household staff. She had come to America years before in a fruitless attempt to track down her husband, a sea captain who ran off with her younger sister. While a member of Congress, Harrison had met her in Washington, where she worked for an acquaintance. When she fell on hard times, he invited her to join his household in North Bend. She spoke fluent English, and she sat at the dinner table as part of the family.

The Harrisons lived simply, but with many niceties that their neighbors lacked. For example, Mr. and Mrs. Harrison each had their own tin bathtubs, both painted black, that were filled with water heated at the fireplace. The tubs were in separate rooms.

Contrary to his campaign image, Harrison didn't drink hard cider. Only sweet cider was served at the Harrison table. The general wasn't a teetotaler, but he preferred imported wine or whiskey when he drank, which wasn't often. Harrison had become an outspoken critic of alcohol. It began with his problems handling drunken soldiers and Native Americans. Then his son William Henry Harrison Jr. became an alcoholic, running up big debts.

At one point, the senior Harrison had run a very profitable distillery at North Bend, producing whiskey from corn. But he shut it down. In 1831, Harrison told a meeting of the Hamilton County Agricultural Society that he regretted ever producing a product "which is so destructive of health and happiness." He said that in doing so he had sinned, "but in that way I shall sin no more." The general's antipathy to alcohol increased in 1838 when William Henry Jr. died from alcoholism at age thirty-six, leaving a wife and two children to be cared for.

To support his large family, Harrison tried various endeavors. After the War of 1812 ended in early 1815, he sought to capitalize on his war fame with a political career. Elected to Congress in 1816, Harrison immediately ran into a sticky issue. Some House members moved to censure General Andrew Jackson for having two British traders hanged during the Seminole wars in Florida. The move failed, but Harrison supported censure for one of the executions, thus earning the lasting enmity of the hot-tempered Jackson.

In 1819, Harrison won election to the Ohio Senate. Later, as his fame began to fade, he lost bids to be governor of Ohio and a US senator. Finally, in 1825 he persuaded the Ohio legislature to name him to the US Senate (state legislatures, not voters, picked senators until 1913). He was joined in the Senate in 1827 by John Tyler of Virginia.

Much of the time, Harrison was angling for higher-paying government appointments. But his sway with his father's friends was wearing thin. President James Monroe spurned the general's bid to be ambassador to Russia. Then, while serving in the Senate, Harrison sought to be appointed US minister to Colombia. It was a plum post that paid $9,000 a year.

By now John Quincy Adams (the son of Harrison's father's friend, former president John Adams) presided in Washington. President Adams complained that Harrison's thirst for lucrative office was "absolutely rabid." He wrote in his diary that the general had become "the greatest beggar and most troublesome of all office-seekers" during his administration.

Nevertheless, at the urging of Secretary of State Henry Clay, Adams reluctantly gave Harrison the Colombia post in May 1828. It took until early February 1829 for Harrison to get to Bogotá. He was there only a month when Andrew Jackson swept into the White House. It was payback time. Just four days after becoming president, Jackson replaced Harrison. The general returned to Ohio, bringing with him a multicolored macaw that flew among the trees at North Bend.

Harrison kept pushing for high-paying government appointments because money had become a pressing issue. He was no pauper, but he wasn't wealthy either. He had made a number of bad investments over the years. Then there was the cost of raising a large family and sending his kids to the best colleges. He also paid to send two sons of another fallen officer at Tippecanoe to West Point. By 1840, though five of his ten children had died, he was helping to support the families of his grown children. Meantime, he was living beyond his means at North Bend in the manner of a wealthy Virginia planter.

In 1834, Harrison took a job as the Clerk of the Hamilton County Pleas Court in nearby Cincinnati, a city of about six thousand people. Reportedly, a son-in-law did much of the work, but the image of a humble clerk worked into Harrison's 1840 campaign image. Whigs told the story of a French writer, Michael Chavier. While visiting Cincinnati, Chavier spotted an older, plainly dressed man at the Main Street Hotel and asked who he was. The Frenchman was shocked to hear that the man was the great General Harrison. He wrote that the old war hero "is poor with a numerous family, neglected by the federal government, although yet vigorous." He still had "the independence to think for himself."

In fact, Harrison's clerk post was no low-paying job. He earned more than $6,000 a year in fees related to court transactions. This exceeded the $5,000 annual salary of the vice president of the United States. (The president himself made $25,000 a year.)

The Democrats stepped up their attacks against the image of Harrison as a poor, log-cabin-living, hard-cider-drinking candidate. Ohio Democratic congressman Alexander Duncan, speaking in the House, complained that Harrison had lived off government jobs most of his life, and was now living high on the hog in his fancy North Bend house. He "does not live in a log cabin, nor does he toil in sweat" to earn a living, the fifty-one-year-old Duncan asserted. "All this story about the log cabin is a falsehood; it is a mean fraud."

Harrison lived "in splendor and luxury" in a fine house, declared Democratic senator Felix Grundy of Tennessee. "Of all the miserable humbugs that I have ever seen or heard of, this exceeds them all."

The Democrats' complaints had little impact. This was a campaign where facts clearly didn't matter much. With Harrison's image as the champion of the poor in place, the Whigs turned to the other side of their campaign strategy: painting President Martin Van Buren as nothing more than the candidate of Washington's rich and powerful officeholders.

6

LITTLE MATTY

As a rule we simply assailed Mr. Van Buren and his administration, charging all sorts of misdemeanors and corruption.

—Whig editor Richard Smith Elliott

At first, President Martin Van Buren and the Democrats were surprised and pleased by the Whigs' nomination of General William Henry Harrison for president instead of Senator Henry Clay, whom they considered a much more formidable candidate. The Whig convention's "mountain in labor has brought forth a mouse," sneered Sam Medary, editor of the *Ohio Statesman.*

President Van Buren, who planned to run for a second term, had already defeated Harrison in 1836 when he was one of the Whigs' regional candidates. Now Harrison was back for a second try, "like a cat which you thought you saw killed yesterday, looking in at your window with a bloody head, to scare you and wake you in the morning," wrote newspaper publisher William Cullen Bryant.

At five foot six inches tall, Van Buren stands as the shortest US president except for James "Little Jemmy" Madison, who stood five foot four in his silk stocking feet. The amiable, fifty-seven-year-old Van Buren was bald and increasingly plump, with clear blue eyes and reddish-gray sideburns that curled all the way down the sides of his face. He was smart but not formally educated. He was quiet, courteous, and fairly formal. He didn't swear, smoke, or chew tobacco. He could be lively and sometimes would spring up the White House stairs two steps at a time.

President Martin Van Buren. *Library of Congress*

Van Buren was the first professional politician to become president. Because of his political prowess, the New Yorker had more nicknames than he could count. He was called "the Red Fox," "the Little Magician," "the Wizard," "the Careful Dutchman," and "Little Matty." He also was known as "Old Kinderhook," after the name of his home village in upstate New York in the Hudson Valley.

In reality, Van Buren was far more representative of the common man than the aristocratic Harrison. He was born in Kinderhook on December 5, 1782, above his father's tavern in a modest wood-frame boardinghouse. His parents, Abraham and Mary Van Buren, were humble Dutch immigrants who also operated a small farm. Growing up, Martin spoke more Dutch than English.

Martin was one of nine children who lived in the house, along with six slaves inherited by Mrs. Van Buren. While slavery was mainly a southern institution, in the late 1700s some northern farmers also owned slaves.

As a small boy, Martin carried cabbage from the family farm to sell to neighbors. As he got older, he worked in the tavern, serving drinks and meals. The tavern and boardinghouse were located on the Old Post Road between the state capital of Albany and the nation's capital of New York City. Politicians traveling between the two capitals often stopped by, including future vice president Aaron Burr and treasury secretary Alexander Hamilton. The house also served as a voting place during elections. Young Martin developed his interest in politics by listening to the conversations of politicians and voters.

The Van Burens couldn't afford to send their son to college. So at age fourteen, he went to work in the office of a prominent local lawyer, Francis Sylvester, to learn the law. Martin showed up for work dressed in clothes made from rough wool that his mother had woven. The young man was a sharp contrast to the well-dressed lawyer, who wore silver buckles on his square-shaped shoes. Sylvester lectured his young protégé on the importance of dressing well.

Martin went missing from work the next two days. When Sylvester finally saw his law clerk on the third day, he had to suppress a grin. Martin arrived wearing a cocked hat and stylish clothing down to his silken hose and silver shoe buckles. Van Buren had borrowed money to pay for the clothes. He was a dapper dresser from then on.

In those days, trials often were held in taverns. One day when Martin was about fifteen years old, Sylvester sent him to deliver some papers to a lawyer in a nearby town. The lawyer was arguing a case before a jury in a local tavern when Van Buren arrived. It was a routine case, and the lawyer asked Martin to make the final argument. The young law clerk did, but he was so short that he had to stand on a chair to be seen by the jurors. The lawyer's client won. It was Van Buren's first legal victory, and the lawyer gave him a silver dollar for his effort.

In 1801 nineteen-year-old Martin went to New York City to work in the law firm of William P. Van Ness, a young lawyer from a prominent family back in Van Buren's home county. Billy Van Ness was a close friend of Aaron Burr, who that same year became the vice president under President Thomas Jefferson. Burr had a home in New York City; he frequently saw Van Buren and took a liking to the inquisitive young man from Kinderhook.

Burr's political career went down the drain in 1804 when he shot and killed Alexander Hamilton in a duel in New Jersey after Hamilton supposedly made some disparaging remarks about the vice president. Billy Van Ness served as Burr's second in the duel. Burr returned to his post as vice president. He was never prosecuted, but his reputation was permanently tarnished.

After obtaining his state law license in 1803 at the age of twenty-one, Van Buren opened a practice with his half brother back home in the Hudson Valley. The timing couldn't have been better. Within a few years, Robert Fulton's newly invented steamboat, the *Clermont*, began running up and down the Hudson River, generating an economic boom in the area. Soon, Van Buren was earning $10,000 a year. He specialized in cases challenging the legality of old land grants held by wealthy people.

By then, Van Buren had begun raising a family. In 1807 he married his childhood sweetheart, blue-eyed Hannah Hoes, a cousin. He called her by her Dutch name, Jannetje. She was known as a kind woman with a pleasant disposition. The couple soon had two sons.

Martin Van Buren's legal success drew the attention of New York politicians. In early 1812, the son of a tavern owner ran for the state senate against an upper-crust incumbent. After he lagged in early returns, Van Buren figured the race was over and boarded a steamboat on the Hudson River for a trip to New York City.

As the boat was passing Catskill, New York, he saw his brother-in-law waving frantically from the shore. A rowboat was heading toward the steamer with news of the latest election returns: Van Buren had won—by only 193 votes out of nearly 12,000 cast.

In the New York legislature, Van Buren—a disciple of Thomas Jefferson—belonged to what was known as the Bucktail Party (so named because members wore deer tails in their hats at conventions). Over the next few years, he became one of New York's most powerful politicians.

Van Buren's main political skill was his ability to find out lawmakers' positions on issues while remaining noncommittal about his own views. Critics claimed Matty would seem to show support for both sides of an issue. "It was said that at a year old he could laugh on one side of his face and cry on the other, at one and the same time," cracked Tennessee frontiersman and congressman Davy Crockett.

After his election, Van Buren moved to the state capital in Albany with his family, including a personal slave named Tom. The slave took the opportunity to run away. Van Buren made no effort to find him, but ten years later he was informed by a man in Richmond that Tom had turned up there. Van Buren agreed to sell the slave for $50 if the man could "get him without violence."

In Albany, Martin and Hannah had three more children. Hannah had no interest in politics and devoted herself to her family. One of Van Buren's close political friends described her as "a woman of sweet nature but few intellectual gifts." A devout churchgoer, she did volunteer work for the poor. "There never was a woman of purer and kinder heart," said one friend. After the birth of the couple's fifth child, Hannah became seriously ill. She died in February 1819 of tuberculosis of the lungs. She was thirty-five years old.

The thirty-six-year-old Martin Van Buren would never remarry. Instead he became married to politics. In 1821, he went to the US Senate, where he quickly emerged as a leader. He was a strong speaker. He spoke so fast that congressional shorthand writers were hard put to keep up in their efforts to make an accurate record of the dialogue.

After his wife's death, Van Buren was rarely linked romantically with any other women. One exception occurred soon after he joined the Senate. The widower attracted the attention of Ellen Randolph, the young granddaughter of Thomas Jefferson. At that time, Van Buren's hair was more blond than red. Miss Randolph shocked guests at a Washington party by asking the Marine band to play a song called "Yellow Haired Lad." Van Buren referred to Ellen as a warm friend, but nothing ever came of the friendship.

Van Buren's mind was focused on the US Senate, where other new members included Andrew Jackson, the military hero from Tennessee. At first Van Buren was wary of the volatile Jackson, who in 1824 was one of several men who mounted presidential campaigns to succeed James Monroe after he had served two terms. Van Buren decided to hitch his wagon to the more stable William Crawford, Monroe's treasury secretary. House Speaker Henry Clay and Secretary of State John Quincy Adams also were in the race.

Jackson won the popular vote but his electoral votes fell short of the majority needed to win. The election was thrown into the House of Representatives, where lawmakers would choose among the top three vote getters: Jackson, Adams, and Crawford. As the odd man out, Speaker Clay threw his support to Adams, who won the White House. Not long afterward, Adams named Clay to be secretary of state, a post widely seen as a stepping-stone to the presidency. Jackson was furious about what he called the Corrupt Bargain, and he never forgave Clay.

As the easygoing Van Buren got to know the hot-tempered Jackson, the two struck up an odd-couple relationship. "Van Buren is as opposite to General Jackson as dung is to a diamond," said Davy Crockett. But the two men had common interests. Both men enjoyed betting on horse races. Jackson also admired the Little Magician's skills in bringing discipline to party politics. Together, they formed the Democratic Party.

Van Buren helped run Jackson's successful 1828 presidential campaign against Adams. To help Old Hickory win in New York, the Little Magician also ran for governor of the state. By then, the eye for fashion that Van Buren had learned as a boy was on wide display. He showed up at a church in Rochester festooned in an elegant cutaway coat with a velvet collar, an orange cravat, a pearl-hue vest, and trousers of a white-duck color with matching hose. His shoes were of Moroccan leather. He topped off the ensemble with a beaver-fur hat with a broad brim.

Van Buren easily won election as governor, but he had served only seventy-one days when President Jackson summoned him to be secretary of state. During his tenure, Van Buren became entangled in a controversy involving not a foreign affair but the Eaton affair of 1831.

Jackson's secretary of war, John Eaton, had just married a pretty young woman named Peggy O'Neal, who had worked as a waitress at a Washington tavern connected to the boarding-house where Eaton had lived. Peggy had a reputation as a loose woman; indeed, it was rumored that her sailor husband had committed suicide after discovering that she was having an affair with Eaton.

The wives of other cabinet members, led by Floride Bonneau Calhoun, the wife of Vice President John C. Calhoun of South Carolina, snubbed Peggy. The snubs outraged President Jackson, whose wife, Rachel, had died just before he took office. He took the side of Mrs. Eaton. So did Van Buren, who personally called on Peggy to offer his support. In the end, at the suggestion of Van Buren, Jackson fired most of his cabinet and sent his friend Secretary Eaton with Mrs. Eaton to Spain as the US ambassador.

Van Buren's involvement with Peggy Eaton was innocent and seemed to be aimed at scoring points with Jackson. When Mrs. Eaton thanked Van Buren for his sympathy, he asked her not to tell President Jackson, knowing full well that she would. Some saw Van Buren's role in the affair as a turning point in his ultimate climb to the presidency. Historian James Parton would later write, "The political history of the last 30 years dates from the moment when the soft hand of Mr. Van Buren touched Mrs. Eaton's knocker."

In the meantime, Van Buren used his clout with Jackson to wangle appointment as the US ambassador to Great Britain. In

London he became good friends with the head of the US delegation, author Washington Irving. Like Van Buren, Irving hailed from New York's Hudson Valley, the locale for his famed stories of "Rip Van Winkle" and "The Legend of Sleepy Hollow."

Van Buren's post in England came to a jarring halt in early 1832 when his old nemesis Vice President Calhoun blocked the official confirmation of his appointment. But Van Buren got the last laugh. First, he returned to Washington with trunk loads of fine British clothing and a fancy British carriage. Then Jackson replaced Calhoun with Van Buren as his running mate in the 1832 election. When Old Hickory swept to victory for a second term, Van Buren became vice president. In 1836, as Jackson's hand-picked successor, Van Buren won the presidency. He was the first president who had been born a US citizen.

But President Van Buren had a short honeymoon. Just after he took office, the nation's economy was hit by the Panic of 1837. It was the biggest economic crash since the birth of the Republic. It would be the most severe downturn until the Great Depression began in 1929.

Some seeds of the 1837 economic collapse were planted when President Jackson had abruptly ordered all federal funds withdrawn from the privately owned Bank of the United States and deposited into state banks, which became known as "pet banks." To cool a real estate bubble in land sales in the West, Jackson required federal land to be purchased only with hard money—gold and silver. He also restricted the use of credit and the paper money issued by banks. (The United States didn't print paper money yet.)

Any kind of money was hard to come by after an economic crash hit England, and the ripples flowed to America in 1837. Britain cut back on its large investments in the United States and curtailed its major purchases of American cotton. US banks began falling like tenpins. Of the nation's 850 banks, 343 went bust in 1837. Unemployment soared. Food riots broke out in New York City.

For those who still had jobs, wages fell by 40 percent or more. Bricklayers who had made $2.00 a day in 1836, now were lucky to earn $1.25 a day. Common laborers saw their pay drop from a dollar a day to sixty-eight cents. In Georgia, young single women complained that monetary awards in breach of promise lawsuits against ex-suitors had dropped in half.

In Ohio, personal economic concerns led Democratic legislator John Brough (pronounced "Bruff") to change his vote on a bill because "I have my bread and butter to look after." It was the start of the phrase "bread-and-butter issue."

President Van Buren couldn't blame his predecessor for economic problems because he himself had been a key part of the Jackson administration. As a small-government Democrat, Van Buren opposed a big federal spending stimulus package. So he did nothing. Van Buren scolded those who were "prone to expect too much from the government." Though jobs were all but impossible to get, the president further alienated voters by declaring, "Damn the panic. If you would all work as I do, you would have no panic."

In response, the Whigs mocked Van Buren by dredging up one of his old letters from when he was in the state legislature in which he had said, with garbled grammar, "Our sufferings is intolerable."

One of Van Buren's solutions was proposed legislation to put all of the government's gold and silver in a new independent treasury. The treasury would collect and pay out public money in hard money. No paper money would be used in government transactions. The public money would be kept in sub-treasuries placed around the country, so it was called the Sub-treasury Bill.

The Whigs assailed the plan as a government scheme to help the rich at the expense of the middle class and the poor. They wanted to restore a National Bank for storing government money and to promote the use of paper bank notes and credit for those who had a hard time getting their hands on gold and silver. The goal of Van Buren's darling plan, the pro-Whig newspaper the *Campaign* said, was "to give him and all his office-holders gold for their salaries and to give the people rags for their labor."

The Whigs adopted a new economic slogan, promising voters higher pay in their pockets and better food on their tables:

"Matty's policy, fifty cents a day and French soup; our policy, two dollars a day and roast beef." In an ominous sign for Democrats, the president took on another nickname: Martin Van Ruin.

The economy wasn't the only cutting issue. Despite the Democrats' small-government philosophy, Presidents Jackson and Van Buren added twenty thousand federal workers by giving jobs to their supporters. It was the spoils system, as in "to the victor belongs the spoils." Many appointees turned out to be corrupt. The Whigs became the first party to run against Washington and its "office holders."

The Whigs referred to the Democrats as the Loco Focos. The name grew out of a dispute between two factions of the Democratic Party at a meeting in New York City. When protesters marched out, they turned off the gaslights to leave their opponents in the dark. But officials continued the meeting by the light of Loco Foco matches, a popular brand at the time. Whigs mainly liked the idea of labeling their opponents as loco.

As the campaign heated up, critics painted Van Buren not as a political genius but as a political hack. Opponents called him a weasel, a crawling reptile, and a political schemer. Van Buren, said an acquaintance of seventeen years, was "heartless, hypocritical, selfish and unprincipled." Former president John Quincy Adams speculated that Van Buren might be the bastard son of his one-time mentor, Aaron Burr.

Even his upstate New York friend Washington Irving deserted Van Buren. When the president refused Irving's request to appoint his brother Ebenezer to a federal post, the author accused Van Buren of "heartlessness in friendship and low mindedness in politics." He publicly backed Harrison in the 1840 campaign.

The numerous nasty rebukes shook the laid-back Van Buren. "Why the deuce is it that they have such an itch for abusing me?" he asked. "I tried to be harmless and perfectly good natured."

The taunts would soon get even worse.

7

PALACE OF SPLENDOR

[Why should the American people] support their chief servant in a PALACE *as splendid as those of the Caesars?*

—Whig congressman Charles Ogle of Pennsylvania

President Martin Van Buren's supporters admired him for his courteous manner and fashionable dress. Critics, however, ridiculed the president as an effeminate dandy. To fit into his finery, Van Buren "is laced up in corsets, such as women in a town wear and, if possible, tighter than the best of them," Congressman Davy Crockett had written. "It would be difficult to say, from his personal appearance, whether he was a man or woman, but for his large and red and gray whiskers."

The Whigs claimed that Van Buren doused his sideburns with expensive imported French cologne. They called him Sweet Sandy Whiskers and said he was no friend of the common man.

The man of modest origins had indeed come to enjoy the finer things of life. A uniformed British coachman drove the president around Washington in a fancy, olive-green carriage, the one that Van Buren had purchased while he was in England. Two majestic, golden-colored horses pulled the coach, which sported shiny gold-colored ornaments, satin cushions, and silver buckles. On Sundays, Van Buren sometimes even rode the carriage to the Episcopal church—just three hundred yards away from the White House across Pennsylvania Avenue in Lafayette Square.

DEMOCRATIC SIMPLICITY.
Or the Arrival of our Favourite Son.

Martin Van Buren's carriage. *Library of Congress*

While the economy suffered, the president continued to give lavish parties at the White House, some for as many as five thousand guests. Said one critic, "The Nero of the White House is feasting and dancing, while the American Rome is burning."

Since Van Buren had no wife, he sometimes enlisted former First Lady Dolley Madison for hostess duties. Then a widow in her early 70s, she was still vivacious and good looking. To display bipartisanship, Van Buren made it a point to invite members of the opposition party, including Henry Clay and former president John Quincy Adams, to his gatherings.

The president and Clay remained friendly rivals. One day a fire broke out in the White House laundry, and fire wagons rushed to the executive mansion. Clay, who happened to be walking nearby, dashed in to see what was going on. Van Buren greeted Clay and assured him that some minor flames had been doused. Putting his hand on Van Buren's shoulder, Clay joked, "We want you out of the White House, Mr. Van Buren, but we don't want you burnt out."

Dinner parties were the most prestigious White House events. Guests gathered in the parlor, which was surrounded by big folding doors. At the appointed moment, servants opened the doors to reveal a long dining table loaded with fish, overdone beef, mutton, or chicken and what one journalist described as "a watery compound called vegetable soup"—all served on fine china. Guests drank champagne and French claret from tall, slender glasses. Puddings, pies, cakes, and ice cream were brought out for dessert, along with Madeira wine. The finest Madeira was called "the Supreme Court," because it was the brand that the justices imported every year to sip as they studied legal cases in the evenings.

At less formal dinner parties, light refreshments such as lemonade were served before the meal. After dinner, the carpet was taken up for dancing to a live band. The floors were chalked to keep the dancers from slipping. President Van Buren himself was known to dance a mean waltz. Later, the ladies and the younger men departed; the older gentlemen stayed to discuss politics with the president over more Madeira. The candles in the windows sometimes burned as late as 2:00 AM.

A few guests to the presidential table were not all that welcome. Some prominent people threatened not to vote for Van Buren unless he invited them to dine at the White House, according to French diplomat Chevalier de Bacourt. Others, after gaining a place at the table, complained the food was bad and sent it back. At least that is what the White House chef told Bacourt's servant, who noted, "It seems that it is not very pleasant to be President!"

Van Buren made improvements to the president's mansion, which was still undergoing repair after the British Navy torched the place in 1814 during the War of 1812. He installed the first central heating system in the White House. The system relied on gravity to send rising heat through the house via ducts from a huge boiler in a basement corridor. Van Buren set aside one basement room (later the China Room) for a live-in fireman, who ran the furnace.

Then Little Matty made the political mistake of seeking appropriations from Congress for further fix-ups.

On the morning of April 14, 1840, Whig congressman Charles Ogle of Pennsylvania took to the House floor to attack an administration request for $3,665 for "alteration and repairs of the President's House." Over three days the tall, dark-haired, forty-two-year-old lawmaker accused Van Buren of turning the White House into a "presidential palace" where he lived like a king.

Ogle proceeded to remark sarcastically on the rooms of this Versailles on the Potomac, questioning spending as he went. He began with the East Room, a stateroom used for presidential receptions. Shortly after taking office in 1829, President Jackson had completely refurbished the room, which is eighty feet long, thirty-seven feet wide, and twenty-two feet high. Wallpaper of a fine lemon color with a rich cloth border adorned the walls. The floor was covered with five hundred yards of a blue and yellow Brussels carpet with a red border. Four new mantels made of brick marble with Italian black and gold fronts were installed. So were three splendid chandeliers, each with eighteen candles.

To help keep the room tidy, spittoons were strategically placed along the east and west walls. Some 150 gilded stars were pasted over the room's arched door. In all, Ogle said, the room was decked out with a "regal splendor" far above any of the grand saloons of England's Buckingham Palace or Windsor Castle.

Yet, in 1839 President Van Buren decided that the lemon color wallpaper was so 1820s and no longer fashionable in high society, Ogle claimed. So he ordered the paper taken down and new wallpaper put up. To document his claim, Ogle leaked a federal document, a bill of sixteen dollars from Henry Snowden to strip the old paper from the walls.

Ogle then cited more bills from S. P. Franklin for the purchase of sixty pieces of new wallpaper at five dollars each, plus thirty dollars to put the paper on the walls. Thus, declared Ogle, not less than $346 of taxpayer money was spent "for the gratification of a womanish but costly whim" by Van Buren to replace the unfashionable lemon with what the president's decorators called a chaste and beautiful silver paper.

The Whig lawmaker then moved on to the mansion's Blue Elliptical Saloon, with its stunning view of the South Lawn. This oval room was filled with fine French furniture and costly gilded ornaments. The expensive French carpet featured the image of a large-as-life bald eagle with a scroll in its beak.

Dolley Madison previously had decorated the room in crimson. President Jackson added a green touch. Not content, Ogle declared, Van Buren had redecorated the room in blue. He spent $1,805.55 for three window curtains, fourteen chairs, and two sofas with silk-covered pillows. This cost, Ogle noted, was enough to build three log cabins. In all, the president spent on the blue room "the sum of $3,805.55 of the PEOPLE'S CASH, SIR, NOT OF HIS OWN." (In his written speech, Ogle capitalized some points for emphasis.)

Despite Ogle's ridicule, it turned out that Van Buren's blue period resulted in his most enduring legacy. This was the beginning of the Blue Room, widely admired as perhaps the most beautiful room in the White House.

Ogle next moved on to the presidential bedroom, where he expressed contempt for the French bedsteads installed there, along with marble-top washstands and dressers, at a total cost of $1,599.50. Ogle's main complaint was that the items were not made in America. "I protest against spending the money of my constituents for Elegant FRENCH BEDSTEADS made in France instead of American wood," he said.

Next he took listeners to the Court Banqueting Room on the first floor. He pointed out a massive gold-plated and sterling silver French serving set that included gilded spoons. "Oh, how delightful it must be," he marveled, for a visitor to eat his foi gras "from a SILVER PLATE with a GOLDEN KNIFE AND FORK. And how exquisite to sip with a GOLDEN SPOON his soupe a la Reine from a SILVER TUREEN. It almost makes my mouth water to talk about it."

Ogle reserved special scorn for the green finger cups acquired for formal presidential meals. Van Buren used these, he said, "to wash his pretty, tapering, soft, white lily fingers after dining on omelets soufflé."

Van Buren's grandiose tastes even extended to the grounds and gardens surrounding the President's House, Ogle said. Here the landscaping apparently was redone in what one might call Dolly Parton style. Level greenery was replaced by beautiful mounds, "every pair of which, it is said, was designed to resemble and assume the form of AN AMAZON'S BOSOM, with a miniature knoll on its apex to denote the nipple."

About the only thing missing, Ogle said, was a colossal bronze equestrian statue of President Jackson "with the little Kinderhook magician mounted on beside him." (In 1853 Andrew Jackson would be memorialized with a statue in Lafayette Square across the street from the White House, mounted on a rearing horse but without Van Buren at his side.)

The Ogle speech sent the Democrats into a frenzy. Van Buren was in such a rage, said George Prentice of the pro-Whig *Louisville Journal*, "that he actually burst his corset."

In fact, most of the charges were false. Even fellow Whig congressman Levi Lincoln Jr. of Massachusetts, chairman of the Public Buildings Committee, took to the House floor to challenge Ogle's claims. President Van Buren, Lincoln noted, had actually spent less per year on the White House than his predecessors.

The administration newspaper, the *Washington Globe*, assailed the Ogle speech as an "omnibus of lies." The solicitor of the US Treasury chimed in that there was "not the least foundation to the charge" that Van Buren had purchased gold spoons used in the White House. Any gilded spoons still in use there had been brought to the mansion by President James Monroe twenty years earlier. Monroe, a former US ambassador to France, had used many of his own French belongings to furnish the White House after it was burned.

The Whigs were undeterred. The Harrison campaign later distributed tens of thousands of copies of Ogle's "Gold Spoons" speech throughout the land (with the reference to Amazon's bosom censored out). New York Whig party boss Thurlow

Weed declared that it was no wonder that Van Buren sneered at Harrison's log cabin. "The man who walks upon Royal Wilton Carpets which cost $4 per yard, reclines upon Ottomans which cost $250, indulges his feet with rugs which cost $30, touches 'Bell Pulls' which cost $107, and enjoys the fragrance of 'Roses' at an expense of $72, must hold the occupants of Log-Cabins in supreme contempt!"

Winning voters, not devotion to facts, was the political goal. The Whig images for the campaign were now set: Harrison sipped hard cider in a humble log cabin; Van Buren drank champagne in his presidential palace.

With the Whig themes intact, the two campaigns headed for an early-May face-off in Baltimore, where both parties planned dueling conventions in the same city at the same time.

8

SHOWDOWN IN BALTIMORE

In no country, in no time, never before in the history of man, was there a spectacle so full of natural glory.

—*Baltimore Patriot* newspaper

Whigs by the thousands rolled into Baltimore, Maryland, on the first weekend of May 1840. One Whig leader called it an avalanche of people. Their destination: The Whig Young Men's Convention, called to ratify the nominations of William Henry Harrison and John Tyler.

On the train, some of the Whigs showed off handkerchiefs imprinted with the face of Harrison and the inscription THE HERO OF TIPPECANOE. Upon arriving in Baltimore, the Whigs quickly headed to the local saloons for a boisterous night of socializing, singing, and guzzling hard cider.

Also arriving this weekend were several hundred sober-sided men going to the Democratic Presidential Convention to nominate Martin Van Buren for a second term. Some of these men also displayed handkerchiefs with references to Harrison. Except theirs said THE COWARD OF TIPPECANOE. Most of the Democratic visitors went straight to local hotels and boardinghouses for a quiet night's sleep before preparing for the nominating convention. Van Buren would be the only candidate considered. The president, of course, would not be attending.

Baltimore had become the go-to city for US presidential nominating conventions. The Democratic gathering was the fifth since the first convention there in 1832. One reason was that the Monument City was only an hour's train ride from the nation's capital in Washington, DC. With a population of 102,000 people, it also was the country's second largest city, behind New York, with a population of 312,000 souls.

The population swelled by tens of thousands of people of all ages for the Whig Young Men's Convention. The gathering had no real official authority. It had been scheduled by the Whigs' Harrisburg convention simply to promote an enthusiastic counter to the planned Democratic meeting in Baltimore. "The steam must be kept up," said New York congressman Millard Fillmore.

At dawn on Monday, May 4, cannons fired to awaken the city for the day's festivities. Nearly twenty-five thousand Whig delegates began taking their places for the Grand National Procession through downtown Baltimore in a two-mile march to the former Canton Race Track, where the outdoor convention was to take place. Some hundred marshals, wearing black silk hats, dress coats, and white pants, were assigned to help keep order along the way.

The procession got going at 9:30 AM. Leading the way were nine open carriages, each pulled by four gray horses and carrying dignitaries such as Massachusetts senator Daniel Webster. A marching band played a popular campaign song; some of the song's words were printed on a huge, white banner in a frame:

> The people are coming from plain and from mountain,
> To join the brave band of the honest and free,
> Which grows as the stream from the leaf-sheltered fountain,
> Spreads broad and more broad till it reaches the sea;
> No strength can restrain it, no force can retain it,
> Whate'er may resist, it breaks gallantly through,
> And borne by its motion as a ship on the ocean
> Speeds on its glory, Old Tippecanoe!
> The iron arm'd soldier, the true hearted soldier
> Old Tippecanoe!

Up to seventy-five thousand cheering people lined the sidewalks along Baltimore Street, which was wide enough for six to ten delegates to march abreast. Some state delegations exceeded a thousand men. On each side of the street, men, women, and children waved from the windows and roofs of buildings. The Whigs' political pep rally was underway.

As in the rally in Columbus, Ohio, many of the state delegates rode in log cabins on wheels. Six gray horses pulled a large cabin from Frederick County, Maryland; up top, a live eagle perched on the branch of a tree. The biggest cabin, from Washington County, Maryland, rolled on six wheels and was drawn by eight horses, each wearing a set of jingling bells. The cabin was big enough to hold forty delegates. Another man sat outside in the back on a barrel of hard cider. On top, a live opossum clung to the branch of a gum tree. Smoke rising from the chimney suggested that perhaps a squirrel was roasting inside.

Several delegates from Allegany County, Maryland, kept the ball rolling. This time it was a twelve-foot-high red-and-white-striped ball with a blue background. The ball was covered by dozens of snappy inscriptions, including "With heart and soul, this ball we roll," "Farewell Dear Van, You're not our Man," and "To guide the ship, we'll try Old Tip."

The Baltimore parade featured the widespread waving of banners, more than a thousand of them by one count. Some were huge. It took six men from the town of Laurel in Prince George's County, Maryland, to carry one banner made with forty yards of silk atop a long pole with a feather at the end. One side of the banner showed a drawing of the Laurel Factory and adjacent buildings with the motto PROTECT AMERICAN INDUSTRY. The other side showed an industrious factory worker being ignored by an indifferent President Van Buren.

Another anti–Van Buren banner, from Bunker Hill, Massachusetts, took up the theme of the Red Fox's supposed gold dinnerware. One side showed a golden goblet overflowing with gold pieces; the other side read, THE GOLDEN HUMBUG. A banner from Cumberland County, Maryland, read, OLD MOTHER CUMBERLAND. SHE'LL BAG THE FOX.

A poster supporting Harrison. *Indiana Historical Society (0130): Bass Photo Co. Collection, Indiana Historical Society*

Other signs celebrated Harrison as a hero. The crowd cheered a banner reading, BUFF AND BLUE, GOOD AND TRUE, FOR TIPPECANOE. One from Bucks County, Pennsylvania, read simply, HUZZAH FOR OLD TIP. Only a few banners displayed mottos on issues; Delaware County, Pennsylvania, proclaimed, TIPPECANOE: NO REDUCTION IN WAGES. A handful of others declared, HARRISON AND REFORM.

The procession stretched for more than two miles as Baltimore Street became a moving mass of humanity. The parade was so long that it took an hour and a half to pass a single location.

It was "really a great and inspiring sight, with its lines of marching men, its log cabins drawn by many horses, its banners predicting the fall of Little Van and the rise of the Log Cabin candidate," marveled one eyewitness, John Parsons, who was passing through town from Virginia on his way to Indiana. "I had not guessed that so much enthusiasm could have been aroused over a comparatively unknown candidate, a backwoodsman, as we of the East are accustomed to speak of him."

The shouts and cheers grew even louder as the procession passed within a block of the Hall of the Music Association, where Democrats were quietly setting up for their convention the next day. A jeer went up as the marchers passed by the hall.

As the procession streamed down Baltimore Street near Howard Street, emotions were running high among supporters of both parties. Suddenly, a gang of young men broke into the parade line. They might have been protesting a particularly gruesome Whig banner showing Van Buren's head being squeezed so tightly in a screw vise that blood was gushing from his eyes, nose, and ears. One of the interlopers carried a long pole, atop which was a stuffed effigy of Harrison dressed as a petticoat general.

A scuffle broke out as Whigs tried to grab the pole. A young marshal, Thomas H. Laughlin, moved to intervene. One of the intruders hit Laughlin over the head with the pole, knocking the marshal to the ground. He didn't move. He was dead. The assailants disappeared into the crowd as spectators stood by in shock. After police arrived on the scene, the procession moved on.

By noon, the parade reached the abandoned Canton Race Track, now a large and open grassy field. Marchers entered under a high arch decorated with flowers. To the right of the entrance stood a hastily constructed log cabin with a stick chimney and a door with the latch opened. Across the lawn was a small fortress modeled after Fort Meigs, with its cannons firing to greet the visitors. A large platform had been constructed for speakers.

The thousands of participants quickly supported the nominations of Harrison and Tyler for president and vice president. Then they settled in to listen to rousing speeches by a half dozen speakers, including Senators Henry Clay and Daniel Webster. Invoking the Whigs' campaign theme, Webster declared, "We have fallen upon hard times, and the remedy seems to be hard cider."

At nightfall, the convention adjourned. But the Whigs weren't done. The next morning they reassembled downtown in Monument Square in front of the five-story Barnum's Hotel. Thousands of people filled the square to listen to still more speeches.

Many of the morning's speakers focused on Thomas Laughlin, the marshal who had died in the parade the day before. Laughlin, who also was a delegate, was a young Baltimore carpenter who left a wife and four young children. The Whigs called for the arrest and prosecution of his killers. Baltimore's mayor offered a $1,000 reward for capture of the assailants.

Some Democratic newspapers, however, cast the event in a different light. The *Ohio Statesman* reported that one of the Whig delegates "fell dead in the street" in a scuffle with some rude boys. "The man, it is said, was subject to fits, and in his rage fell on the pavement and did not recover." The *Washington Globe* noted that "the heartless throng" of Whigs barely waited to see what had happened before marching on.

In Monument Square, the assembled Whigs approved a resolution to raise money for Laughlin's family and asked for donations. Then they adjourned until five o'clock so that all could attend Laughlin's funeral that afternoon. After the gathering resumed at Monument Square, it was announced that an astounding $10,000 had been raised for the Laughlin family. This was equivalent to more than $200,000 in twenty-first-century cash. Police later arrested a man for the killing, but a jury acquitted him.

The speeches went on until eleven o'clock. The Whigs finally headed home with their determination further fueled by the killing of a fellow Harrison supporter. For Whig leaders, the rousing

Baltimore rally was a sure sign that the campaign was resonating among the people.

Meantime, only a few blocks away from the boisterous Whig triumph in Monument Square, the Democratic Convention had quietly begun.

9

A DEMOCRATIC SPLINTER

I have not solicited a re-nomination, nor shall I decline it.

—Democratic vice president Richard Mentor Johnson

The roars of Whigs in Baltimore's Monument Square could be heard inside the nearby Music Hall as Democrats opened their presidential nominating convention at noon on Tuesday, May 6, 1840. But the noise only underscored the determination of Democratic Party leaders to show that their gathering was nothing like the unseemly circus show down the street.

"We wish no deceptive parade of log cabins and empty cider barrels," said sixty-two-year-old Tennessee senator Felix Grundy, the keynote speaker. "We desire to address ourselves to the intelligence of the people."

With the nomination of President Van Buren a foregone conclusion, the 248 delegates from twenty-one of the twenty-six states were restrained, in sharp contrast to the Whigs' enthusiasm. The president, of course, remained in Washington. His son John attended as an unofficial observer and was alarmed by the widespread apathy about the event. What was lacking, he lamented, was "a universal sense of the necessity of action and organization."

The Democrats filled the void by attacking William Henry Harrison and the Whig campaign tactics. Senator Grundy painted General Harrison as a pale imitation of General Andrew Jackson, who rose to the presidency as a military hero from the War of 1812. Grundy asserted that Harrison's log cabin image was all smoke and mirrors. The Whigs "have a candidate whom they want to make president, and of whom four years ago very little was heard; but within the last few months no mortal man has ever grown so vastly as he," Grundy declared. "From a plain honest clerk of a county court . . . he has grown to be an astonishingly great man." Yet nobody could find out what his opinions were on any subject.

Newspaperman Sam Medary, wearing his hat as head of the Ohio delegation as well as that of editor of the *Ohio Statesman*, agreed. His paper had reported that the Whig gathering in Baltimore was made up of geezers wearing glasses and "young dandies in hunting shirts, made by their mothers for the occasion. The ridiculous parade of log cabins and hard cider through the streets here produced nothing but disgust."

Grundy stated that he had gone into the streets to view the Whig spectacle first hand and found it nothing more than a parade of empty promises. "The remark of a rough-looking laboring man, who passed by where I stood looking at the show, forcibly struck me," Grundy said. "This is all a cheat. I struck my hand upon the head of one of the cider barrels, it sounded entirely hollow, and I am sure there was no cider in it."

Democrats zeroed in on a Whig banner that read, We Stoop to Conquer. The message reflected the goal of Whig leaders to take the campaign down to the people. Democrats portrayed it as the condescending view of rich Whig bankers who had never seen the inside of a log cabin. Denouncing the Whig "animal show" in Baltimore, Ohio congressman Alexander Duncan chided, "Now if we deducted all bank presidents, bank lounging loafers and all the idle dogs that paraded the street on this occasion, how many log cabin men would there be left?"

The next day, a Wednesday, the Democrats got down to business. They noted that the Whigs at their Harrisburg convention had failed to adopt a party platform. So the Democratic convention pointedly approved a nine-point platform stating the party's principles. In summary, they were:

1. The Federal Government has limited powers. These are derived solely from the Constitution, and it is dangerous to exercise doubtful constitutional powers.
2. The Constitution doesn't give the federal government the power to initiate and carry on internal improvements across the states.
3. The Constitution doesn't give the federal government authority to assume the debts of states resulting from making local internal improvements or other purposes.
4. The federal government can't promote one branch of industry or one part of the country to the detriment of another. Every citizen and every section of the country has an equality of rights and privileges.
5. The federal government should raise no more money than is required to defray the necessary expenses of government.
6. Congress has no power to charter a National Bank, which would be deadly hostile to the best interests of the country, dangerous to our Republican institutions and to the liberties of the people, and calculated to place businesses under the control of a concentrated money power.
7. Congress has no power under the Constitution to interfere with state institutions, such as slavery. The efforts of abolitionists or others to induce Congress to interfere with slavery would lead to alarming and dangerous consequences that would diminish the happiness of the people and endanger the stability of the nation.
8. Government money should be kept separate from banking institutions to ensure the safety of government funds.
9. The principles embodied by Thomas Jefferson in the Declaration of Independence and sanctioned in the US Constitution are the cardinal principles of the Democratic Party. Every attempt to abridge those rights is to be strongly resisted.

Cheering delegates unanimously passed each resolution. Then New Hampshire governor Isaac Hill took the floor for what amounted to a nomination speech for President Van Buren. Hill's long talk was a snoozer, filled with overwrought rhetoric. In one single, disjointed sentence, he declared, "The firmness of Mr. Van Buren, and the calm, temperate wisdom of his measures, have thus far overcome every obstacle, and triumphed over all the efforts of an opposition, more active, more inveterate, more powerful, and more unscrupulous as to means and ends, than any preceding Democratic Administration ever had to encounter."

Without casting a ballot, the convention by voice vote unanimously approved Van Buren's nomination as their presidential candidate. But then the love fest hit a serious snag.

The delegates' first and only disagreement, surprisingly, was over whether to nominate Vice President Richard Mentor Johnson for a second term. To some, this would seem to be a no-brainer. After all, Old Dick was the poster boy for the War of 1812. And Democrats considered the fifty-nine-year-old Johnson, not Harrison, to be the Hero of the Thames, since he was thought to have killed Chief Tecumseh at the Battle of the Thames River.

Johnson, however, had become a controversial figure, especially in the South. After the war, he openly lived on his Kentucky plantation with a family slave, Julia Chinn, as his common-law wife. Julia ran the family operation when Johnson was away. They had two daughters, Adeline and Imogene, who took Johnson's last name. Julia Chinn died of cholera in 1833. Johnson, then a congressman from Kentucky, created a stir when he sought to introduce his young daughters into Washington society.

Van Buren had made Johnson his running mate in 1836 on the recommendation of President Jackson. After Van Buren won, the controversy about Johnson's domestic life nearly cost Old Dick the vice presidency. He failed to win enough electoral votes, but the Senate approved him—barely—for the veep post, marking the only time in US history that the vice presidency was decided by Congress.

Then after the economic panic began, Johnson took a nine-month leave of absence. A vice president didn't have much to do, so he was hardly missed. And Johnson had to deal with financial problems at his Blue Spring Farm plantation. To bring in money, he opened a tavern and a spa there. Postmaster General Amos Kendall was sent to check up on the vice president in August 1839.

While there he received a letter from a local Kentuckian who reported that Johnson was a happy tavern keeper, giving personal attention to chicken and egg purchasing and watermelon selling. But, the letter writer added, the vice president "openly and shamefully lives in adultery with a buxom young negro" woman named Parthene. The slave was "a young Delilah of about the complexion of Shakespears [sic] swarthy Othello," said to be eighteen or nineteen years old and "quite handsome." Kendall included the letter in his report to President Van Buren.

Southerners called for Johnson to be dropped from the 1840 race. Even former president Jackson conceded that the old hero would have to go. In a letter to Van Buren, the spelling-challenged Jackson wrote that Johnson would be "a dead wait [sic] upon your popularity." But Van Buren was reluctant to abandon his vice president.

The Whigs reveled in the Democrats' dilemma. New York congressman Francis Granger wrote Thurlow Weed that the Democrats "ache to drop 'Old Dick,' but in my opinion, dare not." He was partly right.

The convention decided simply not to nominate anyone for the number two spot. Nobody at the convention publicly stated why Johnson was being snubbed. Delegates voted to let states choose from four regional candidates, including Johnson. The others were James Polk of Tennessee, Littleton Tazewell of Virginia, and Thomas Earle of Pennsylvania. It was the first and only time since conventions began that a major political party didn't nominate a vice presidential candidate.

As the convention ended, Democrats sought to paper over their veep split by contrasting the proceedings of the two parties in Baltimore. One party kept the city in a whirl with its marching, banners, cider barrels, and rolling balls. The other "made no inflammatory appeals, held no parade of unmeaning contrivances, resorted to no clatter of barrels and tin cups." The Democrats expressed confidence that the people would go with reason over revelry.

For their part, the Whigs scorned the Democratic gathering as the Office Holders' Convention. They turned to song to ridicule the dance over choosing Van Buren's running mate:

> *Pretty little Martin, tiptoe, tiptoe,*
> *Pretty little Martin, tiptoe fine,*
> *Couldn't get a candidate for Vice-President,*
> *Couldn't get a candidate to please his mind.*
> *Old Dick Johnson he wouldn't answer,*
> *He was too rough for a President so fine;*
> *Pretty little Martin tiptoe, tiptoe,*
> *Couldn't get a candidate to please his mind.*

After their own success in Baltimore, the Whigs were ready to take the Tippecanoe and Tyler Too circus nationwide.

10

TIPPECANOE AND RALLIES TOO

The prairies are on fire.

—Multiple Whig newspapers

Log Cabin fever spread across the nation. In city after city, town after town, crowds flocked to Whig presidential rallies in huge numbers as never before.

If one could imagine a whole nation declaring a holiday lasting several months in "the wildest freaks of fun and frolic, caring nothing for business, singing, dancing, and carousing night and day," said journalist Nathan Sargent, then "he might have some faint notion of the extraordinary scenes of 1840."

More than sixty thousand people jammed into Boston for a five-mile parade from Boston Commons to Bunker Hill. The parade was so long that when the head of the column reached the hill, the rear had not yet begun to move. More than twenty-five hundred horsemen led the parade; one of them carried a big painting of General Harrison on horseback leading his army. Some forty carriages carried surviving soldiers from the Revolutionary War and other battles. The Ohio delegation marched with a sign that read, THE NATION WILL REST IN PEACE UNDER THE SHADE OF HER BUCKEYE. The *Bay State Democrat* reported that "song singing, huzzahing, drinking and carousing appeared to be the order of the night."

Rallies were just as lively in small towns. More than six thousand people turned out in Sharpsburg, Maryland, rallying under such mottos as "Martin Van Buren, you won't do. The people's choice is Tippecanoe." In the Sharpsburg town square sat a full-size log cabin with a chained live bear on the roof. In Erie at the northeastern tip of Pennsylvania, a parade marshal noted that the far end of the parade line was forming in New York State. One flag in the parade used creative spelling for the sake of rhyme: WITH TIP AND TYLER, WE'LL BURST VAN'S BILER.

A mile-long parade in Auburn, New York, featured a 551-pound loaf of bread measuring seven feet long and two and a half feet wide. In Utica, New York, a Harrison parade that stretched over nine miles was led by 110 horsemen dressed as farmers, each wearing a hunting shirt and a red sash around his middle. They were followed by 417 double wagons drawn by horses or oxen.

Thousands poured into the streets in Philadelphia to hear speakers tout Old Tippecanoe and deplore the policies of Martin Van Ruin. One of the Whig speakers, Frederick William Thomas, was a friend of a young author named Edgar Allan Poe. The thirty-one-year-old Poe may even have been in the crowd that day. In any case, he was a Tippecanoe man. "I battled with right good will for Harrison when opportunity offered," he later wrote to Thomas. The only downer for the Whigs that day was that the Harrison ball, which had been rolled over from Baltimore, fell apart in the parade—much to the delight of Democrats in the crowd.

In late May more than thirty thousand people descended on the sixteen-acre Tippecanoe Battlefield in Indiana where Harrison had earned his nickname in 1811. Harrison himself was invited to attend the two-day affair, but he declined. To go would be improper, he said, because of his position as a presidential candidate.

People began arriving the day before, moving through nearby Lafayette, Indiana. They came by foot, by horseback, in carriages, inside log cabins on wheels, and by canoe. Five steamboats on the Wabash River overflowed with passengers coming to the event. By the day the celebration began, thirty-two hundred wagons were parked on forty acres near the battleground. Tents were pitched all around.

The procession to the battlefield from Lafayette began early on a Friday morning. Leading the way were survivors of Harrison's forces along with militiamen from across Indiana. Marching bands with fifes and drums added to the festive atmosphere. Near the battlefield, a tent three-fourths of a mile long was erected to hold thirty thousand people. With sunny skies, however, most gathered outside to listen to speakers, some of whom stood on the roofs of portable log cabins. Participants dined on free stew and bread and swigged hard cider. There was music and dancing. In the evening, fireworks lit up the sky.

At one point, a steamboat arrived at the river dock and unloaded still more barrels of hard cider, recalled a young man named George Washington Julian. He had ridden 150 miles on horseback through mud and swamps to attend the "monster meeting." In keeping with the backwoods theme of the Harrison campaign, drinks of the hard cider were handed out in gourds instead of glasses. "The people seemed to be supremely happy," said Julian, who later became an Indiana congressman.

These huge public rallies marked a major turning point in presidential campaigning. Previously, campaigns mostly had been conducted in small meetinghouses and via newspaper articles, with scant effort to reach the common man. The Whigs were out to court the masses. For their part, voters were frustrated and angered by the economic hard times. Many were ready to join in a call for change.

The campaign rallies also became a form of entertainment. Hardworking farmers and industrial workers enjoyed their limited leisure time. When the opportunity arose, they were eager to take in rousing political gatherings that were like three-ring circuses. "Nothing attracts a crowd so rapidly as the knowledge that there is a crowd already," noted New York's Whig governor, William Seward. "And when it was known that there was to be not only a crowd, but music, festivity, flags, decorations, and processions, eloquence of famous men, and keen political humor, few could resist the infection."

POLITICAL BARBECUE OF 1840.

Tippecanoe and Tyler Too rally. *Indiana Historical Society (0483): Bass Photo Co. Collection, Indiana Historical Society*

Whig organizers founded Tippecanoe Clubs in nearly every town, housing them in log cabins built by local men. The festive cabin raisings were complete with food, dancing, and songs. As one minstrel sang at a cabin raising in Easton, Maryland:

> *Come, all you Log Cabin Boys,*
> *We're going to have a raisin',*
> *We've got a job on hand,*
> *That we think will be pleasin'.*

Nearly ten thousand people turned out for a cabin raising in St. Louis, where laborers marched with a banner reading, WE WANT WORK. The cabin raised in Richmond, Virginia, was large enough to hold fifteen hundred people.

Democrats countered that the cabin raisings weren't the product of working men but rich Whigs posing as champions of the poor. In Cincinnati, a Democratic newspaper jeered a Whig log cabin raising by men wearing ruffled shirts and black gloves to protect their delicate fingers. The paper claimed that it took twenty-seven bankers to budge a log that six strapping Democratic workers could have moved with ease.

The Whigs referred to the cabins as reading rooms, where voters could meet to read educational pamphlets and discuss politics. Democrats dubbed them dens of drunkenness and debauchery, because the clubs served up free-flowing hard cider to daily crowds. The Tippecanoe Club on Broadway near Prince Street in New York City measured fifty feet wide and a hundred feet long, and boasted a thirty-foot bar with a spruce log for a foot rail and a hard cider barrel at one end. A New York preacher predicted that more than ten thousand men would be made drunkards within the year.

A mandatory feature of any Tippecanoe log cabin was the presence of "coons," as the raccoon was a symbol of the backwoods. Sometimes live raccoons scurried around in cages inside the cabins. In others, raccoon skins were nailed on outside walls. The latch of the cabin was always kept open, just as General Harrison had promised the latch at his home would always be open for his former troops.

It seemed the whole country was caught up in the frenzy. Schoolboys ran through the streets shouting "Huzzah for Harrison." Parents named their newborn babies Harrison, Tippecanoe, or even North Bend. Twin boys were named Harrison and Tyler. One couple named their newborn triplets William, Henry, and Harrison.

Farmers called their teams of two horses Tip and Ty. One farmer joked that when his hens laid eggs, they cackled, "Tip-tip! Tip-tip! Tyler." At an outdoor rally in Richmond, Virginia, a pickpocket being marched off to jail jumped on a box to deliver an impromptu speech for Tippecanoe and Tyler Too.

A popular participant in many parades was Big Jim Porter of Kentucky. Standing seven feet eight inches tall, he was advertised as the world's tallest man. He appeared dressed in a hunting shirt with bright colored fringes and a large coonskin hat. Over his shoulder he carried a rifle that was eight feet long. No matter how crowded the parade was, you couldn't miss Big Jim.

In Dresden, Ohio, just west of Columbus, Whigs manufactured their own Harrison ball to keep rolling. It was unveiled in the

July Fourth parade in nearby Zanesville. The ball had a diameter of thirteen feet, representing the original thirteen colonies. It revolved on an axle through the center and was supported by a black frame. To cut down the wear and tear, the ball was carried on a wagon pulled by four black horses. The ball was a light cream color with a sky blue line for the equator. It featured such slogans as OUT WITH THE SPOILERS, DOWN WITH THE TYRANTS.

After the parade, the ball was presented to the Tippecanoe Club of Zanesville. The ball kept rolling in more Whig parades in the region before ending up in Henry Clay's hometown of Lexington, Kentucky.

Free food also was a big part of the allure. Most rallies featured tables full of meats, potatoes, breads, pies, and more. At a rally in Wheeling, which was then in Virginia, tables groaned under the load of three hundred hams, fifteen hundred pounds of beef, eight thousand pounds of bread, a thousand pounds of cheese, and forty-five hundred pies. One favorite was a dish called Burgoo, which was made by adding chopped vegetables to a tasty squirrel stew.

The public campaign celebrations shocked the Democrats. Pennsylvania senator James Buchanan marveled that the people had "abandoned their ordinary business for the purpose of electioneering." Even *Ohio Statesman* editor Sam Medary conceded that he had never seen anything like this; it seemed as though every man, woman, and child preferred politics to everything else, he said.

Democrats blasted the parades. "These popular movements have been nothing but idle and ridiculous pageants, with displays of cider barrels, coon skins and gourd shells, and every variety of low and contemptible mummery, characterized by scenes of noise and disorder, or vulgar songs in praise of their mock hero, with coarse and ribald abuse of his opponents and often by drunkenness and debauchery," scolded a letter writer in the Democratic *Detroit Free Press*.

Some people who lived in towns invaded by the Whig hordes weren't too happy about the celebrations. "It seems as though men, women, and children would become insane," complained the resident of one western town. "They are raising their Harrison flags, and surround them by companies at night and day. Such noises I think I never heard from human beings as are made in the night."

Added a resident of Fairfield, Ohio, "Our village has been in turmoil for three days. I heared [*sic*] them two miles distinctly whooping and yelling, as if some infernal demons were let loose."

Even some old-fashioned Whigs such as former president John Quincy Adams were uneasy with this new rabble-rousing style of politics. "Where will it end?" asked Adams, who worried that it could even lead to civil war. Henry Clay also preferred a campaign based on issues instead of such passion. But even Clay finally conceded that passion had become the driving force of the campaign. And it just might drive the Whigs to the White House.

"You are no doubt certain that General Harrison will be our next President," a young West Point cadet who was the adopted son of Ohio Whig senator Thomas Ewing wrote to his father in the spring of 1840. "I do not think there is the least hope of such a change, since his friends have thought it proper to envelop his name with log cabins, gingerbread, hard cider and such humbugging, the sole object of which is plainly to deceive and mislead his ignorant and prejudiced but honest fellow citizens, whilst his qualifications, his honesty, his merits and services are merely alluded to." The young cadet was future Civil War general William Tecumseh Sherman.

Some Whigs did stress serious issues. In a meeting in Boston's North End, there were no parades but strictly appeals based on reason alone. Speakers addressed the needs of the working class for jobs and better wages, while charging Van Buren with favoring the wealthy. "Take care of the laborer, take care of the poor, and the rich will take care of themselves," said a speaker from Roxbury.

To keep the momentum going, Whig leaders kept coming up with new gimmicks. Tall flagpoles were put up next to many Tippecanoe Club cabins. Soon towns were competing to erect the tallest pole. In Washington, DC, a "Harrison Pole" rose 107 feet. Then Whigs in Jefferson, Maryland, put up one climbing to a height of 143 feet. The competition hit its zenith when Whigs in Wheeling put up a pole 230 feet high topped with an American flag waving in the breeze.

For the Democrats, the Harrison Poles were the last straw. The poles obviously were a knockoff of the Hickory Poles that Democrats had created in the 1828 and 1832 campaigns for General Andrew "Old Hickory" Jackson. Indeed, the Whig rallies emulated the torchlight parades and barbecues that had marked Jackson's campaign. In those days, Democrats had generated enthusiasm by planting "hurrah boys" in the crowd to stir onlookers by shouting, "hurrah, hurrah." This grassroots campaign tactic had been initiated by none other than Martin Van Buren, back when he helped run Jackson's campaign.

But in 1840 the Whigs, for the first time, made grassroots outreach the entire centerpiece of a presidential campaign. While the Democrats had used some of these tactics before, the Whigs were doing them bigger and better. "We have taught them how to conquer us," lamented the *Democratic Review*.

The *Review* recognized that something new was happening in America's body politic: "This must be called the Log Cabin and Hard Cider campaign and must unquestionably stand without a parallel in our past political history. It presents a totally new phase in our party politics, a new experiment upon our institutions. . . . They have struck upon a new idea."

But the Whigs, the *Review* charged, were bamboozling the ignorant masses. "The plan of operations was organized at the Harrisburg Convention, and has been zealously carried out ever since, throughout every section of the country. It consists in avoiding all public expositions of their principles, of the views and intentions which they would bring with them into power if successful."

Democrats argued that the carnival tactics were even duping people to vote for John Tyler, a man who only recently was a member of the opposition party. What were they thinking? To which some Whigs replied with these lyrics:

And we'll vote for Tyler, therefore,
Without a why or wherefore.

The Democrats could hardly respond with big rallies of their own after trashing the Whig gatherings as demagogic sideshows. And renaming the former Hickory Clubs as Van Buren Clubs would just emphasize the difference between the charismatic war hero Jackson and the bland Van Buren.

The Whig rallies continued to grow even larger. As many as sixty-five thousand people took part in a state Whig convention in Syracuse, New York, in early September. The featured attraction was a parade that one reporter described as a living sea of heads, banners beyond counting, a bevy of bands, and log cabins on immense wagons pulled by as many as eighteen horses. It was a procession the like of which had never been witnessed in the state of New York. Another pro-Whig reporter gushed that the gathering's "grandeur surpasses the power of description. I am oppressed and subdued in the august presence of the people, who are here in their majesty."

Indeed, newspapers searched to find new ways to express this phenomenon. "The prairies are on fire," wrote a Cleveland paper, "and the whirlwind they create will be felt east of the mountains." It was the beginning of the idiom a "whirlwind campaign."

Helping to fuel the excitement was the presence of a group of people who were a new force in presidential politics. Hint: they wore dresses.

11

THE FIRST GENDER GAP

This way of making politicians of their women is
something new under the sun.

—A Georgia Democrat

It was a sign of change that couldn't be missed. At the big Whig
rally in Baltimore, a woman reached out of a window overlooking
the parade and waved a bright red petticoat.

All along the parade route, windows were crowded with ladies
who looked "with delight upon the scene to which their own presence with waving handkerchiefs and fluttering veils give a bright
adornment," the *Baltimore American* reported.

While marching in a Harrison rally in New York City, former
New York mayor Philip Hone was struck by the flood of feminin-
ity along the route. "The balconies and windows were filled with
women, well-dressed, with bright eyes and bounding bosoms,
waving handkerchiefs, exhibiting flags and garlands, and casting
bouquets of flowers upon us," Hone wrote in his diary.

Women became openly involved in presidential politics for the
first time in 1840. The Whigs actively encouraged female participation in the campaign. Not that women could vote, of course.
Who could imagine such a thing? But they could influence the men
who would be casting ballots in the coming election.

Some single Whig women teased their suitors that they wouldn't
marry a man who voted Democratic. In Tennessee, young women
wore sashes embroidered with the words WHIG HUSBANDS OR
NONE. Some even carried out the threat. In Bristol, Maine, a
young woman who was engaged to a local fisherman told him
the wedding was off unless he agreed to vote for the Whig ticket.

To do otherwise showed a lack of either intelligence or patriotism that she couldn't ignore. The young man swung to the Whigs, the *Providence Journal* reported.

A Richmond newspaper told of a Miss Bond, "a warm Harrison woman" in Port Clinton, Pennsylvania, who wouldn't say yes to her beau unless he declared for Old Tippecanoe. Miss Bond persuaded her boyfriend to go with her to hear a pro-Harrison speaker. After the speech, the man proposed on the spot. The speaker drank to their health and advised them to build a log cabin immediately. They were married that same evening.

Some Whig women zeroed in on men who already were Whigs. In Wheeling, Virginia, Frank Smith, a Whig bachelor, fell for his cherry-cheeked cousin Tilly, who "like all other pretty girls was a thorough-going Harrisonite." Too shy to talk about love, according to a newspaper story, they talked politics instead.

"I bet you that Harrison will be elected," said Tilly.

"Oh, but I would bet that way myself," replied Frank.

Tilly insisted he take the bet. So he asked what she wanted to bet.

"Myself."

"Against what?"

"Yourself."

Frank was somewhat puzzled by the wager. But Tilly spelled it out. "If you lose," she said, "I will win you, and if I lose you will win me."

"Done, done, done. Give me your hand—Hurrah for Tip, Ty and Till," said Frank.

Whether true or not, the article made a point. As women threw their support behind Harrison, said Tilly, "I certainly think that our sex should . . . receive a share of" the attention for his success.

One Whig woman with a deep interest in the election was twenty-one-year-old Mary Todd of Lexington, Kentucky. In late 1839, Mary moved in with her married sister Elizabeth Todd Edwards and her sister's husband in Springfield, Illinois. Mary had heard about a skinny young bachelor who was working with her brother-in-law, a lawyer. One night she attended a ball celebrating the start of the state legislative session. She spotted a tall, thin, clean-shaven young man. He was the bachelor she had heard about, and his name was Abraham Lincoln.

As a Whig state lawmaker, Lincoln was the manager of the dance. He soon noticed Mary too. Introducing himself, the lanky Abe told Mary that he wanted to dance with her "in the worst way." And that's just how he danced, Mary later joked.

Mary and Abe soon became an item. The thirty-one-year-old Lincoln was a Harrison elector who would cast one of Illinois's votes in the Electoral College should it go for Old Tippecanoe. Mary shared his interest in the presidential campaign. She attended Whig meetings in Springfield and joined in Harrison songs.

One night when Lincoln dropped by the Edwards house to see Mary, her sister offered him a glass of sherry. When Lincoln declined, Elizabeth teased that he wouldn't have refused a glass of hard cider to drink a toast to Harrison. "No," Lincoln replied, "for I was brought up in a log cabin and raised on hard cider." Mary and Abe would marry in 1842 in the parlor of the Edwards home.

The wily ways of young single Whig women raised flags for Democrats. Warned one Democratic newspaper, "*Young men and Bachelors look out!* unless you want to wear ragged stockings, cook your own victuals, and tend your own children, have care how you connect yourself with a brawling, female politician. If you would have your house a hell, and your home a curse, marry a 'feminine Tippecanoe,' one who is aiding and exciting the animosities, and participating in the political strife of the day."

In the campaign, the Whigs also wooed married women, urging them to sway their politically straying husbands. Samuel G. Goodrich, a Massachusetts Whig state senator, gave speeches based on a supposed conversation between a Democratic-leaning man and his common-sense Whig wife. When the husband praised Democrats, his spouse innocently asked why. After all, hadn't the Democratic government's policies caused the man's wages to drop so much that he couldn't pay his bills?

Man: "I never thought of all this before. There is something wrong somewhere."

Woman: "There is indeed, my husband. . . . I think you, with too many others in the country, have been grossly cheated and deceived. A set of men who only wished to enjoy power, and office, and spoils have been entrusted with the reins of government, and they have driven us over a precipice."

Man: "Well, wife, I am afraid you are right; but what can I do?"

Woman: "Well, there's no danger in trying change. Here it goes: Hurrah for Harrison and better times!"

Even if women couldn't persuade their husbands to vote Whig, many wives found new courage to at least challenge their spouse's political views. When pro-Harrison marchers passed near a house in northern Ohio, a man came out and began shouting for Van Buren. Suddenly, his wife crept up behind him, put her hand over his mouth, and with the other hand waved a banner for Harrison as the crowd roared its approval.

Whig women were also celebrated in song:

> *The beautiful girls, God bless their souls,*
> *The country through, will all to a man, do all they can*
> *For Tippecanoe and Tyler Too.*

Whig speakers singled out women. Some of the rhetoric was more patronizing than informative, but for the first time politicians were paying attention to the female point of view. Near the end of a three-hour speech in Portland, Maine, former Mississippi congressman Seargent S. Prentiss directed his words to the ladies in the audience: "When you fair daughters come forth to encourage us by your smiles and your presence, we feel ourselves doubly armed." Prentiss praised female involvement in the campaign, saying, "It is your right and your duty to come forward in a time like this, and say by the interest your presence manifests how much you have at stake in a contest like that to come."

Massachusetts senator Daniel Webster, one of the great orators of the day, gave several speeches exclusively to female audiences. More than a thousand women turned out for one Webster speech at the Tippecanoe Club in Richmond, Virginia. In his talk, Webster gave short shrift to issues, a move he deemed to be a compliment to the ladies present. "I know you hardly expect me to address you on the popular political topics of the day," he said. "You read enough, you hear quite enough on these subjects."

Instead, Webster discussed the virtues of motherhood and its impact on the political system. "The rough contests of the political world are not suited to the dignity and to the delicacy of your sex," he said. But women have the intelligence to know how important it is to instruct their children in the value of good government and public morals. "That is a subject on which the moral perceptions of woman are both quicker and juster than those of the other sex," Webster declared. So good mothers "will impress upon their children the truth that the exercise of the elective franchise is a social duty of as solemn a nature that man can be called to perform."

The pro-Whig *National Intelligencer* was so impressed that it published Webster's entire speech and praised the senator for recognizing the "vast influence" of women. The anti-Whig *Richmond Enquirer* wasn't so positive: "Are the ladies of Virginia so destitute of religious and moral instruction that they need a thorough politician to enlighten them on the subject of raising their children?"

If so, the Whigs were to blame, argued Democratic newspapers. The Whig mothers of the land have forgotten their homes and children, lamented the *Spirit of the Age* newspaper in Woodstock, Vermont. "They ride around in log cabins, guzzle hard cider and attend coonskin powwows. God help a boy of one of these mothers."

Many women supported Van Buren, of course. But the Democrats frowned on open female involvement in politics as improper and downright scandalous. Women of the day dressed conservatively, covered from head to toe in bonnets, floor-length dresses, and blouses with puffy long sleeves. But those shameless Whig women! Vice President Richard Mentor Johnson said he was shocked to see some Whig ladies wearing ribbons embroidered with the words HARRISON and TYLER across their breasts.

Johnson's views on female participation in politics represented those of most Democratic males. The rights of women were secured through the "coarser sex," their husbands and brothers, he argued. "It is the right of a woman to maintain a modest retirement in the bustle of politics and of war," he said. "She does not appear at the polls to vote because she is privileged to be represented there by man. She does not serve on juries . . . because it would be a degradation of her dignity. She does not take up arms and meet her country's foes because she is a privileged character, and man is her substitute who represents her in all these drudgeries."

Democrats contended that the Whigs were simply using women as a decorative diversion from the drunkenness and debauchery of their log cabin and hard cider campaign. There was some truth to the charge. Whig organizers believed the presence of women added an element of beauty, virtue, and sobriety to the boisterous campaign. In short, they were political eye candy.

The high visibility of the fairer sex at Harrison rallies was no accident. Whig organizers sent "To the Ladies" invitations for wives to join their husbands at political meetings. They brought wagonloads of women to rallies. In Bennington, Vermont, it took twenty-five horses to pull one wagon filled with more than a hundred ladies. Political advance men handed out free handkerchiefs for women to wave. The waving hankies not only added a feminine touch at rallies; they were also sure to be noticed by newspaper reporters writing about the events.

Recruitment of women also had a practical benefit. The monstrous Whig rallies required monstrous meals, and women were the ones who cooked the food. At a Harrison rally in Zanesville, Ohio, celebrants downed more than eighteen tons of meat, pies, and cider. At a barbecue in Concord, New Hampshire, more than sixty-three hundred men were served a sit-down dinner in a huge tent.

Whig women were expected to house, host, and feed many of the thousands of people who poured into town for rallies. After all, it was the woman of the house who did the cooking and the cleaning to accommodate guests. For a rally in Richmond, "every

Whig house in the city is to be crammed. We expected to have 10 or 12 sleep here, to say nothing of the stragglers in to dinner," a woman named Mary Steger wrote to a friend. "It is no easy task in this filthy place to keep a three-story house clean."

Eliza Davis of Worcester, Massachusetts, was the wife of US senator "Honest John" Davis, a Whig who now was running for governor. When the Whigs scheduled a state convention in Worcester, Eliza agreed to house about two dozen committee members and feed them a log cabin meal. At the last minute, she also agreed to feed the band members from the small town of Harre following the parade. Eliza was on her own; her husband was away in Washington during the event.

More than thirty thousand delegates rolled into town for a massive Tippecanoe parade of log cabins and marching bands. After the parade ended, Eliza rushed home to finish preparing for her visitors. Instead of the few people she expected from Harre, suddenly more than two hundred band members from the small town were pouring into her living room with banners, drums, and trumpets in tow. "My heart sank within me—how on Earth should I feed them?" Eliza later wrote her husband.

The invaders soon mowed through Eliza's prepared food of beef a la mode, tongue, ham, boiled beef, and leg of veal and bread. They downed the cakes she had made. They guzzled rivers of beer, wine, and hard cider. Somehow, after Eliza scrambled to dig out food from her cabinets, everybody got fed. As the two hundred delegates from Harre left, they lined up outside the house and serenaded Eliza with "Hail Columbia."

The experience only deepened Eliza's loyalty to the Whig cause. "I shall be a lover of the people, shall ever believe and trust them," she wrote her husband.

The letter moved Senator Davis to tears. He showed it to his colleague Senator Webster, who also was touched. Then a Whig congressman mentioned the letter in a speech, but erroneously stated that Webster also cried when reading the missive.

This was too much for the cynical Democratic press. "Boo-hoo-hoo," mocked the *Ohio Statesman*—under the headline THE

GREAT WHIG BOOBIES. The Davis and Webster tears, the paper asserted, were pathetic ploys to make fools out of the voters. Another newspaper speculated that Davis was crying because the visitors had devoured all of his wine and cake. Whigs, on the other hand, praised Eliza's commitment to the campaign.

Most Whig women didn't seem to mind going to such lengths for the cause. They were grateful finally to be a part of the political process. The traditional role of women, especially married women, was to clean, cook, and raise kids without voicing any independent opinions. Priscilla Cooper Tyler, the twenty-four-year-old daughter-in-law of Whig vice presidential candidate John Tyler, complained to a visiting French diplomat that in America "married women are never invited anywhere" or allowed to talk to anyone about anything outside of the home. In most places, she said, married women were treated as pariahs. Priscilla, a former actress, actively campaigned for the Harrison-Tyler ticket.

Self-described "Harrison Women" were everywhere in the Whig campaign. They began visiting the initially all-male Tippecanoe Clubs. They dubbed their bonnets Tippecanoe Hats. They sewed banners to be carried in the big parades. The Whig Ladies of Alexandria, Virginia, presented a banner to the local Tippecanoe Club with the motto GEN. WM. H. HARRISON, THE GLORY AND HOPE OF OUR NATION. Many Whig women praised Harrison as the protector of women and children from Indian attacks back when he was governor of the Indiana Territory and a general in the War of 1812.

As the campaign rolled on, women became another symbol of the Whigs' populist campaign. "Women are the very life and soul of these movements of the People," proclaimed the *Cincinnati Gazette*. And before long, the female contributions went far beyond cooking and waving handkerchiefs from the sidelines.

12

PETTICOAT POWER

We have been pained ... to see our fair countrywomen unsex themselves and stepping across the threshold to mingle in the fight.

—Democratic *North Carolina Standard*

While sitting in a train car ready to depart from Baltimore in early 1840, British writer James Silk Buckingham was shocked to see something unlike anything he had ever witnessed while touring the United States. A well-dressed woman, "with gay bonnet, veil and shawl," entered the train carrying a small basket. As she walked down the aisle, she reached into the basket and began handing out copies of a political pamphlet

"It is a good Harrison paper," she explained. The title of the anti–Van Buren paper: "A History of the Present cabinet ... Gather all your strength ... Draw their teeth in time, unless they should devour you ... An Exposition of Martin Van Buren's Reign."

Buckingham was flabbergasted at the sight of a woman openly pushing her political views. "My first impression was that the woman was insane," he wrote later. Some fellow passengers informed him that the woman was known to make a living by writing political pamphlets. The pamphlet she was distributing was not anonymous but signed by the author, Lucy Kenney.

"Yes, that is my real name," she told Buckingham. And she would never change it for any man.

The woman, who could be no more than thirty years old, was eccentric, but her general demeanor was respectful and orderly, Buckingham said. "She was under no influence from wine or other stimulants." People who knew her well declared her to be of perfectly sane mind and irreproachable morals, though "a great oddity" and "unlike the rest of us."

Lucy Kenney, a single woman from Fredericksburg, Virginia, had begun writing in the 1830s in favor of slavery. She also wrote for President Jackson and then President Van Buren. When she asked to be paid for her work, Van Buren offered her one dollar. Kenney was insulted, so when the Whigs offered her $1,000 to write for them, she switched allegiances.

In 1840, Kenney became the first woman to write political pamphlets for a presidential campaign. In *The Strongest of All Government Is That Which Is Most Free: An Address to the People of the United States*, she praised Harrison as an honest and upright man who would restore the country to "peace, plenty and prosperity." (Earlier, in *A Letter Addressed to Martin Van Buren, President of the United States*, she had predicted that the American people would "hurl you from the place you have gained by false pretenses and substitute one more worthy, and one whose time and talents have always been devoted to his country.")

Many women were starting to find their voices on serious issues. Females in New England were active in the antislavery movement. In 1840 a group of them traveled to London to the World Anti-Slavery Convention, which refused to seat them because of their gender. Some of these women became Whig activists. Quaker abolitionist Sarah Pugh called herself a "flaming Whig partisan."

Now, for the first time, women organized political meetings, and some even spoke at them. In Vandalia, Illinois, Harrison supporter Jane Field gave a fiery speech to the Fayette County Whig delegates to the state party convention, declaring, "When the sound of war whoops on our prairies was the infant's lullaby, our mothers reposed in security for Harrison was their protector . . . we would indeed be traitors to our sex if our bosoms did not thrill to his name."

Elizabeth Clarkson, a longtime friend of Harrison, headed a group of women in Brookville, Indiana, in an open campaign for the general. The women took part in local political meetings and pro-Whig demonstrations. "Mother Clarkson" rode on horseback to lead four hundred women to one Harrison barbecue seventy-five miles away. Another time she presented a flag on behalf of the Whig Ladies of Southern Indiana at a Whig meeting of five thousand men. Clarkson then delivered a pro-Harrison speech while holding her baby son in one arm.

At a log cabin dinner celebrating the raising of a Harrison Pole by women in Roseville, Ohio, several of the women offered "lady toasts." The remarks were not exactly scintillating. But the very fact that women were publicly speaking at a political gathering made them newsworthy. "Harrison. We love him because he first loved us," said one Mrs. H. Little. "He who protected the widow and orphans in 1813 will not be by them forsaken," added a Mrs. Combs.

Some women wrote campaign songs, such as this one by a woman in Virginia:

> *Down with the Locos*
> *Dark hocus-pocus*
> *The banner of liberty*
> *Floats through the sky.*

Whig women were ready to do or die for Old Tip. At a rally in Springfield, Illinois, some restive horses began running loose, endangering people nearby. One woman cried out, "If there's to be any killed, let it be the ladies, for they can't vote."

Nearly one thousand women joined their husbands at a July Fourth meeting of the Log Cabin Boys of Michigan in Kalamazoo. After several hundred women attended a Whig gathering in Ravenna, Ohio, the state's sixty-seven-year-old Democratic senator, Benjamin Tappan, called ladies who went to political meetings women of "doubtful reputation."

One group of women in Cincinnati led a one-day trip to Harrison's home in North Bend. Three steamboats were needed to hold the passengers, including male guests. One man brought along a barrel of hard cider. A band played, and the group was in high spirits when the boats landed near Harrison's home.

Crowds of people now regularly gathered at the landing spot. They cheered and waved flags as the visitors descended from the boats and walked up the rough road to Harrison's home. The general himself came out to greet the visitors and gave a short talk. He paid particular attention to the ladies. The women presented the general with a special gift: a live eagle that had been caught near Fort Meigs. Some women also gave him wildflowers.

The visitors could plainly see that Harrison's home was no log cabin as his campaign claimed, but that was overshadowed by seeing the old hero in the flesh. As one woman wrote later, "Indeed, to see him actually called from his home in the forest, where he dwells with such quietness and peace, to receive the plaudits of the people as their candidate for the Presidency, seemed to me one of the most glorious, ennobling scenes that could be conceived of, and republican institutions never stood higher in my humble estimation, than at that moment."

The Lowell Mill girls who worked in the textile factories in Lowell, Massachusetts, actively supported Harrison as a champion of the working poor. Women made up the majority of the eight thousand workers at the mills. They typically earned two dollars a week working from 5:00 AM to 7:00 PM six days a week. Fifteen-year-old worker Harriet Jane Hanson Robinson later wrote that the working women attended Whig meetings and promoted Harrison "to show how wide-awake and up to date" they were. One of the mill girls was moved to write an article on women's rights in the first edition of a publication that became known as the *Lowell Offering*, which was written entirely by women who worked in the mill.

At rallies, many Whig women not only waved from the sidelines but joined in the parades, shocking Democratic men. Ladies filled about a half-dozen open wagons with about fifty women per wagon in a Buffalo, New York, parade. When the wagons rolled by a local tavern, a gang of men pelted the women with eggs.

In a parade in Indianapolis, Indiana, several women rode in a large canoe, setting off angry shouting and fistfights among some men in the crowd. The *Indiana Democrat* disapprovingly noted the increased appearance of women in the political arena. "This is all wrong and entitled to censure," the paper said. "Woman has no right to vote under our laws and Constitution. Therefore her appearance at a political meeting, or her participation of any kind in political strife, must be considered improper."

"Ladies are better mending their stockings or making puddings than becoming politicians," scolded the *New York Herald*.

The *Tennessee Whig* wondered where these new demands by women would end. "They now claim the right of wearing drawers, and the next thing will be the breeches."

The criticism didn't deter Whig women. In Seneca Falls, New York, twenty-two-year-old Amelia Bloomer helped her new husband, Dexter Bloomer, edit his pro-Whig newspaper the *Seneca Falls County Courier*. She began attending Whig political gatherings at the local log cabin headquarters. She made political badges and wrote campaign slogans for Harrison marchers. Her husband termed the campaign the turning point of his wife's life.

In 1848, Amelia Bloomer would attend the Seneca Falls Convention for women's rights. The next year she began publishing the *Lily*, a magazine that advocated temperance and women's rights. It also promoted women's fashions. Bloomer championed a new type of loose-fitting pants for females to wear beneath their dresses. Prominent women's rights activists began to wear the pants, which become known as bloomers.

Women's rights activist Elizabeth Cady Stanton, who organized the 1848 Seneca Falls Convention, cited the 1840 election as the start of women's involvement in politics and government. Abraham Lincoln had talked about the possibility of allowing women to vote as early as 1836: "I go for all sharing the privileges of the government, who assist in bearing its burdens. Consequently I go for admitting all whites to the rights of suffrage who pay taxes or bear arms (by no means excluding females)." Women would not actually get the right to vote for another eighty years. But in 1840 many women began thinking that one day they would be able not only to vote but even to hold elective office. Who knows? Perhaps a woman could even be president someday.

Meanwhile, the voices of woman weren't the only new means of communication the Whigs were relying on to spread the good news about Tip and Ty. An even broader audience would be exposed to their message thanks to the influence of a new, highly partisan newspaper.

13

READ ALL ABOUT US!

[The Log Cabin *newspaper] was the best campaign paper ever published.*

—*New York Times* founder Henry Jarvis Raymond

The Harrison campaign created a completely new kind of propaganda machine in 1840. The groundwork had been laid just about two years earlier.

In late 1837, Albany, New York, newspaper publisher Thurlow Weed decided to start a weekly newspaper to promote his political protégé, red-haired William Seward, as the Whig candidate in the 1838 race for governor of New York. Weed knew just the man he wanted for the job: the editor of a popular newspaper in New York City. The editor's name was Horace Greeley, and his publication was the *New Yorker*.

So Weed went down to New York City to meet Greeley for the first time. When the Whig boss arrived at the newspaper's attic office at 30 Ann Street, he encountered a tall, light-haired but balding, disheveled young man with round eyeglasses on his nose working at a printer's case. When Weed asked to see the editor, the man replied that he was one and the same.

The rail-thin Greeley was deeply interested in American politics and culture as well as health fads. He took cold-water baths and was a follower of the Rev. Sylvester P. Graham, a vegetarian who invented the Graham cracker.

Over a presumably meatless dinner at the City Hotel, the twenty-seven-year-old Greeley agreed to publish the proposed new publication out of Albany during the election campaign for a salary of $1,000. He decided to call the paper the *Jeffersonian*.

The pro-Whig paper began in February 1838, with Greeley commuting weekly to Albany by steamboat from New York, where he continued to publish the *New Yorker* newspaper (which had no connection with the later *New Yorker* magazine.) The *Jeffersonian* was a big success; Seward won the election easily.

Now both Weed and Greeley were anxious to put out a similar newspaper for the 1840 presidential race. Drawing on the theme of the young campaign, Greeley suggested calling the paper the *Log Cabin*. It would be the first national newspaper devoted entirely to a presidential campaign.

Most people in those days got their news from newspapers. There were more than fifteen hundred papers across the country, and the number was growing every week. Most of the papers made no pretense of being objective; they were either rabidly Democratic or Whig. "As for the country press, two thirds of it is a nuisance and a positive curse, a mere mouthpiece for demagogues, who are ravenous for spoils. This is a sad truth, but it is a truth none the less," said Greeley.

The reliability of these journals also left something to be desired. "If they do not lie from dishonest motives, their avidity to have something new and in advance of others leads them to take up everything that comes to hand without proper examination," said Whig politician Philip Hone.

Two of the biggest dailies were in Washington, DC. The *National Intelligencer* was pro-Whig, and its editor, William Seaton, also was the mayor of the District of Columbia. The *Washington Globe* was the mouthpiece for the Van Buren administration. The *Globe* was created in the Andrew Jackson administration in late 1830 by Amos Kendall, a close Jackson adviser who had published a newspaper in Frankfort, Kentucky. Kendall recruited one of his editors, Francis P. Blair, to be the publisher. The *Globe*'s motto was "The world is governed too much."

Blair soon became one of the nation's most powerful publishers and a leading member of President Jackson's Kitchen Cabinet of unofficial advisers. To be close to the president, Blair built a large house directly across the street from the White House. The

Blair House later would be used to house foreign dignitaries during visits to the US president.

Blair also owned a 250-acre estate a few miles north in Maryland, where he would take his family during Washington's steamy summer days. He called the estate Silver Spring; the site later would become a suburban town by the same name. Kendall meantime became President Van Buren's postmaster general and chief political hatchet man. Whigs called him the president's head devil.

About the only nonpartisan paper was the weekly *Niles' Register*. The national paper was published out of Baltimore, where it had been started by Hezekiah Niles. After Niles died in 1839, an old friend, Jeremiah Hughes, took over the paper and continued its even-handed reporting. The paper essentially reprinted articles from both Whig and Democratic newspapers, thus providing balanced national coverage.

Greeley's *Log Cabin* newspaper was different from the others. Its pages were devoted entirely to the presidential campaign of William Henry Harrison. The first edition of the eight-page weekly paper was published May 2, 1840. The logo at the top of the front page was a picture of a log cabin with a cider barrel attached. Nearby a farmer was plowing the field next to a pole with a flag waving at the top. On the flag were the words HARRISON and TYLER.

In the paper, Greeley declared that the *Log Cabin* "will be a zealous and unwavering advocate of the rights, interests and prosperity of our whole country, but especially . . . cultivators of her soil. . . . [It] will be the advocate of Freedom, Improvement and of National Reform, by the election of Harrison and Tyler, the restoration of purity to government, of efficiency to the public will, and of Better Times to the People."

Greeley vowed that the *Log Cabin* would be the champion of the working person. Most important, it would be "devoted to the dissemination of Truth, the refutation of Slander," and the vindication of one of the country's "noblest and most illustrious Patriots." It would "champion the common people who dwell in rude and humble cottages."

The paper was sold for two cents a copy—or three cents if put up in wrappers ready for mailing. Greeley made no apologies for the cost: "Is not this paper worth two cents? No? Well, then don't take it."

The first edition's front page featured an engraving of a middle-aged Harrison and a summary of his biography under the headline AN EXCELLENT RECORD. Below that article was a letter from a Cincinnati clergyman who knew Old Tip. He praised Harrison's record as a war hero, a farmer, and an educated citizen. "On many accounts, I think him better fitted for the station of President of the U.S. just at this juncture of affairs than any other man in the country," the clergyman concluded.

The second page featured a "Poem to the Soldier of Tippecanoe." Next to the poem was a report of a Springfield, Illinois, meeting of old soldiers who had served under General Harrison. All vouched for his bravery in battle.

Page three recounted a "Thrilling Log Cabin Incident" during a cabin raising in Erie, Pennsylvania. The cabin raisers were approached by a group of men dressed as Native Americans, waving tomahawks. The "Indians" all surrendered as volunteer prisoners of war. Turned out they were all previous supporters of President Jackson who were now backing Harrison. Future editions included a listing of Jackson and Van Buren supporters who switched to Old Tippecanoe. They were called former Van Jacks.

The *Log Cabin* also reported on some national and foreign news. The initial edition noted that the king of Holland had yielded to the opposition of his children and subjects and had abandoned plans to marry a countess—whereupon "there is great rejoicing."

The maiden edition of the *Log Cabin* was a smash hit. More than thirty thousand copies quickly sold out, as did another ten thousand that Greeley hurriedly printed up. Apparently readers felt they were getting their two cents' worth. Greeley's only problem was getting them to pay up. A notice in one edition read, "All persons who have obtained credit for The Log Cabin under whatever circumstances will greatly oblige us by remitting the amount coming to us immediately."

By July, circulation surged past the sixty-thousand mark. Readers were treated to descriptions of Harrison's military victories at Tippecanoe, Fort Meigs, and the Battle of the Thames. The paper reported on Whig parades, cabin raisings, and anecdotes. One edition, for example, noted a backwoodsman in the Far West who welcomed travelers to stay overnight at his log cabin with a sign that read, "Oats and chop for the horse, and for the rider. Hog hominy and hard cider. The politics of Harrison rules this garrison. Those of Van Buren is beyond all enduring."

The paper berated the small-government Democrats for mocking the unemployed as penniless loafers. At a time when thousands couldn't find jobs or bread to eat, the paper said, "their miseries are outraged by the taunting inquiries—Why don't you work? Why are you constantly begging help of the Government? Go about your business and not be troublesome."

The stories tried to show a growing support for Harrison. Even the Mormons, who had been known to back President Van Buren, were getting on board, the paper reported. Mormon leader Joseph Smith had visited the White House, and the "cavalier reception" he received from Van Buren reportedly led Smith to convert his followers to Old Tip.

Adopting features from his *New Yorker* newspaper, Greeley printed nonpolitical poems to add a touch of culture. One was entitled "To My Cigar":

> *Yes, social friend. I love thee well.*
> *No learned doctor's spite;*
> *I love thy fragment, misty spell.*
> *I love thy calm delight.*

There were even advertisements. "Stammering cured," boasted one ad. In another, M. Levitt, a dentist at 260 Broadway in New York, promoted "the insertion of incorruptible artificial teeth," based on his unique application of the principle of atmospheric pressure. The teeth were "much recommended by those that wear them."

Greeley had promised not to use the paper for personal attacks on President Van Buren. But naturally he couldn't resist. The *Log Cabin* said, "Whenever you find a bitter, blasphemous Atheist and enemy of Marriage, Morality, and Social Order, there you may be certain of one vote for Van Buren."

The publisher found a tongue-in-cheek way to remind readers of the president's fancy carriage: "Mr. Van Buren's coach is his own, bought of his own money, and he has a right to ride it where he thinks proper."

Greeley built up the impression that a tide of voter support was growing for Harrison. One week's paper told of a Van Buren supporter who visited Cleveland and dined at a local hotel. He asked an elderly woman there how politics stood in Ohio. The woman replied, "Oh, I don't know much about it, no how; but there don't appear to be but only two parties in this state, as far as I know. . . . Let me see: one they call the Tippecanoe Party and the other Harrison Democrats I believe."

The *Log Cabin* newspaper was so popular that it spurred both parties to start more campaign newspapers. On the Whig side, there was the *Log Cabin Hero* newspaper in St. Louis. In Illinois, Abraham Lincoln supported the *Old Soldier* newspaper, proclaiming, "Every Whig in the state must take it." Ohio alone had seventeen party newspapers. They included the *Straight Out Harrison*, the *Cleveland Axe*, and Elyria's *Old Tip's Broom*. In Kentucky, a Whig newspaper was called simply the *Campaign*.

The Whig papers were part of a national strategy to flood voters with tales of abuse by the Van Buren administration. Said pro-Whig *Harrisburg Intelligencer* editor Richard Smith Elliott, "Strangers reading our Whig journals would have supposed the United States, under the presidency of Mr. Van Buren, to be in the grasp of the most shameless scoundrels on Earth."

The Democrats countered with their own newspapers. President Van Buren himself suggested the creation of a Democratic paper in Thurlow Weed's hometown of Albany, New York. The result was the *Rough-Hewer*, whose stated goal was to dispel Whig falsehoods—which it did mainly by printing falsehoods of its own. Other papers that sprang up included the *Democratic Rasp* in Newark, Ohio, and the *Log Cabin Humbug* in Maysville, Kentucky.

The *Globe* rushed to counter the *Log Cabin* with the *Extra Globe*, devoted entirely to the Van Buren campaign. Jackson adviser Amos Kendall, now fifty-one years old, resigned as postmaster general, citing supposed health problems, to coedit the *Extra*. The new periodical listed its goals under the headline WHAT WE INTEND:

- That no freeman who prizes the right of self government can support General Harrison for the Presidency, after his refusal to answer the reasonable inquiries of his countrymen as to his political opinions upon the most exciting topics of the day:
- That every freeman who prefers a Government of principle to one of excitement, should separate from a party who openly cast reason and men to the winds, and are attempting to carry an election by appealing to man's worst passions and most sordid appetites:
- That the refusal of Harrison to answer questions, the interposition of . . . "log cabins" and "hard cider," rolling balls and canoes upon wheels, pictures, and banners, great assemblages, and long processions, with loud huzzahs and senseless declamation, as substitutes for reason and argument, are gross insults to a free people, which ought to be indignantly resented and rebuked at the polls.

In contrast to the lively *Log Cabin*, the *Extra Globe* was heavy handed in its relentless attacks on Harrison and the Whigs. To emphasize its outrage, the charges were often printed in all capital letters, accusing the Whigs of "THE LOW PRICES HUMBUG," "WHOOPING AND YELLING," and "DOWNRIGHT LYING."

The *Extra Globe* devoted most of one edition to countering the image of Van Buren as the candidate of the rich. Instead, the paper sought to start its own image campaign showing the president as the real face of the common man.

"The son of a farmer, he is an example to show that the son of any farmer in the country may aspire to, and arrive at, its highest honors," the *Extra Globe* reported. "Imbibing the pure principles of Democracy in his rural occupation, he is an example of one who has been faithful to those principles in every station of life. Not allured from them by the possession of power, nor driven from them by the combination of the entire wealth of the country, he is just such a man as the Democracy needs, to lead them on in the present crisis."

The *Extra Globe* soon claimed a national circulation of fifty thousand. For the first time, political parties were using mass communication to woo voters. For their part, voters clearly were anxious to drink in the flow of information, however biased it might be.

To counter the claims that Harrison wasn't running on issues, Greeley published a list of the candidate's goals in the *Log Cabin*.

1. One presidential term
2. A retrenchment of the patronage and powers of the federal executive
3. No intermeddling of offices of the federal government in the elections of the states and people
4. Rotation in office
5. A sound and uniform currency alike for the government and the people

"Fellow citizens," Greeley asked, "are these principles sound, just and positive? Or are they nothing but a coonskins and hard cider?"

Despite the new competition, the *Log Cabin* ran far ahead of the field, generating even more enthusiasm for the campaign. The weekly issues ran rapidly up to eighty thousand copies. Greeley claimed he could sell one hundred thousand if he had enough printing and mailing facilities.

In the process, Greeley made another contribution to the energy of the Whigs. He helped put the campaign to music.

14

SING US A SONG

I shall never forget [some of the Whig songs].
They rang in my ears wherever I went, morning
noon and night.

—A Democratic newspaper editor

You didn't have to listen hard to hear America singing in 1840.
All across the country, Whig songs were in the air. They were the
ultimate singing commercials. Voters knew the words by heart,
and Old Tip was on their lips:

> *Old Tip's the boy to swing the flail,*
> *Hurrah, hurrah, hurrah!*
> *And make the locos all turn pale,*
> *Hurrah, hurrah, hurrah!*
> *His latchstring hangs outside the door,*
> *As it has always done before;*
> *The people vow he shall be sent*
> *To Washington as President,*
> *Hurrah, hurrah, hurrah.*
> *In all the States no door stands wider,*
> *To ask you in to drink hard cider,*
> *But any man's "given to grabbin',"*
> *Ne'er can enter his log cabin,*
> *Hurrah, hurrah, hurrah.*
> *So here's three cheers for honest Tip.*

The Whigs made music a central theme of their down-to-the-
people campaign. The party established Tippecanoe glee clubs
in nearly every town. Printing presses were carried on wagons in

campaign parades to print up copies of Tippecanoe songs so they could be handed out to the crowd as the wagon rolled along. Whigs sang at their political meetings. They interrupted Van Buren meetings with Harrison songs as well, sometimes causing the gatherings to break up in fistfights. They sent troubadours such as Titus of Toledo around to towns. They even hired singers to jump into stagecoaches and sing Whig songs to the passengers as a sort of traveling political advertisement.

The songs had an electrifying impact on the campaign. Since times were hard for most people, many of them decided they might as well laugh as cry, said writer Dorus Martin Fox. "They did laugh and sing loud and long until the music of their voices reverberated through every valley to every hilltop in the land."

Many of the new ditties were, of course, anti–Van Buren songs. One of the most popular went:

> *Old Tip he wears a homespun suit.*
> *He has no ruffled shirt, wirt-wirt!*
> *But Mat has the golden plate.*
> *And he's a little squirt-wirt-wirt.*

After singing the final line, the singer often would spit tobacco.

Whigs sang about the need for change—and not always with the best of grammar. As in this song:

> *Things ain't now as they used to was been*
> *Folks ain't now as they used to have been*
> *In the good old days when Matty Van*
> *Ruled over the land like a feared man*
> *And his mighty rule no one denied*
> *But now they are leaving foxy Van*
> *And all for Harrison am settling*
> *Oh Martin mourns and Martin grieves*
> *For the good old days of Adam and Eve.*

Horace Greeley helped fuel the music fest by publishing songs—complete with the musical notes—on the back page of each edition of the *Log Cabin*. The May 16 edition featured "The Wolverine's Song" about William Henry Harrison:

> *They call him a granny—they say he is poor,*
> *And lives in a cabin befitting a boor!*
> *And they say that he never drinks Port or Champagne*
> *But Cider as hard as his dwelling is plain!*
> *Well, what if he does? Still his table is spread*
> *With such as his purse will afford, and a bed*
> *Though coarser than Martin Van Buren's 'tis true*
> *Is kept for the stranger by Tippecanoe!*
> *Huzzah for Tippecanoe.*

At first, Greeley's boss, Thurlow Weed, objected to devoting so much space to music. "Our songs are doing more good than anything else," Greeley told Weed. "Really, I think every song is good for five hundred new subscribers." Weed ended up singing some of the songs as he took to the campaign trail to back Harrison.

Yet Greeley conceded that the songs themselves weren't all that great. "I know the music is not worth much, but it attracts the attention even of those who do not know a note," he said. In other words, the songs had a beat, and you could campaign to them.

Greeley wrote some song lyrics himself. He also sang the songs during campaign stops at train stations in New York. Apparently, the scrawny, eccentric Greeley cut quite a figure.

"His dress, his figure, with the white hat set several degrees farther up his head than usual, and the old white overcoat hanging free and clear from his shoulders gave him an appearance that was grotesque," said one eyewitness. "But his beating time beat everything else of the kind I ever saw before or since. It was not enough for Mr. Greeley to use one arm in this important task; the occasion was grand enough to demand both; nor was it fitting that they should move mechanically and together. So far from this, when one went up, the other was more likely to be going down, and as the song grew more inspiring, he found it necessary to call in to the aid of his arms, his right leg."

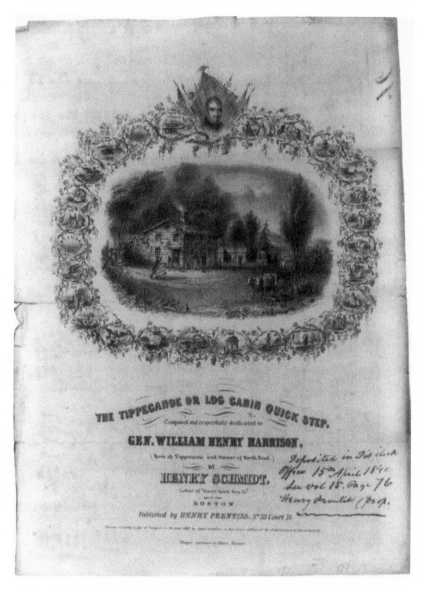

Tippecanoe sheet music. *Library of Congress*

Greeley published *The Log Cabin Song Book*, which quickly sold out at two thousand copies. So did a second edition twice the size of the first, seventy-two pages long with fifty-five Tippecanoe songs plus illustrations. "In short, it is the genuine article, and the bare sight of it is enough to give a Federal office-holder a touch of hydrophobia," Greeley wrote in the *Log Cabin.*

The second songbook featured such songs as "Harrison and Liberty," "Our Hero Farmer," and "The Hero of the Thames." Dozens of other songbooks also sold briskly. Among the featured songs: "The Harrison Two Step," "The Hurrah Song," and "A Tip Top Song About Tippecanoe."

Many of the songs were aimed at specific audiences. One was "The Working Man's Election Song":

> *Van Buren cannot be the Working Man's friend*
> *He has left him nothing to do*
> *But to starve or to beg, his Country defend*
> *And to work for Old Tippecanoe*
> *To Work for Old Tippecanoe*
> *To Work for Old Tippecanoe.*

Most of the campaign songs were words written to popular tunes. Several went to the tune of the "Star Spangled Banner." One was the "Harrison Song," which went in part:

> *Oh say have you heard how in days that are past,*
> *Bold sons of the West with brave Harrison leading,*
> *At the bugle's shrill call and the trumpet's loud blast,*
> *To the battlefield rush'd where our frontiers lay bleeding;*
> *Hark! with the loud acclaim, How they shout at the name,*
> *Of the hero predestin'd to guide them to fame!*
> *Oh! the name of our Harrison, long may it stand*
> *The boast of our country, the pride of our land!*

The popular New Year's Eve anthem "Auld Lang Syne" was another favorite tune. One song was called "Log Cabin and Hard Cider Candidate":

> *Should good old cider be despised,*
> *And ne'er regarded more?*
> *Should plain log cabins be despised,*

Our fathers built of yore?
For the true old style, my boys!
For the true old style?
We'll take a mug of cider, yet,
For Old Tippecanoe.

Another campaign song set to the "Auld Lang Syne" tune was "The Farmer of North Bend." All together now:

Can grateful freemen slight his claims
Who bravely did defend,
Their lives and fortunes on the Thames,
The farmer of North Bend?
The farmer of North Bend, my boys,
The farmer of North Bend,
We'll give a right good hearty vote
For the farmer of North Bend.

A few songs rose to a higher artistic level. The singing campaign attracted the attention of James Percival, a widely known poet acclaimed for his poems on liberty. Percival was also the main editor of Noah Webster's new *Webster's Dictionary*. The poet had joined a Sing-Sing club in New Haven, Connecticut, and he became active in putting his own lyrics to Harrison songs.

One of them was "Success to Tippecanoe," written to the tune of "The Campbells Are Coming":

The Day is all over; the Battle is done;
The Field it is conquered; the Victory won:
We've carried our Leader triumphantly through;
Then peal your huzzahs for Old Tippecanoe; . . .
CHORUS.
Old Tip is a coming from Ohio!
Old Tip is a coming from Ohio!
Old Tip is a coming—he's let his Log Cabin!
Old Tip is a coming from Ohio!

Number one on the Whig hit parade, of course, was the "Great Commotion," the song about Tippecanoe and Tyler Too that Zanesville, Ohio's A. C. Ross was moved to create after attending the Columbus convention. Back home, Ross kept thinking about writing the song while singing in his church choir. As the minister delivered a sermon, Ross blocked out in his mind a version of what would become the famous campaign song.

The next Saturday night, Ross was scheduled to unveil his new song at the Tippecanoe Glee Club, which was meeting at the Zanesville Court House. But at the last minute he decided not to sing because he wasn't happy with one of the verses. "Let me hear the line," one of the members asked. Ross replied, "Van, Van, you're a nice little man." "Thunder," the club member responded, "make it Van is a used-up man."

The rest was presidential campaign history. When Ross sang his new song, the audience went nuts, cheering and shouting. The original song had twelve stanzas and went in part:

> *What has caused the great commotion, motion, motion.*
> *Our country through?*
> *It is the ball a rolling on, on.*
> *For Tippecanoe and Tyler, too—Tippecanoe and Tyler, too;*
> *And with them we'll beat little Van, Van, Van.*
> *Van is a used-up man;*
> *And with them we'll beat little Van.*
> *Like the rushing of mighty waters, waters, waters.*
> *On it will go.*
> *And in its course will clear the way*
> *For Tippecanoe, and Tyler, too.*
> *Don't you hear from every quarter, quarter, quarter,*
> *Good news and true,*
> *That swift the ball is rolling on*
> *For Tippecanoe and Tyler, too.*
> *Let them talk about hard cider, cider, cider,*
> *And log cabins, too,*
> *'Twill only help to speed the ball*
> *For Tippecanoe and Tyler, too.*

The latch-string hangs outside the door, door, door,
And is never pulled through
For it never was the custom of
Old Tippecanoe, and Tyler, too.
Little Matty's days are number'd, number'd, number'd
Out he must go
And in his chair we'll place the good
Old Tippecanoe and Tyler, too.

The song initially became a regional hit. Then in early September Ross attended a Whig meeting at Lafayette Hall in New York City. When the Whig speakers were late, officials asked if anybody in the audience could sing a campaign song until the orators arrived. Ross raised his hand. Immediately, he was lifted hand-to-hand above the audience to the stage like a fan at a rock concert.

Ross broke into the first few lines of his song:

What has caused the great commotion, motion, motion
Our country through!
It is the ball a rolling on, on . . .

By now the crowd was on its feet, cheering. Ross sang on, and on, adding impromptu verses to his original twelve.

Whig newspapers across the country published the entire song. "Van is a used-up man" became another widely used campaign slogan.

The Whig songs divided families. Democratic husbands and fathers were outraged when their wives and daughters joined in the singing. "We know of daughters being locked up to prevent their singing Whig songs," said journalist A. B. Norton.

Democrats ridiculed the Whigs musical tactics. Under the headline SINGING FOR THE PRESIDENCY, the *Extra Globe* charged that the Whigs were using songs to cover up the lack of discussion on issues. The Democrats tried to organize their own glee clubs and write their own songs, but they found little enthusiasm and few memorable songs. Most were lame imitations of the spirited Whig songs, such as the Democratic version of the great commotion:

> *What has caused this great commotion, motion, motion*
> *Our country through?*
> *It is the ball a rolling on*
> *And Tippecanoe and coon skins too—Tippecanoe and*
> *   coons too;*
> *And we shall elect little Van, Van, Van*
> *And we shall elect little Van, Van, Van*
> *Van is a re-elected man.*

Clearly the Democrats' songs were no match for the Whigs'. The *New York Evening Post* editorialized, "We could meet the Whigs on the field of argument and beat them without effort. But when they lay down the weapons of argument and attack us with musical notes, what can we do?"

Like Horace Greeley, Whig editor Richard Smith Elliott admitted that the Whig songs weren't exactly elegant but were exactly suited to their purpose. "The plain language, homely allusions and cant flings at our adversaries were sweet morsels to the Whig palate," Elliott said. "We strained our throats in vocal efforts never before equaled."

At the same time as the Whigs were promoting their message across the country through song, they were also marketing the campaign's log cabin symbol far and wide—even at the family dinner table.

15

THE MARKETING OF A CANDIDATE

ALL you Tips who want Log Cabin Breast Pins, Tippecanoe pencils or Combs are requested to call at JAS. W. FAULKNER'S Watch and Jewelry Store [and] buy them cheap for Cash.

—Ad in the *Log Cabin* newspaper

William Henry Harrison and log cabins not only were on the lips of singing Whigs in 1840. They also were on about every kind of item, from dinner plates to walking canes. Long before radio and television, the Whigs marketed their candidates like soap—literally—with Tippecanoe Shaving Soap, which was a real product.

"Log cabins were everywhere; in parlor pictures; in shop windows; worked in jewelry; hung to watch chains; displayed on harness, and worn by pendant from ears of patriotic dames and damsels," said Whig strategist Richard Smith Elliott. The campaign items weren't just souvenirs. The log cabin symbol or Harrison's image adorned items used by average people nearly every day as a constant reminder of the Whig message.

In later years, accounts of the campaign asserted that the most famous campaign product was a bottle shaped like a log cabin and filled with whiskey, produced by Philadelphia distiller E. G. Booz. Legend has it that the popularity of the Booz Bottles led to the nickname *booze* for liquor.

Legend has it wrong on both counts. The bottles, while perhaps symbolic of the 1840 campaign, actually weren't sold until at least 1860. That's when Edmund G. Booz operated his whiskey company at 120 Walnut Street in Philadelphia. The bottles were made by the Whitney Glass Works of Glassboro, New Jersey, which had a plant next door at 118 Walnut Street. The confusion arose because the date 1840 was stamped on the cabin roofs of the amber glass bottles. "Perhaps the '1840' indicated the date the whisky was distilled," one bottle historian speculated. As for the term *booze*, it had been around for years in various languages and spellings. But the popularity of the Booz Bottles likely did expand use of the term in America.

There really were popular log cabin bottles for whiskey in the campaign, however. The Mount Vernon Glass Company in New York made one of them in 1840. The bottle was a deep olive green color and made of lead glass. Above the door on one side was the word Tippecanoe. Over the door on the opposite side were the words North Bend. Whigs also could sip their whiskey or hard cider out of flasks shaped like a log cabin.

The Harrison campaign spread the log cabin symbol into the minds of voters through scores of products. When a voter cleaned up his plate at dinner, he often was staring at the log cabin image imprinted right on the dish. Whigs drank their coffee using cups and saucers with the log cabin imprint. They poured milk out of a pewter pitcher or tea from a teapot with a picture of a log cabin on it. They walked using log cabin canes with barrel-shaped ceramic heads inscribed with the words HARD CIDER. They wiped their noses with a campaign handkerchief featuring a picture of a log cabin and the words HARRISON AND REFORM.

As much as the log cabin was a marketing symbol, so were images of Harrison himself. The general's face was on a brandy snifter, a snuffbox, writing paper, and a hairbrush. Whig women wore kerchiefs with pictures of General Harrison on horseback. The Whigs distributed log cabin campaign buttons and ribbons with Harrison's face on them. One ribbon of light green silk showed Harrison's mug between two flags and an eagle above, with the saying POOR MAN'S CABIN. Harrison's face also adorned campaign medals in silver, copper, bronze, glass, and tin.

True, there were ribbons and medals featuring Van Buren, but not as many as for Old Tip. Democrats charged that many of the Whigs' pieces of political Americana weren't made in the USA but

Log cabin handkerchief. *Library of Congress*

were produced by foreign workers, especially in England. "While our great manufacturing corporations are discharging from their employment all the supporters of the Democracy and reducing the wages of the rest . . . their English rivals are flooding the markets" with Tippecanoe products, the *Extra Globe* thundered.

The Democrats were right in many cases. Men could shave with "superior razors," made with blades inscribed with the words TRY ME ONE TERM. The razor showed Harrison welcoming two old comrades to his log cabin. It was made by Wm. Graves and Sons of the Scarf Works in Sheffield, England.

Many of the log cabin dinner plates also were British made. One tip-off was when the plates pictured a two-story log cabin, which was common in England, rather than the one-story American cabin.

The most popular log cabin china set was produced in England by John Ridgeway, who later became the potter for Queen Victoria. This was called the Columbian Star set, featuring a one-story log cabin with a blue border of large stars in a galaxy of small ones. The first consignment was sent to a New York City merchant named Henry Winkler. What made these plates unusual was that they were the first decorative dishes made for everyday use. They sold for only seven and a half cents a plate and were used in Whig households for years.

Harrison was everywhere. There were at least twelve biographies. One 300-page book, *The Life and Times of William Henry Harrison* by S. J. Burr, sold for thirty-seven and a half cents. Harrison got royalties from one of the books, *A Memoir of the Public Services of William Henry Harrison* by James Hall. Colonel Charles Todd, Harrison's old friend and campaign manager, published a biography of the candidate. The Whigs also printed a ninety-six-page *Tippecanoe Text Book* detailing Harrison's life and accomplishments. The book was meant mainly for Whig speakers, but sold like hotcakes to the public.

Another bestseller was the *Harrison Almanac for 1841*. Sprinkled between reports on the phases of the moon each month and predictions of four solar eclipses expected in 1841 were stories about Old Tippecanoe. They included "Harrison's Kindness to an Old Irishman in Distress," "Harrison's Humanity in War," "Harrison's Self-Devotion," and "Harrison's Generosity to a Captured Enemy."

Dozens of posters and engravings promoted Harrison as a military hero and the Farmer of North Bend. Many of these posters were quite elaborate, with the glowing text surrounded by as many as a dozen drawings of Harrison. One poster of "Log Cabin Anecdotes" portrayed Harrison on horseback with twelve vignettes about his life. There were "Harrison charging in battle at the Thames," "Harrison giving his horse to a Methodist minister," and "Harrison saving the life of a Negro."

General Harrison campaign poster. *Library of Congress*

Other posters showed General Harrison as the Washington of the West. On one he was pictured as an American Napoleon Bonaparte, even tucking his hand into his military jacket in the familiar Napoleonic pose. In all of the posters, Harrison was shown as a young man, not the sixty-seven-year-old candidate he was at the time.

Some of the campaign posters were quite artistic. One color lithograph showed General Harrison on a white horse in battle at Tippecanoe. The lithograph was one of several published in New York City by twenty-seven-year-old Nathanial Currier, who specialized in political prints. Another dramatic Currier print depicted Harrison as a dashing figure dressed in a black suit and cape against a purple-colored sky.

William Henry Harrison portrait by Nathanial Currier. *Library of Congress*

After the election, Currier would expand into color prints on a broad array of subjects. A bookkeeper named James Ives joined the company in 1850. His marketing skills were so successful that he later became a partner in the firm, which became known as Currier & Ives.

Political cartoons also were popular. Most of the cartoonists apparently were Whigs, since the anti–Van Buren drawings greatly outnumbered the anti-Harrison ones. A favorite theme was President Van Buren being chased out of the White House. One cartoon called "Matty's Dream" pictured the president fleeing in his nightshirt as he was pursued by a winged barrel of hard cider with Harrison's head. Another showed Van Buren as a fox fleeing hounds shaped like cider barrels while Harrison looked on from the steps of the White House.

One of the most popular cartoons depicted an angry Van Buren walking down the steps of the White House. He was muttering the infamous quote from his days in the New York legislature, "Our sufferings is intolerable," while Harrison peeked out of the window from inside. Harrison was saying, "Show the Gentleman out . . . and give him a glass of cider before he goes."

The Log Cabin and Tippecanoe craze meant that the Whigs often did not have to pay to advertise their messages; private companies did it for them. An ad in the *Burlington (VT) Free Press* read, "HARRISON GOODS. We invite attention to our assortment of the Goods, amongst them Gold Miniature Log Cabins for Lockets, gold log cabin Watch Keys, Goldplated Log Cabin Pins. Log Cabin Medals, Tippecanoe Shaving soap, Tippecanoe Canes, Song Books, Text Books, Almanacs . . . Boy's life of Harrison, a new kind of Log Cabin Letter Paper, and various other goods in this line at the Variety store, PANGBORN &, BRINSMAID."

One company advertised Log Cabin Emollient to soften skin, "efficiently removing all pimples and pucks in a few days." A Tippecanoe Extract was promoted as "a compound of the finest essences and a most delicate perfume for handkerchiefs, gloves and the air, leaving a rich and durable fragrance."

The People's Line—Take care of the Locomotive
Sold at 104 Nassau, and 18 Division Streets, New-York.

Pro-Harrison cartoon. *Library of Congress*

Tippecanoe Shaving Soap was advertised as "the most valuable preparation yet discovered to afford ease and comfort in shaving." (The Democratic *New York Morning Herald* retorted about the shaving soap, "We took it to our barber, Jem Grant, who tried it and says it was no great affair. And if everything that is marked with the Tippecanoe brand is no better than this shaving soap, why the less said about it the better.")

Democratic newspapers mocked the Whig merchandising for trying to woo the common people with such fancy doodads as Log Cabin gold-plated buttons, a silk Tippecanoe handkerchief, and Log Cabin champagne. Scoffed the *Illinois Free Trader*, "We expect before the farce is ended, we will see some of our dandies with 'Log Cabin Ruffle Shirts' and 'Log Cabin Silk Stockings.'"

The Democratic sniping did nothing to slow the Tippecanoe marketing juggernaut. Indeed, the advertising rhetoric intensified as more private companies sought to take advantage of the attention-getting Whig campaign. One ad in the *New York Evening Signal* proclaimed, "If General Harrison had been murdered in his bed! And Martin Van Buren accused of his murder. It could not have caused a greater sensation than Jones's Bunker Hill Shaving Cream has."

With the Whigs' message everywhere, the Democrats regrouped to strike back.

16

GOING NEGATIVE:
THE DEMOCRATS FIGHT BACK

*I am the most persecuted ... individual now
living.*

—William Henry Harrison

Jarred by the early success of the log cabin and hard cider carnival
of the Whigs, Democratic leaders sent out a new strategy: forget
about defending President Van Buren. Attack Harrison.

As usual, the *Extra Globe* was not subtle about the message:

> DEMOCRATS, now is the moment to charge! Democratic editors,
> abandon your defensive warfare and charge home upon the
> enemy! . . . Hold up to solemn scorn the Federal candidate
> STANDING MUTE before a nation of freemen! Ask the people
> whether they will surrender themselves to this DUMB IDOL at the
> bidding of the priests who surround him!

Democrats renewed their focus on Granny Harrison's advanced
age. They began a whispering campaign hinting that the old general, at age sixty-seven, was in such poor health that he might not
survive the campaign.

At least one Democrat went public. "In my judgment," said
Congressman L. W. Tazewell of Virginia, "General Harrison is
both physically and intellectually incompetent to perform the
many, varied, arduous, and important duties which must devolve
upon every President of the United States."

For the first time in a presidential contest, the Whigs trotted out
a physician to vouch for a candidate's physical and mental fitness.

Dr. Daniel Drake, Harrison's doctor in Cincinnati, wrote a long letter to a Louisville newspaper stating that he recently had examined the general and was surprised by his "vivacity and almost youthfulness of feelings. . . . His intellect is unimpaired. Body vigor as good as that of most men of his age. Subject to no disease but periodic headaches." Harrison himself wrote a supporter to say, "My health is indeed better than it has been for many years." Issuing a doctor's report on the physical health of a presidential candidate eventually would become standard practice.

Picking up on the Whigs' hard cider theme, the Democrats also accused Harrison of being a drunk. Once again emulating their opponents' song-singing, the Van Buren forces put the drinking charges to music:

> *Hush-a-bye baby, Daddy's a Whig*
> *When he comes home, hard cider he'll swig*
> *When he has swug, He'll fall in a stu*
> *And down will come Tyler and Tippecanoe.*
> *Rockabye, baby, when you awake*
> *You will discover Tip is a fake.*
> *Far from the battle, war cry and drum*
> *He sits in his cabin a'drinking bad rum.*

Not only was Harrison a drunk, Democratic newspapers declared, he also used "SHOCKING PROFANITY." The latter charge stemmed from an incident in which an acquaintance of Harrison saw the general on a Cincinnati street soon after Democratic senator James Buchanan of Pennsylvania had given a speech attacking Harrison. The general "commenced cursing Buchanan," the acquaintance wrote in a letter to a newspaper. Harrison, the man claimed, called Buchanan "a DAMNED SCOUNDREL," adding, "GOD DAMN HIM, he was a lawyer and knew better."

Then there was the sex—or alleged sex. Democratic newspapers reported that the old Indian fighter had sired three illegitimate children with a Winnebago squaw. According to the papers, the woman had attempted to obtain government payments offered to help support half-breed children. The story was completely fabricated. "Now it happens that I have never seen a squaw of any tribe for upwards of 28 years and never, that I know of, one of that tribe in my life," Harrison responded.

The Democrats' trailblazing opposition research dug up more dirt. Under the headline HARRISON THE SEDUCER, the *Ohio Statesman* dredged up a fifteen-year-old allegation that Harrison had led a young woman astray at his home in North Bend, Ohio. "Perhaps there has not been in the state of Ohio a more melancholy and dastardly case of seduction than this," the article said.

According to the story, during the summer and fall of 1825, the Harrisons had temporarily moved into Cincinnati, and the general had given use of the home in North Bend to a Doctor Brower with his family, including their daughter. "Miss Brower was a young, artless girl, and Gen. Harrison marked her for his prey" during his overnight stays back at the farm, the paper said.

The newspaper couldn't bring itself to say exactly what Harrison supposedly did with the young girl. "It is an act of such a deep and damning nature that virtue must ever blush in crimson when the brazen destroyer passes in view," the article said. As for Miss Brower, she "is still living, a solitary monument of ruined virtue of this black and dastardly act, which ten thousand lives of penitence cannot wash out." At the time of the controversy, Harrison wrote a letter to a local newspaper declaring that he did not have sexual relations with that woman, Miss Brower.

(The Democrats may have missed one possible sex scandal. In the 1940s, Walter White, the African American executive director of the NAACP from 1918 to 1942, said that Harrison was his great-grandfather. White said that his great-grandmother, Dilsia, was one of Harrison's slaves and that his grandmother was one of six children she had with the general. According to the family story, Harrison didn't want "bastard slave children" around during the 1840 presidential race, so he gave them to his brother. There is no mention of Dilsia in any writings about Harrison, but she could have been one of the slaves that he brought from Virginia. At any rate, the story did not emerge during the campaign.)

Harrison's political foes even accused him of being under the spell of witchcraft. One reason not to vote for Harrison was that he was "a man who believes in ghosts and witches," said one critic, adding that such a man "ought to die in obscurity."

Democrats repeatedly charged that as a lawmaker Harrison favored the whipping of white men and women who failed to pay their debts. The white debtors could even be sold into slavery in order to pay back what they owed. The *Globe* raised the specter of a law that "exposed the bare backs of women and of children to the lash." The charge was a grossly exaggerated version of proposed debt bills that had been backed by members of both parties but had never become law. The allegation failed to gain traction with voters.

The Democrats often played the race card. They said that abolitionists and slaves supported Harrison. The *Delaware Gazette* warned that Harrison would move to "place the BLACKS on an EQUALITY with the WHITES." An Ohio newspaper declared that, if elected, Harrison would use $28 million of surplus federal revenues to set slaves free "to overrun our country."

Harrison played both sides of the issue. In letters to abolitionists, he noted that as a youth he had joined a Quaker humane society in Richmond, Virginia, dedicated to abolition. In comments to proslavery backers, he insisted that the society's devotion to things humane had nothing to do with abolition. In fact, his view on slavery was no different from that of President Van Buren— or slaveholding presidents Washington, Jefferson, and Madison: slavery was an evil institution, but the federal government had no right under the Constitution to force states to end it.

Antislavery forces opposed both Van Buren and Harrison. Their supporters formed a third party, the Liberty Party, and nominated James Birney of Kentucky, a former slaveholder, to run as its candidate for president. But countering the Whig excitement was an uphill battle. One Birney backer lamented in a letter to abolitionist leader William Lloyd Garrison that seven-tenths of the voting abolitionists were politically intoxicated in their enthusiasm for Harrison and reform.

One of the most surprising attacks against Harrison was that he had been a supporter of America's second president, John Adams. At this point in American history, Adams no longer was idolized. To the contrary, to be aligned with John Adams was akin to being a fan of Attila the Hun. Adams was widely reviled for presiding over an American "Reign of Terror" after backing the notorious Alien and Sedition Acts. Among other things, the acts made it illegal to criticize the president and other government officials. Many Americans were fined and even jailed under the law. When President Adams was parading through Newark, New Jersey, in July 1798, a drunk in a local tavern heard the salute of cannon shots and was overheard remarking, "There goes the President, and they are shooting at his arse." The man, the pilot of a garbage scow, was fined $150 and sent to the slammer. Fortunately for Harrison, the first Adams was one of the few Founding Fathers with whom he'd had little contact.

Adopting another Whig tactic, the Democrats distributed anti-Harrison cartoons. One showed President Van Buren standing on the bank of a stream as Harrison, in the form of a donkey, flopped around in the shallow waters with a barrel of hard cider tied to its tail. Van Buren wished the donkey "a quick voyage, take care you don't spill your valuable cargo." It was lame, but it was about all the Democrats had.

Equally lame were Democratic attempts to come up with a catchy phrase like Tippecanoe and Tyler Too. The best they could do was a story about a man who was asked if he planned to vote for the Whig candidate. The voter responded by stating Harrison's name spelled backward: "No Sirrah."

Indeed, just about everything the Democrats came up with seemed to backfire, just like the log cabin slur by the Baltimore newspaper that had inspired Harrison's campaign image. In the spring of 1840, some Democrats in New York City formed a group to campaign for Van Buren's reelection. They called themselves the O.K. Club, a reference to one of Van Buren's nicknames, Old Kinderhook, and to a then-obscure joke about the misspelled abbreviation for "all correct." Part of the group's strategy was to disrupt Whig meetings. One night a gang of club members broke into a Whig meeting shouting, "Down with the Whigs, boys. O.K.!"

Newspapers picked up the expression "O.K.," which became a popular catchphrase. The problem for the Democrats was that the Whigs pretty much confiscated the term, using "O.K." to mock the Democrats every time Van Buren suffered a setback. The phrase has lived on.

Democrats continued to replay all of Harrison's military campaigns, casting him as a fighting failure. They called him a Petticoat General, citing an incident in Chillicothe, Ohio, after the War of 1812. Supposedly, the ladies of the town had presented a sword to one veteran of the war and sewn a petticoat to give to Harrison. The story fell apart when townspeople declared that the event never happened. The woman who was said to have sewn the petticoat swore on her deathbed that she never did any such thing.

When Democrats called Harrison a coward, Whigs responded, where was Martin Van Buren during the war? While Harrison was in battle, Van Buren sat out the War of 1812 as a state legislator in New York. The only time Little Matty ever carried a gun was when he was vice president. One day after an assassination attempt on President Jackson, Van Buren concealed two small pistols in his coat while presiding over the US Senate.

The Whigs even wrote a song about Van Buren's war record. They called it "Little Vanny":

> *He never was seen in a battle,*
> *Where bullets and cannon shot flew;*
> *His nerves would be shocked with the rattle*
> *Of a contest like Tippecanoe!*

Whig newspapers accused the Democrats of plotting to deny Harrison the presidency even if he were elected—they would claim the election to be a fraud and retain Van Buren in office. The Whig papers in Cincinnati even speculated that the Democrats were plotting to kill Harrison should he win.

At one point, the Democrats came up with what they thought would be the silver bullet that would shoot down Harrison's campaign: evidence that Old Tip had once supported creating a standing army. This was the third rail of American politics at the time. In the American Revolution, citizen soldiers had won freedom against a standing British army. Americans vowed that never again would there be a national army stronger than state militias. They cemented that vow in the Bill of Rights; the Second Amendment to the US Constitution states, "A well regulated Militia, being necessary to the security of a free State, the right of the people to keep and bear Arms, shall not be infringed."

Years ago Harrison had proposed drafting adult men to serve in a professional army. Like many military men, the general became concerned that state militias often were not well trained and not reliable. Nor would they be a strong enough force to thwart a major enemy. If elected president, Democrats warned, Harrison would act on his plan to create a national army just like the British forces that oppressed America in the 1700s.

It was around this time that President Van Buren's tone-deaf secretary of war Joel Poinsett publicly proposed a major reorganization of the state militias. His plan called for drafting at least a hundred thousand able-bodied white males from twenty to forty-five years old for militia service, with a total anticipated force of two hundred thousand men. The drafted men would undergo annual training. They would be provided with a musket, bayonet, knapsack, and a cartridge box with at least twenty-four cartridges. Beyond that, they would have to provide their own guns and ammunition.

The Poinsett plan set off a firestorm. Though the plan would keep men under state control, Whigs quickly charged that Poinsett wanted to create a national standing army of two hundred thousand men. The plan would make Van Buren a new king with soldiers at his command. Van Buren backed away from the proposal as quickly as he could, saying he never approved such a plan. The idea, he said, was as preposterous as proposing to create, at public expense, a menagerie of two hundred thousand wild beasts. But it was too late. The Poinsett plan caused severe damage to Van Buren's campaign.

(Secretary Poinsett's proposal eventually faded away, but his name lived on because of his horticultural hobby. As America's first minister to Mexico in the 1820s, he became intrigued with a bright red flower that the Mexican people called the Christmas Eve flower, which was displayed on that holiday. Poinsett brought the flower back to the United States. By the 1830s, the flower had become popular in America as the Poinsettia.)

Finally, the Democrats discovered an opening. A Democrat in Oswego, New York, had sent a letter to Harrison asking his opinion on several political issues. The man, who ran a bowling alley, received a response, not from Harrison but from a member of a committee for the Whig candidate.

The Democratic press jumped on the case. The Whigs didn't even trust Harrison to answer his own mail. Instead, the general was merely a puppet with a conscience committee pulling the strings.

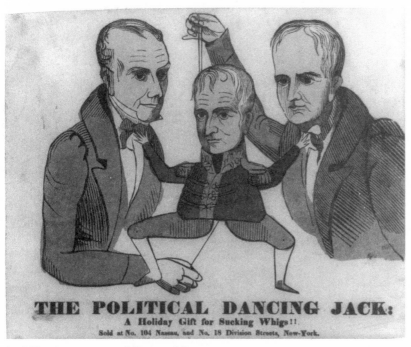

Anti-Harrison cartoon. *Library of Congress*

The *Washington Globe* purported to be shocked, shocked that Harrison wasn't answering his own mail. Under the headline HORRID BARBARITY, the opposition newspaper declared, "We are credibly informed—though we can scarcely believe it, the fact appears so monstrous and is incredible—that the keepers of Gen. Harrison's conscience have carried their barbarous caution so far as to shut up the old gentleman in an Iron Cage."

Democratic papers derided Harrison as General Mum. They joked that the Whigs kept their candidate muzzled and on a short leash. But once again, a Democratic slur was about to bite back at the Van Buren campaign, this time personally led by Old Tippecanoe himself.

17

GENERAL MUM SPEAKS

*When was there ever before such a spectacle . . .
as a candidate for the Presidency, traversing the
country, advocating his own claims for that high
and responsible station? Never!*

—*Cleveland Advertiser*

As the 1840 campaign moved into full swing, William Henry
Harrison sat seething in his North Bend, Ohio, home. The proud
general ached to get out and refute the charges that he was a senile
granny and a coward. But he knew that a presidential candidate
campaigning for himself would be improper.

So Harrison used the traditional campaign tactics of the day: he
answered letters, with the expectation that some responses would
be printed in newspapers. One letter writer, for instance, sought
out the general's views on duels. Harrison, in a long and rambling
response, said that he was against them. For the most part.

Dueling hardly was a cutting political issue. Democratic charges
that Harrison was ducking substantive debate increasingly got under
his skin. Now the ridicule that he was General Mum kept in an Iron
Cage by his keepers was the final straw. He couldn't take it anymore.

So when a letter arrived inviting him to speak at a celebration in early June to commemorate the 1813 siege of Fort Meigs,
Harrison accepted. His decision must have sent shockwaves
through the ranks of his political handlers. The last thing they
needed was for their aging candidate to be talking in public and
going off message.

But Harrison was determined. His advisers hoped that at least
he would follow the earlier advice of Nicholas Biddle, the president

of the Second Bank of the United States, who said that a Harrison candidacy should focus strictly on his image as a military hero: "Let him say not one single word about his principles, or his creed—let him say nothing—promising nothing. Let no Committee, no Convention—no town meeting ever extract from him a single word about what he thinks now or what he will do hereafter."

Harrison wasn't about to mess with the log cabin and hard cider image that had already gained so much political traction. When he took leave for Fort Meigs, he left his tall silk hat at home and packed his broad-brimmed farmer's hat. He wore a plain frock coat and a black vest. He left Cincinnati on the southern border of Ohio on June 4, 1840, in a stagecoach that would roll over the bumpy roads first to Columbus, a hundred miles away in central Ohio. Then he would travel another 140 miles to Perrysburg near the state's northern border.

The Whigs spread word of the trip, and large crowds greeted Harrison in towns along the way. The candidate got his first taste of presidential campaigning. He shook so many hands that his right hand got sore. So he began wearing a glove.

After arriving in Columbus at about 5:00 PM on a Friday, Harrison went to the local Tippecanoe Club log cabin, where he mingled with hundreds of "log cabin boys" for two hours. The cabin, which was sixty feet long, had been built on State Street between High and Third Streets. Then he checked into the National Hotel (soon to be renamed the Neil House) in the center of town for a good night's sleep before starting out for Perrysburg.

The next morning Harrison was leaving the hotel at about nine o'clock. A crowd had gathered outside. The general began making a few informal remarks. And then, without intending to, he launched into a full-blown speech. So it was that on June 6, 1840, on the steps of the National Hotel in Columbus, Ohio, William Henry Harrison gave the first presidential campaign speech in history.

His main goal was finally to answer his critics. "The story goes that I have not only a committee of conscience-keepers but that they put me in a cage," he said with a smile as the crowd laughed.

Harrison meeting poster. *Library of Congress*

He explained he couldn't keep up with the letters sent to him, at least twenty-four a day. It was costly, too—at that time, it was the person who received the mail who often paid the postage, not the sender. So he had begun turning over some letters to a friend, who directed the writers to statements Harrison had made on various subjects over the past decades. In other cases, Harrison said, he still responded personally.

Harrison said he was mortified by the personal attacks on his character and military record. He welcomed honest debate, he said. "But that political warfare which seeks success by foul detraction, and strives for ascendancy by the ruin of personal character, merits the indignation of honest men."

The old general specifically deplored the charges against his military record. "These charges were not made by my companions in arms, by the eyewitnesses of my action, by the great and good and brave men who fought by my side or under my command," he said. "They tell a different story."

Harrison even defended President Van Buren against personal attacks on him. "Nay, I have often defended Mr. Van Buren against what I believed to be the misrepresentations of my own mistaken friends and others," Harrison told the crowd. "Fellow citizens, if Mr. Van Buren be the better statesman, let us say so—I shall be the last man to raise an objection against it."

Like many presidential candidates to come, Harrison complained that the press took many of his prior comments out of context. "It seems almost incredible, fellow citizens," he said, "but it is true that from a long speech, filling several columns of a paper, two short sentences have been taken from different parts of it," separated from their original meaning, and published throughout the land under his name.

Harrison spoke for about a half hour, drawing cheers from the growing crowd. One of the onlookers was thirty-nine-year-old Sam Medary, editor of the anti-Whig *Ohio Statesman*. "We were charged with smiling as the General was speaking. If so, it was the smile of pity for our Whig friends," Medary wrote afterward.

Medary's report ran under the headline THE CAGED HERO LOOSE IN PART. His article said, "Gen. Mum was not actually set loose, but the rope only a little lengthened like that of a pet possum to exercise his limbs."

After the speech, Harrison rode in a carriage drawn by four white horses to a farewell ceremony conducted by the mayor of Columbus as a brass band played "Hail Columbia." At that point, the general switched to a fancy stagecoach provided for his personal use by the stage-line owner for the trip north. As the coach approached the nearby town of Worthington, an escort of soldiers rode up on horses with sprigs of buckeye trees in their bridles.

Traveling on the stagecoach with Harrison was a reporter from the *Buffalo (NY) Journal*, who noted the early perks of presidential campaigning. Harrison continued his travels by stagecoach free of charge. What's more, "the General himself has not been charged for a meal on the whole route."

Harrison, who had promised his wife that he wouldn't make appearances on Sundays, took the next day off in Delaware, Ohio. Then he resumed his stagecoach ride north to Belleview, where he boarded a train for only the second time in his life. The train headed for Sandusky, Ohio, fifty miles away, at a brisk speed of twenty miles per hour.

On the late afternoon of June 9, Harrison was taken by boat to the small village of Toledo on the Maumee River. From there he went by steamboat to Fort Meigs, about an hour away at Perrysburg. The town was named after Oliver Hazard Perry, the commodore who had won the Battle of Lake Erie in 1813 and then carried Harrison and his troops across the lake to fight the British. Perry had died from yellow fever in 1819 at age thirty-four.

Harrison boarded a steamship, the *Sandusky*, which along with the *Commodore Perry* led a fleet of sixteen ships up the river with bands blaring from many of them. Harrison waved to a waiting crowd from the top of the *Sandusky* as it approached Perrysburg at about six o'clock. "There he stood on the upper deck as shout after shout arose from the mouths of thousands," wrote the *Buffalo Journal* reporter.

Harrison landed to a salute of seventeen guns from the Buffalo Flying Artillery. He rode in an open carriage to the site of the old fort, high on the right bank of the Maumee River, where he was greeted with another seventeen-gun salute. Inside the fort, a huge log cabin had been built with trees from each township in Wood and Lucas Counties. Tired from his long trip, Harrison went to stay overnight at the home of a local judge.

Meantime, thousands of people had arrived to party at the Fort Meigs site. A delegation from Richland County, Ohio, came from a hundred miles away in 123 wagons. Another delegation came in 500 wagons. About three thousand people arrived by boat from Detroit, where a traveling young writer named Herman Melville had watched them board, amazed by the enthusiastic turnout. Maybe it was something like seeing a white whale.

Tents were put up everywhere. By 9:00 PM at least twenty thousand people were on the grounds. People listened to speakers, sang Tippecanoe songs, and swigged hard cider. About midnight, a mock attack by a hundred men portraying Native Americans began, and mock soldiers fought them off.

Crowds reassembled starting at ten o'clock the next morning for a day of speeches. The feature attraction was General Harrison. There at Fort Meigs, on June 11, 1840, a sunny Saturday, Harrison gave his first formal presidential campaign speech.

It must have been an overwhelming moment for the old hero. From the speaker's stand, he looked out toward the old fort where he had battled the British in 1813, and the fields where earlier he had fought Native Americans under "Mad Anthony" Wayne. He was surrounded by a sea of thirty thousand to forty thousand people, including many who were his old comrades in arms. He spoke without notes. There were no microphones, so it's unlikely all could hear him. But it didn't matter.

Harrison instinctively adopted techniques that would become staples of presidential campaign addresses to come. Early on, he spotted an old soldier, one General Hedges, sitting near the front. Harrison quickly captured the crowd's sympathy by inviting his old colleague to join him on the speaker's stand: "You have stood by my side in the hour of battle, and I cannot bear to see you at so great a distance now," Harrison said. Several men carried General Hedges to the stage. The crowd went wild.

Harrison also used some stage props. At one point in his speech, Harrison indicated that he could use something to "wet my whistle." Someone passed up a jug of hard cider, from which Harrison took some swigs, much to the delight of his audience.

(A Democrat in the crowd later claimed that both the invitation to Harrison's old colleague and the cider drinks were staged by the candidate and his handlers. When Harrison's cider sips drew cheers, the man said, "you could plainly see him chuckling at the temporary effect it produced.")

Harrison spoke for two hours, mainly reminiscing about past battles. "Not for one moment did he falter," wrote the *Buffalo Journal* reporter. "The trumpet-like tones" of his voice rang out as clear at the close of the speech as it had at the start.

The closest the candidate came to discussing issues was warning about the Democrats' unquenchable thirst for more political power. "If the ladies whom I see around me were near enough to hear me, and of sufficient age to give an experimental answer, they would tell you that no lover is ever satisfied with the first smile of his mistress," he said. It was necessary, then, to watch the Van Buren administration "to see that it keeps within the bounds of the Constitution and the laws of the land."

After Fort Meigs, Harrison traveled by boat across Lake Erie to Cleveland. Despite a bout of seasickness, he spoke for nearly two hours from the plaza of the American House hotel before a crowd of some five thousand people. Then he headed home via the Erie Canal to North Bend, stopping to make more speeches along the way.

Thousands turned out to hear him in Newark, just east of Columbus. A marching band and local officials escorted Harrison from the canal to the courthouse at the center of town. Along the way farmhouses were decorated with flags, "and on one occasion especially, we noticed some handsome ladies waving their handkerchiefs from the balcony, while there was suspended a small keg of hard cider and a gourd hanging below it," the *Dayton Journal* reported. "His remarks were in a style as happy as those delivered at Fort Meigs and Cleveland," the paper said.

The idea of a presidential candidate campaigning for himself sent shockwaves through the nation. "What a prodigy of garrulous egotism!" scolded the *Globe*, which counted eighty-one "I's" in Harrison's Fort Meigs speech. Commented another Democratic newspaper, "The precedent thus set by Harrison . . . appears to us a bad one."

But Whigs hailed the speech-making. Both Harrison and the voters clamored for more.

18

OLD TIP ON THE CAMPAIGN TRAIL

*General Harrison is going from town to town,
behaving like a . . . blubbering child.*

—*Ohio Statesman*

William Henry Harrison's first speech-making tour got cut short.
Following his triumph at Fort Meigs, his original plan was to campaign his way back home, but that changed after he arrived by
stagecoach in Springfield, Ohio, in the early afternoon of June 25.

He rode into town in an open, horse-drawn carriage. Reaching
the top of a hill, he could see more than fifteen thousand jubilant
people below, filling the main street and anxiously waiting to see
and hear him. More than five hundred banners waved in the breeze.

But before heading down to the village to give his speech,
Harrison stopped at a local residence, where he was handed a letter with terrible news: his son Benjamin, a physician, had died from
tuberculosis at age thirty-four. He was the fourth of Harrison's
sons to die in recent years. As the news quickly spread to the
townspeople, the joyful crowd turned somber. When Harrison
continued his ride through the town, the onlookers greeted him
with respectful silence. The carriage nudged through the street
crowds without stopping.

Harrison returned home to North Bend to find that his griev-
ing wife, Anna, was ill. He put his presidential campaign on hold.

Meanwhile, he had reached out to Henry Clay, seeking a meeting, perhaps to get campaign advice. "I would be gratified to see
you," Harrison wrote in a letter dated June 21. "But the meeting
must appear to be accidental. Can you arrange such a one? [P.S.]
I am in excellent health."

There is no record that the meeting ever took place. In any case, after a month away, Harrison resumed campaigning on July 28 in Greenville, Ohio. This was where he had signed peace treaties with Native American tribes. Harrison addressed more than fifteen thousand people from a stage that had been set up on a hillside. It was the biggest crowd ever seen in the town, attracting people from both Ohio and nearby Indiana.

In person, voters could see that Harrison was not the young general pictured in campaign posters. His jowls sagged and his hair was graying. A member of the reception committee at Greenville recalled that Harrison looked tired and worried. "Nobody expected to see such a common and plain old gentleman," he said.

But Harrison's lively manner soon put all worries aside. "Fellow citizens, you have undoubtedly seen it oftentimes stated in a certain class of newspapers that I am a very decrepit old man, obliged to hobble about on crutches; that I was caged up, and that I could not speak loud enough to be heard more than four or five feet distant," he told the crowd. "You now perceive, however, that these stories are false."

Indeed, "there is nothing old granny about him," one eyewitness later wrote a friend. The man, a carriage maker from Warren, Ohio, described the candidate. "He is about 5 feet 9 inches in height, very slender and thin in flesh with a noble and benign expression of countenance and keen penetrating eyes. He is not bald but gray and walks very quick and seems to be as active as a man of 45." Harrison's talks stirred his supporters, the Warren man wrote. When a local Democrat yelled out that Harrison was a coward, an old man on crutches sprang up and hit the heckler with one of his crutches, knocking him to the ground.

Critics complained that Harrison never spoke on issues or said specifically what he would do as president. "In vain we look in this Greenville speech for any declaration of PRINCIPLES. On that point he firmly adheres to his policy of concealment," said the *Extra Globe*.

Harrison explained in his speeches that he believed people running for public office shouldn't make promises. Why?

William Henry Harrison in 1840. *Library of Congress*

Because "then the battle will no longer be to the strong, to the virtuous, or to the sincere lover of his country; but to him who is prepared to tell the greatest number of lies"—meaning that those who make pledges often have no intention of keeping them.

The general stuck with the myth of his log cabin home, though sometimes seemingly with a wink as if discussing an inside joke between himself and his listeners. "It is true that a part of my dwelling house is a log cabin, but as to the hard cider . . ." he said in Columbus. The crowd's laughter drowned out his final words.

Soon he dropped the "part of" phrase. At Greenville, he talked about living with his family in "the peace and quiet of our log cabin at the Bend."

Harrison continued to crisscross Ohio, drawing huge crowds like an aging rock star on a concert tour. He seemed to want to show that he had the energy to be president. He would thrill the throng when he rode his white horse right up to the speaker's stand. Other times the general would ride up to his speeches in a horse-drawn open carriage with a collapsible top and two double seats facing each other. The driver sat in a raised seat outside the carriage. Old Tippecanoe would stand up and wave to the crowd from his Tip-mobile.

Many folks traveled for days just to hear the old general speak. Crowds continued to grow. They reached a peak in Dayton, Ohio, on September 10 at one of the biggest public events of the year: the celebration of Commodore Perry's victory on Lake Erie on September 10, 1813, in the War of 1812.

Hordes of people began pouring into Dayton days before the big event. Harrison arrived on the evening of September 9 and stayed at a private residence. At seven the next morning, marching bands and carriages began a procession into downtown Dayton with General Harrison riding in the middle on his horse. People lined the streets as more than six hundred Tippecanoe banners and flags waved. Many of the banners stretched across the streets from the roofs of stores and factories; others were raised on flagpoles outside private homes.

There were log cabins rolling on wheels, some filled with men in hunting shirts. Inside others were singing boys and girls. One cabin had a live wolf draped in a sheepskin, representing Harrison's opponent as the proverbial wolf in sheep's clothing. Once again Harrison backers rolled a big leather ball down the street for Tippecanoe and Tyler Too. Over a thousand carriages, three abreast, filled the streets. The procession ran for more than two miles.

General Harrison went to the National Hotel on Third Street to prepare for his speech. At one o'clock, the procession regrouped and moved to the stand where the speech-making by Harrison and others would take place. As the general waited on the stand, he looked out over the largest sea of people ever to attend a political event in America up until that time.

The event was a magnet for people ranging from political junkies to pickpockets. Sitting in the crowd was young George Julian, who had traveled from Indiana to see Harrison speak. "He was the first 'great man' I had seen, and I succeeded in getting quite near him," the future Indiana congressman said. "And while gazing into his face with awe which I have never since felt for any mortal, I was suddenly recalled from my rapt condition by the exit of my pocket-book."

Crowd estimates ranged from at least sixty thousand people to more than a hundred thousand. Either figure was astonishing, given that Dayton's population was only about six thousand. But three civil engineers calculated the crowd by counting the number of people who stood on a quarter of an acre. They calculated the audience as ten acres of people. All ten acres roared as Harrison stood up to speak.

"I rise, fellow citizens," he began. The crowd interrupted him with prolonged cheering. A transcriber of the speech later interjected, "The multitude was here agitated as the sea when the wild wind blows upon it, and it was full five minutes before the tumult of joy at seeing and hearing the next President of the United States could be calmed."

Again showing a natural instinct for campaign speaking, Harrison began with some self-deprecation. He was not a professional speaker, he said. "I am an old soldier and a farmer, and as my sole object is to speak what I think, you will excuse me if I do it in my own way."

By now, Harrison was beginning to feel freer to expound on issues. "Methinks I hear a soft voice asking: Are you in favor of paper money? I am," he said, to shouts of support. He also favored a system of credit because "the two systems are the only means under heaven by which a poor, industrious man may become a rich man without bowing to colossal wealth."

Then, ignoring the fact that many of his major supporters were bankers, Harrison added, "But with all this I am not a bank man. Once in my life I was, and then they cheated me out of every dollar I placed in their hands. And I shall never indulge in this way again."

The audience erupted with acclamation. "General Harrison was a forcible speaker, and his voice, while not sonorous was clear and penetrating," said E. D. Mansfield, a spectator at the speech.

Harrison spoke for two hours, long enough to prove his endurance. "I have detained you, fellow citizens, longer than I intended," he concluded. "But you now see that I am not the old man on crutches, nor the imbecile they say I am, not the prey to disease [a voice cried here, 'Nor the bear in a cage'] nor the caged animal they wittily described me to be."

The crowd stood, cheering and shouting. Or as the transcriber put it, "The multitude swayed to and fro as the leaves of the forest in a storm of wind." The huge turnout sparked the battle cry, "As Ohio goes, so goes the nation." The motto would be claimed by another state later in the election year.

The general moved twenty-two miles on from Dayton to speak in Lebanon, Ohio. Cheering crowds lined the road along the way, waving flags and banners. People in carriages and on horseback fell in behind Harrison's carriage to form a cavalcade a mile long.

Near Piqua in the Miami Valley, Harrison met up with one of his oldest friends, Colonel John Johnston. The sixty-five-year-old colonel was the delegate who had ridden his horse to the Harrisburg convention. He and Harrison had served together in Ohio, Indiana, and the War of 1812. The two men had supper before Harrison gave an hour-long speech to a large crowd. By the end of the day, the candidate had ridden his stagecoach fifty miles and had given three speeches. After the final speech, Johnston took Harrison to stay overnight in his farmhouse.

The two old friends sat up late talking. Asked how he was doing, Johnston said he had kept out of debt, but barely. Harrison asked why Johnston didn't do as some other military officials had done: use government money to speculate and make a fortune. The colonel said it was because Harrison had always urged his officers not to use public money for private purposes. So if there was anybody to blame for him not making a fortune, it was Harrison himself. Old Tip laughed.

Harrison continued making speeches into late October. More than fifty thousand people turned out to hear him in Chillicothe. A procession six miles long escorted the general, who stood in his carriage and waved to the crowd. Another twenty thousand were at Urbana in his home state, including at least five thousand women described as the "fair daughters of Ohio."

In Cincinnati, Harrison rode in a parade three miles long that snaked its way through the Queen City. Whigs estimated the crowd there at near one hundred thousand people. As the carriage passed Miss Staughton's "female academy" at Third and Vine Streets, the students stood with flags representing different states. The "Misses," the Cincinnati paper reported, then "sang most sweetly a Harrison song, and all the ladies joined in the chorus."

Even some of Harrison's supporters began to worry that he was taking on an exhausting schedule. In a final flurry of speeches in mid-Ohio he went to Chillicothe and Lancaster on September 18, then the next morning rode by carriage thirty-eight miles to Somerset, where he spoke for three hours. He rested on Sunday, then went on to speak at Circleville and Columbus. Finally, he returned to Cincinnati in a twenty-one-hour stagecoach ride.

"If General Harrison's friends had one particle of common sense, they would take him home and keep him there," said the opposition *Ohio Statesman*, which lamented, "The other day he was General Mum, now he speaks too much."

Even Harrison sometimes fretted about the long-term impact of his campaigning for president. "Indeed, sometimes I fear that upon me will fall the responsibility of establishing a dangerous precedent to be followed in future time," he said in Chillicothe.

By the end of the campaign, Harrison had given more than two dozen speeches. All were in Ohio, but most were transcribed, published, and distributed nationwide. In addition, when it came to speaking for his campaign, Old Tippecanoe was no Lone Ranger.

19

STUMP SPEAKERS

*This practice of itinerant speech making has
suddenly broken out in this country to a fearful
extent.*

—John Quincy Adams

Thousands of speakers, including three heavy hitters, took to the
speaking circuit for William Henry Harrison in 1840. The Big
Three were US senators Henry Clay and Daniel Webster and an
Illinois lawmaker named Abraham Lincoln.

Stump speakers had been common in campaigns in prior years.
(The name arose because at first speakers literally stood on tree
stumps in fields in order to be seen.) But the Whigs took it to a
whole new level. The party had more than five thousand speakers
traveling to cities and towns in every state. They were known as
"slang whangers."

In the South, the major speaker was Senator Clay of Kentucky,
regarded as perhaps the finest orator in the land. The tall, thin
Clay spoke fervently, and the "gentle scents of his mellow voice
were persuasive and winning," recalled journalist Benjamin
Perley Poore. "He gesticulated all over. The nodding of his
head, hung on a long neck, his arms, hands, fingers, feet, and
even his spectacles, his snuffbox, and his pocket-handkerchief,
aided him in debate. He stepped forward and backward, and
from the right to the left, with effect. Every thought spoke; the
whole body had its story to tell, and added to the attractions of
his able arguments."

At first, Clay wasn't keen on being a mere stump orator for
the man who had defeated him to win the party's nomination. He

thought General Harrison was honest and patriotic enough, but prone to vanity and egotism with an intellect far below his own. He also disliked the circus atmosphere of the campaign, preferring to debate policies. But the Kentuckian realized that by being a team player, he would boost his own chances to win the top spot on the ticket in 1844, since Harrison, if elected, had vowed to serve only one term.

So Clay threw himself into the fray. At a big rally in Baltimore, he declared, "We are all Whigs. We are Harrison men. We are united. We must triumph."

Despite illness, he gave at least eleven speeches for Harrison and was an important influence in the campaign. For the most part, Clay avoided the backwoods imagery of the Harrison campaign and spoke about issues, such as the independent treasury. He also often avoided mentioning Harrison, citing him only once in a long speech in Hancock, Virginia. Nevertheless, he made clear his desire for a Whig victory in the election.

Clay's major speech came in Nashville, Tennessee, in mid-August. Tennessee was a swing state that the Whigs had hopes of winning. Clay said he received an invitation from 350 ladies in Nashville, "and, that, of course, could not be withstood." Tennessee also was the retirement home of Clay's political foe, former president Andrew Jackson, whose Hermitage Plantation was not far from Nashville. That, too, could not be withstood.

The rally became one of the largest in the South. At sunrise, a gun was fired from the Tippecanoe Club log cabin on lower Market Street. At 7:00 AM, two guns were fired from the cabin to signal the formation of the procession. The parade began at nine o'clock, led by a marching band and the usual collection of rolling log cabins, canoes, and banners carried by delegations from fourteen states. The Harrison ball from Zanesville, brought in by steamboat, rolled through the streets.

Clay's speech was the highlight of the day. The witty Kentuckian was in top form. Clay told the crowd that he had hoped to meet with an old friend, Tennessee's Democratic senator Felix Grundy, who was a lawyer. But Clay said that he was told that Grundy was out making speeches on behalf of President Van Buren. "'Ah,' I said, 'at his old occupation—defending criminals!'"

Clay playfully asked his audience what subject he should speak about, "the ruining currency, upon the protestations of business, the stagnation of trade and destruction of commerce? Or shall I speak of the wasteful extravagances of the present powers that be?" So he decided to speak on just about all of them, including those woes started by former president Jackson.

From his perch at the Hermitage, Jackson was dismissive of what he called the Whigs' campaigning of "coons, log cabins, and big balls." He predicted that Van Buren would win Tennessee. Old Hickory was whistling Dixie, though the song itself hadn't been written yet.

In the North, Whigs relied on the other great orator of the day, fifty-eight-year-old Daniel Webster of Massachusetts. The balding, stern-looking Webster, with his coal-black and receding hair, dark, bushy eyebrows, and deep voice, had a biblical aura. Newspapers referred to him as Godlike Daniel Webster, as if Godlike were his first name. The eloquent orator also knew almost every word in his cousin Noah Webster's new dictionary.

It was Senator Webster who gave the campaign one of its themes—one that would continue for campaigns through the years. "Every breeze says change," he declared. "The cry, the universal cry, is for change."

Webster usually dressed impeccably in satin-lined coats, ruffled shirts, and diamond stickpins. But on an eight-state tour for the Log Cabin campaign he adopted more informal wear—a coat of coarse linsey-woolsey, a wide-brimmed farmer's hat, and knee-high boots. He wouldn't stand for any doubts about his common-man status. "The man that says that I am an aristocrat is a liar," he said.

At Saratoga, New York, Webster invoked the log cabin as the symbol of the history and the patriotism of average Americans. "I was not myself born in one, but my elder brothers and sisters were born in the cabin" in New Hampshire, the humble cabin of his hardworking father, Webster told the crowd.

"That cabin I honor, for the sake of the venerable man who dwelt in it," declared Webster, his voice breaking. "That log cabin I annually visit, and thither I carry my children, that they may learn to honor and to emulate the stern and simple virtues that there found their abode; and when I or they forget that cabin and what it teaches and recalls, may my name and their names perish from among men forever."

When he finished, there wasn't a dry eye in the house.

Another speaker, Hugh Swinton Legare, a wealthy politician from South Carolina, went even further to invoke the backwoods image. The former editor of the academic *Southern Review* and a man educated in the classics, the short, forty-three-year-old Legare normally was the picture of a Southern gentleman of high manners. But on the campaign trail, the sophisticated Legare took to wearing a coonskin cap, swigging hard cider, and partying hard with log cabin boys. He derided Van Buren officials as "the small-beer statesmen who now conduct the affairs of government." Legare campaigned in five states, winning over crowds as he went.

The opposition *Ohio Statesman* declared that Legare's main features were "a very large mouth, a loud boisterous voice, fool enough to make any statement put into his noodle and swear it, and of sufficiently infamous character not to be injured by lying or perjury."

Former Mississippi congressman Seargent Smith Prentiss became one of the Whigs' most popular speakers, even though he talked with a slight lisp. He walked with a cane, though he was only thirty-two years old. Senator William C. Preston of South Carolina also was a frequent speaker, billing himself as the great-nephew of that lauded patriot Patrick Henry. (Give me Harrison or give me death?)

Local politicians were among the most influential speakers in their respective states. One of them was them was Abe Lincoln. He was one of four Harrison electors in Illinois who would cast the state's electoral votes should their man win. Lincoln traveled the state, speaking at rallies and in local debates.

One of the biggest rallies was in Springfield, where more than fifteen thousand people came from all over the state. "They came in carriages and wagons, on horseback and on foot," one eyewitness recalled. "They came with log cabins drawn on wheels by oxen, and with coons, coon-skins, and hard cider. They came with music and banners; and thousands of them came from long distances." Lincoln, wearing jeans, spoke from the back of a horse-drawn wagon.

Abe showed a flair for the dramatic in his campaign speeches and debates. In reply to a Democratic debater who claimed that Van Buren would win the election, Lincoln declared, "I know that the great volcano at Washington, aroused and directed by the evil spirit that reigns there, is belching forth the lava of political corruption . . . while on its bosom are riding, like demons on the wave of hell, the imps of that evil spirit." He concluded, "I cannot deny that all may be swept away. Broken by it I too may be; bow to it I never will." The Whigs published a version of the speech as a national campaign document.

Lincoln addressed the Harrison age issue head on. "When an individual's hairs have grown grey, and his eyes dim in the service of his country, it seems to us, if his countrymen are wise and polite, they will so reward him as to encourage the youth of that country to follow his example."

During the campaign, Lincoln frequently debated another Springfield lawyer, Democrat Stephen A. Douglas. It was a preview of the Lincoln-Douglas debates to come during their 1858 race for the US Senate. Already, Abe knew how to get under Douglas's skin. In one debate, Douglas challenged the veracity of claims that Lincoln had made against Van Buren. Lincoln supported his charges by reading from a book on the life of Van Buren. Douglas angrily grabbed the book and threw it into the crowd, saying, "Damn such a book."

Lincoln often discussed issues in his speeches, but he wasn't above joining in the Whigs' antics. In Lincoln's debate with Colonel Dick Taylor, the colonel claimed he was speaking for the common man and accused Lincoln of being an aristocrat. At this, Lincoln pulled open Taylor's coat and pointed to the ruffled shirt he was wearing, along with a fancy watch. Lincoln said that while Taylor was going around wearing ruffled shirts and kid gloves, he himself had been working on a flatboat with "only one pair of breeches" made of buckskin. "If you call this aristocratic, I plead guilty."

In Ohio, politician Tom "Wagon Boy" Corwin loved plunging into the Whig carnivals for Harrison as he also ran for governor. At a big rally in Warren, near Cleveland, he showed up in Corwin's Buggy, drawn by eighty-two oxen. Another wagon was filled with sixty women and pulled by eight to ten pairs of horses, each pair guided by a boy in a jockey uniform.

Corwin campaigned from one corner of the state to the other. "I have made more than one hundred regular orations to the people this summer," he later claimed. "I have addressed at least seven hundred thousand people, men, women, children, dogs, Negroes & Democrats inclusive." One Democratic critic called Corwin "the most famous stump speaker of his time."

In Kentucky, General Leslie Combs took to the hustings for Harrison, his commander in the War of 1812. Combs combined the two themes of Old Tippecanoe's campaign. He dressed in a hunting shirt like the one Harrison wore when he first met him, crisscrossed by a military sash. The dashing Combs enchanted crowds with old battle stories.

Even John Eaton, the former secretary of war whose wife had relied on the support of President Jackson and Secretary of State Van Buren to weather the Eaton affair, switched over to Harrison. In Pennsylvania, Eaton gave a speech favoring reform under Harrison, declaring that Old Tip was "the right way."

The Clays and the Websters drew attention. But early on Whig strategists longed for an anti–Van Buren speaker who could talk on the level of the common man, somebody like frontiersman Davy Crockett. Unfortunately, Crockett wasn't available. Remember the Alamo? Crockett was one of those who had defended the fort in San Antonio in March 1836 when the Mexican Army wiped out everybody inside. Crockett was forty-nine years old when he was killed.

There was only one Davy Crockett. But then, out of nowhere, just the man that the Whigs were hoping for suddenly appeared.

20

THE BUCKEYE BLACKSMITH

*With horny hands and fluent speech, coarse wit
and coarser invective, [he] rallied the masses."*

—Colonel Alexander K. McClure

John W. Bear, a nearly illiterate forty-year-old blacksmith from
Pickaway County, Ohio, never dreamed how his life would change
when he decided to go to the big Whig rally in Columbus in
February 1840. Bear was standing by the alternate speaker's platform
in the center of town when some friends urged him to make a speech.

"Bear, a speech from Bear," his friends shouted. Before he
knew it, the crowd had hoisted him up to the speaker's stand,
where he stood in a panic, staring out at about twenty thousand
people. Suddenly, he recognized in the crowd the face of the editor
of the opposition newspaper, the *Ohio Statesman.*

"Gentlemen, I see before me my old and worthy friend Sam
Medary," Bear declared. Then he proceeded to recount a dream
in which he told the devil that he was planning to go to the Whig
convention in Columbus. Hearing that the Whigs were united
behind Harrison, the devil ordered two of his assistant devils to
go make trouble to divide them. But first the devil asked what Sam
Medary was up to these days.

When told that Medary was editor of the local Democratic
paper, the devil called out to his underlings, "Come back boys,
come back. If Sam Medary is at the head of the *Ohio Statesman,*
and can't lay the Whigs out of it, all the devils in hell can't do it.
So it is no use of your going."

The crowd went wild. Medary stomped off in a rage. The next
morning Whig officials tracked down Bear and asked him to speak

again at the main platform. Medary had blasted the Pickaway blacksmith in his newspaper, but once again, a Democratic attack backfired. Bear was suddenly a Whig hero.

When the blacksmith was introduced that afternoon, he was prepared with props. He stepped forward dressed in his black leather apron, rolled up his sleeves, and announced to the crowd, "Gentlemen of the convention, I have a very dirty job to do." With that he gingerly picked up a copy of the *Ohio Statesman* with his blacksmith tongs, read a short paragraph, dropped the paper to the ground, and wiped his feet on it. Then he washed the tongs with soap and water. "This caused the wildest excitement I ever saw," he said later.

After that the Whigs decided to send Bear on the road. He was just the man to speak to working people on their own level. Over the next several days, he spoke in Chillicothe, Dayton, and Cincinnati, where he met William Henry Harrison in person. The Whigs then sent him off on a multistate speaking tour, leaving his wife and young daughter back home. The Whigs supplied the blacksmith with talking points, which local officials regularly updated.

John W. Bear, the Buckeye Blacksmith. *The Life and Travels of John W. Bear*

Bear spoke in Kentucky, Pennsylvania, and New York. Soon his fame spread. He could barely read, but he was not ignorant. He had studied politics and current events, and he spoke with a homespun directness. He also made people laugh, while mocking Van Buren and supporting Harrison. In Kentucky, the editor of the Louisville newspaper dubbed him the Buckeye Blacksmith.

This was just one of the ways in which the presidential campaign of 1840 gave rise to Ohio's nickname of the Buckeye State. Local references to the inedible, chestnut-like nuts of the state's many buckeye trees date back to the days of the Iroquois, when many deer roamed the area. The mahogany-colored nuts have a black spot, looking like a buck's eye. The Iroquois name for the nut was *hetuck*, or buckeye.

But it was the 1840 campaign that crystallized the moniker for the state, Ohio historian William Farrar wrote in the 1880s. During the campaign, Farrar said, "the name Buckeye became a fixed sobriquet of the State of Ohio and its people, known and understood wherever either is spoken of, and likely to continue as long as either shall be remembered or the English language endures."

It began with the march to Columbus in February 1840, when men of Marysville in Union County used the logs of buckeye trees to construct their Harrison log cabin on wheels. "The Log Cabin Song," which had been written for the march, not only praised General Harrison but also celebrated the workers' efforts. Copies of the lyrics were passed out during the Columbus parade, and soon the whole state was singing to the tune of "Highland Laddies":

> *Oh where, tell me where, was your buckeye cabin made?*
> *'Twas built among the merry boys that wield the plow and*
>   *spade,*
> *Where the log cabins stand, in the bonnie buckeye shade. . . .*
> *Oh what, tell me what, is to be your cabin's fate?*
> *We'll wheel it to the capital and place it there elate,*
> *For a token and a sign of the bonnie Buckeye State.*

The nickname was picked up in numerous other campaign songs, such as "Buckeye Boys":

> *Come arouse ye, arouse ye, my brave Buckeye boys,*
> *Take the axe and to labor away;*
> *The sun is up with ruddy beam,*
> *The Buckeye blooms beside the stream:*
> *Come, arouse ye, arouse ye, my brave Buckeye boys.*
> *Love ye not, love ye not, O my brave Buckeye boys,*
> *To the rally with Tippecanoe;*
> *For the hero, patriot, brave and free,*
> *Waits to assert your liberty.*
> *Love ye not, love ye not, O my brave Buckeye boys.*
> *To the polls, to the polls, then my brave Buckeye boys,*
> *To the rescue then haste ye away.*
> *The cup we fill—the hard cider pass,*
> *In friendship round, until the last;*
> *With a shout, with a shout, go the brave Buckeye boys,*
> *With Old Tip to the White House away.*

Newspapers began calling Harrison the Buckeye State candidate. The nickname was included in more songs about him:

> *Hurrah for the father of the Great West*
> *For the Buckeye who follows the plow.*

The name got a further boost when Ohioan Alexander Ross, the writer of the "Great Commotion" song with the chorus of Tippecanoe and Tyler Too, went to a major Whig meeting in New York City. When asked who he was, Ross answered, "I am a Buckeye from the Buckeye state." The crowd roared back, "Three cheers for the Buckeye state." Newspapers spread the story across the country.

The buckeye emblem was permanently hammered into the state's image by men and boys in Ross's hometown of Zanesville, Ohio. The town was located on the National Road, which ran from Cumberland, Maryland, to Springfield, Ohio, heading to

Wheeling, Virginia, which was the jumping-off point to the West. Each day the Zanesville men and boys would gather sticks from local buckeye trees to make canes. They sold the buckeye canes to travelers, who spread the buckeye name to their home states.

Whigs across the country came to Zanesville to stock up on buckeye canes for local political rallies. Whig organizers in one town in next-door Pennsylvania needed enough canes for delegates who would march in a parade two miles long. They took home more than fourteen hundred buckeye canes.

The buckeye tree wouldn't become Ohio's official state tree until 1953. But the die was cast in 1840 by the likes of the Buckeye presidential candidate William Henry Harrison and John W. Bear, the Buckeye Blacksmith.

The Buckeye Blacksmith became increasingly famous as he traveled around the country. The Whigs dressed Bear up in some fine new clothes. This caused him some problems. Skeptics wondered if this well-dressed man was really a poor blacksmith. Everywhere he went, someone would challenge him to prove himself: "Make us a horseshoe." So Bear often used his occupation as part of his performance.

For a speech in Philadelphia before twenty-five thousand people, he set up a blacksmith's forge, bellows, and tools on a large platform. Then he took off his coat, rolled up his sleeves, and put on his apron. First, he forged a nail. Then he hammered out a perfect horseshoe. Holding up the horseshoe with his tongs, he said he would like to nail it on the jackass who said he was not a blacksmith.

On July 1, he was in Washington, where Whig politicians greeted him like a celebrity at the US Capitol. He also went to a party at the Pennsylvania Avenue home of former president John Quincy Adams, a fellow Whig. Adams asked Bear what prompted him, a poor blacksmith, "to take such a stand in this campaign as you have taken?"

Bear quipped that it was probably the same reason that prompted Adams to take an active role in politics. "It was to distinguish myself. I know of no other reason." Adams laughed and told the blacksmith, "I think that you are able to hold your own with any of us."

The Democrats, however, didn't think he was so funny. "If low and vulgar ribaldry, stale jokes, and the manners of the Harlequin, be eloquence, then indeed was the Buckeye Blacksmith eloquent," said the *Washington Globe*. "The Whigs are so proud of their prize that they are carrying him about for exhibition as though he were a bear in fact as well as in name."

The *Extra Globe* began running stories that back home in Ohio, Bear was wanted by the law as a thief and a fraud. One story alleged that Bear, as the elected constable of Salt Creek Township in Muskingham County, Ohio, had embezzled money and procured a horse without paying for it. He also allegedly borrowed a wagon and sold it to pay a gambling debt.

The charges outraged Bear's friends back in Ohio. One man wrote the *Extra Globe*'s editor, Amos Kendall, "In your dirty, lying paper this week I see you attempt to make the Buckeye Blacksmith out a rascal, by publishing damned lies." The letter writer went on to say that if the *Extra Globe* didn't take back its lies in the next edition, "I will be in Washington, and take your damned life, if I am hung for it the next day."

When Bear visited Easton, Pennsylvania, in late July, Democrats distributed a circular with the sworn testimony of a Bear neighbor that the blacksmith had left a suffering wife and six starving children back home. Bear was handed the circular just before he was scheduled to speak. As it happened, the Whigs had brought Bear's wife and daughter to see him in Easton. When Bear stood up to speak, he introduced his family. "Ladies and gentlemen," he said, "you have seen my suffering family . . . do they look like they are starving?" Then he drove his political nail home: "What do you think, brother working men, of a party that stoops so low to carry a point?"

Bear often faced jeers and sometimes even danger. In Baltimore three men approached him and threatened to throw him in the Chesapeake Bay. Bear drew a pistol and scared them off. In Ellicott Mills, Maryland, local Democrats disrupted his speeches by running a whistling locomotive back and forth on a rail behind his speaking platform. Near Millerstown, Pennsylvania, thugs pushed a big rock over cliff in the path of his carriage.

The Buckeye Blacksmith was credited with making 331 campaign speeches, the most of any Harrison surrogate. Among the Whig speakers, "none did better work," said Whig editor Richard Smith Elliott. "He moved the masses at his will."

Bear's success prompted the Whigs to send out other tradesmen to speak for Harrison. A blacksmith from St. Louis campaigned through the Midwest "striking while the iron is hot" against Van Buren. The Whigs even recruited a blacksmith from Van Buren's hometown of Kinderhook, New York. A shoemaker named E. W. Kellogg also took to the road with amusing tales. "Bear and Kellogg make a full team, the regular Davy Crockett line," said the *Cleveland Axe*.

Another shoemaker speaker was Henry Wilson, billed as the Natick Cobbler, from Natick, Massachusetts. Unlike the Buckeye Blacksmith, Wilson was well educated and a serious, articulate speaker who strongly opposed slavery. He later went on to a successful political career.

One of the most influential voices for Harrison wasn't a speaker. He was Seba Smith, a folksy humor writer in Maine who wrote under the name Major Jack Downing. In one story, the major told of a fox chase after that old fox Martin Van Buren.

"The first thing next to be done was to select a good, long-winded leader of the chase, one who would not give out, and whose horn could be heard furthest. And so we all agreed upon Old Tip, and we got him pretty well mounted, and he sounded his horn, and its echoes went up and down rivers, and across valleys, and over mountains, till folks all about creation got well acquainted with the sound."

Then one day, Downing continued, the chase was on, and the frightened fox tried to escape by running to Old Tip's log cabin. Wrote the storyteller:

I was standing near the door and I seed him coming, and now thinks I, here he goes for Log Cabin mercy and hospitality, and I opened the door and in he streak'd. And just then came up Old Tip all of a lather.

"He is safe," says I, "General, we have got him snug at last."

"Well," says the General to his friends, "fellow citizens the chase is up; the old fox is in my possession ... He is not in condition just now to be held up by the tail as he has had a hard run and is considerably soiled. But he'll do no more harm."

With that, wrote Downing, everybody joined in three cheers for Tippecanoe and Tyler Too. "And thus ended one of the greatest fox chases ever heard tell'd of afore, and I have only told a very small part of it."

The Democrats also sent out speakers, though not as many as the Whigs. In contrast to a lowly blacksmith, one of the Democratic stumpers was former president Andrew Jackson. Old Hickory had never campaigned for himself, something he believed was beneath the dignity of a presidential candidate. But at age seventy-three, he traveled around Tennessee for Van Buren, speaking, shaking hands, signing autographs, and kissing babies.

Jackson declared that he had never admired Harrison as a military man. In speeches, he warned: cast your votes for Harrison, "and your Constitutional liberties are perhaps gone forever."

In Queens County, New York, twenty-one-year-old writer Walt Whitman was a Van Buren supporter. "How are politicks [sic] getting along down your way?" he wrote a friend in August 1840. "Is hard cider in the ascendant; or does democracy erect itself on its tiptoes and swing its old straw hat with a hurrah for 'Little Matty'?" Whitman, who later would publish his collected free verse poems in Leaves of Grass, took the Democratic side in a debate against a Whig. He mainly accused his opponent of being a liar.

The Democrats' most active speaker was Vice President Richard Mentor Johnson. Though Old Dick hadn't officially been nominated as Van Buren's running mate, he emerged as the last candidate standing after the other three men dropped out.

The sixty-year-old hero of the Battle of the Thames was in great demand. Still handsome, graying hair and all, he cut an imposing figure and always wore a bright red vest. The jovial Johnson drew large, enthusiastic crowds wherever he went.

Johnson never specifically claimed that he was the man who downed the Shawnee's great chief. But his campaign slogan said it all: "*Rumpsey, Dumpsey. Johnson killed Tecumseh.*" In Ohio, Johnson joined up with Senator William Allen, who was known as "Fog Horn" Allen because of his deep voice. Before introducing Johnson, Allen would boom that Harrison was a coward and then introduce Johnson as the real hero of the Thames. Allen would shamelessly hold up Johnson's scarred hand to show the crowd, and have him roll up his shirt to show more scars.

Off on his own, though, Johnson undercut the charges challenging Harrison's bravery. In Wheeling, when asked if Harrison was a coward, Johnson replied, "You might as well ask me whether I was a coward, for in the battle of the Thames there were no cowards. Every man did his duty from the general down."

In a speech in Congress nine years earlier, Johnson had praised Harrison. "Of the character of Gen. Harrison I need not speak—the history of the West is his history," Johnson said. "During the late war, he was longer in active service than any other general officer, he was perhaps oftener in action than any one of them and never sustained a defeat."

Johnson tried to persuade Van Buren to take to the campaign trail, but the president refused. Instead, he stayed in Washington and conducted a traditional campaign of letter-writing. This was an early version of what would become known as a Rose Garden strategy, an incumbent candidate staying put in the White House and acting presidential.

Johnson's barnstorming did put the pressure on Harrison's running mate, John Tyler, to join the speakers' circuit. The dignified Tyler hated the idea, but in late August he reluctantly began a speaking tour that took him from western Virginia through Pennsylvania and into Ohio.

In Pittsburgh and Steubenville, Ohio, he ran into some heck-
lers. After his address in Pittsburgh, an opposition editor described
Tyler as a graceful but bland speaker. "There is nothing forcible
or striking in his speech," the editor wrote. "No bright thoughts,
no well-turned expressions; nothing that left an impression on the
mind from its strength and beauty—nothing that marked the great
man." But Tyler's two-hour speech in Columbus drew praise from
his followers.

Sometimes speakers got carried away in the heat of the political battle. One day emotions ran hot as General Levin Coe, a
Democrat, debated a Whig in Somerville, Tennessee. The two
men got into a nasty spat over the issue of a national bank, of all
things. Coe drew a pistol and shot his debater, wounding him. His
rival was forced off the campaign trail to recover from the wound,
but Coe continued his speaking tour alone.

Usually, however, Democratic speakers calmly focused on
issues in hopes of overcoming the antics of the Whigs. At one
debate, Tennessee Democrat James Polk spoke for an hour on serious matters. After he finished, his Whig opponent quickly "elec-
trified" the crowd simply by pulling a coonskin from his pocket,
stroking it gently, and exclaiming, "Did you ever see such fine
fur?"

And thus the huge Whig campaign rolled on, but now their
opponents began to raise some sensitive financing questions.

21

MONEY TALKS

A diabolical scheme has been hatched ... to carry the Presidential election by the use of money.

—*Extra Globe*

WHERE DOES THE MONEY COME FROM?

That was the headline in the *Extra Globe*. Where were the Whigs getting the millions of dollars to pay for log cabins, monster rallies, free meals and hard cider, armies of speakers, campaign literature, and trinkets of every description? "The log cabins would not have been erected—the carousals and drunken revels would cease—the Tippecanoe songs would lose their music—the Whig agents and cohorts would lose their employment ... if there was no money raised to pay for them," the *Extra Globe* charged.

No campaign finance disclosure laws existed in 1840. But inquiries into who was behind the cash flow brought out the usual suspects. One was New York Whig party boss Thurlow Weed, the publisher of the *Albany Evening News* and a national strategist for the Harrison campaign. His power was lubricated by the money of New York businessmen. Or, as Weed called them, the "merchant princes."

Weed made it his business to make sure that the state legislature passed laws wanted by his merchant friends and rejected "unjust" ones. He rationalized his actions by stating with a straight face that his businessmen pals never asked for any laws that were wrong or opposed any that were right. In return, Weed was quick to remind his friends of his help when he came calling for donations to federal and state elections. On these occasions, he said, his friends "responded liberally and cheerfully."

Did they ever. Weed was known to collect heaps of cash in satchels. In 1839, one group of New York City merchants chartered a steamboat for a nighttime voyage to Albany to deliver to Weed $8,000 in cash wrapped in a bandana handkerchief. Weed stepped up his campaign-money solicitations for the 1840 campaign. He also was able to get an assessment on workers building the Erie Canal to help pay for publishing the *Log Cabin* newspaper.

Weed's merchant friends included two of New York's wealthiest men, shipping magnate Stephen Whitney and banker Moses Taylor. He also was tight with manufacturer Roswell Colt, who owned the Paterson, New Jersey, factory where his cousin Samuel Colt was making his first revolvers. Other big New York donors included the four Harper brothers, who ran the book-publishing company Harper & Brothers. Shipping owner Moses H. Grinnell hosted fundraising events. New York textile manufacturer Joseph Hoxie not only donated money but also went on the campaign trail to lead crowds in singing Tippecanoe songs.

Weed's cohort Horace Greeley fretted that the constant appeals for money for political purposes would drive the rich out of politics. His worry would prove to be quite unfounded.

Massachusetts textile firm owner Abbott Lawrence gave Harrison $5,000 in personal "loans," equal to more than $100,000 in twenty-first-century dollars. In Pennsylvania, Nicholas Biddle, the former head of the Second Bank of the United States, was a prime political giver. Biddle generally donated to lawmakers in both parties, sealing their support on legislation by loaning them money; Daniel Webster was into him for over $90,000. But in the 1840 election Biddle had a personal beef with the Democrats, for he had headed the Bank of the United States when Jackson yanked out federal money.

Meantime, on July 4 the Democratic-controlled Congress passed President Van Buren's plan to establish an independent treasury and sub-treasuries. The Whigs, Biddle hoped, would kill the program and restore the national bank as the federal depository.

Thad Stevens was another money generator in Pennsylvania. He demanded rebates from canal contractors in the state to help pay for Whig operations. In Delaware, several members of the wealthy Du Pont family were ardent Whigs. In the West, land speculators and settlers who backed internal improvements such as roads sided with the Whigs. Growers of sugar cane in Louisiana and hemp in Kentucky supported the Whigs, because the party supported a high tariff on imported competition.

The money drive culminated with a huge rally on Wall Street in late September. More than forty thousand people, including many merchants and stock traders, gathered near a stage set up in front of the Merchants' Exchange at the corner of Wall Street and Williams Street. Some people stood at the top of surrounding buildings. Ladies waved handkerchiefs from the windows.

The speakers complained that Van Buren's handling of the economy was a disaster. Merchants had adopted several principles: the nation's financial system needed a mixed currency of hard money, paper money, and credit; the federal government had the constitutional right to regulate money; Van Buren's sub-treasury plan would concentrate federal money in the hands of the federal government, where it could be used by "a weak and wicked executive" and, in general, add to the administration's "general incompetency at home and abroad."

The speaker of the day was Senator Daniel Webster. According to an eyewitness, Englishman Archibald Maxwell, the crowd was "as compactly wedged together as salted herrings" at a fish market. But, as the great Webster spoke, the crowd quieted so you might have heard a minnow drop.

This time the subject had substance. Webster talked nothing about log cabins or hard cider. Instead he spoke for two and a half hours on the need for a stable currency system that included hard money, paper money, and credit.

"What we need is some currency which shall be equally acceptable in the Gulf of Mexico, in the Valley of the Mississippi, on the Canada frontier, on the Atlantic Ocean, and in every town, village, and hamlet of our extended land," he said to the cheers of the merchant crowd. Not once in his long speech did he mention the name of William Henry Harrison.

Across the square, Democrats held their own, smaller Wall Street rally. It featured multiple simultaneous speakers, with as many as four speaking to knots of people at the same time. They all had a common theme, however: the rich Whig merchants and bankers were trying to buy the election.

The *Extra Globe* spelled out the charges in an article headlined THE GOVERNMENT FOR SALE:

The erection of log cabins all over the country, as places of rendezvous, has required a large expenditure. These, like the barracks of an army were to afford quarters for the vicious and depraved, who were to be debauched with liquor, and stimulated with lying and inflammatory harangues, and with vulgar and ribald songs, and corrupted with money when that should be found necessary. By these means they have been prepared to be taken into the Whig service as bands of hired mercenaries.

With this corruption fund, hundreds of agents have been employed and paid large sums to traverse the country, to distribute pamphlets and speeches filled with the most scandalous falsehoods, and to put in circulation all sorts of lying statements to agitate and alarm the public mind, and produce a high state of excitement.

It is the corruption fund that has enabled them to carry on their business of publishing their tracts and speeches, to an extent surpassing everything which been witnessed in this country. It is by the agency of money that they are enabled to charter steamboats, and pay the expenses of transporting the vagabonds and ferry hirelings from state to state to give fraudulent and illegal votes.

It is by a profuse expenditure of money that they have got together the multitudes at their conventions, as the expenses of the greater portion have been paid from the Whig fund. It is by the agency of money that all the operations of this faction have been carried on since the Harrisburg convention.

It is the money to be shared as the spoils of office which stimulates the profligate and noisy partisans and expectants, who have taken the field as leaders and stump orators of the party.

It is the expectation of making money which has enlisted with such intemperate zeal the speculators, stockjobbers, broken merchants, and men of ruined and desperate fortunes, who are in hopes, by hook or by crook, in some way to retrieve their circumstances by blowing up the bubble of the credit system again.

It is the hope of making more money that induces the gambling merchants and capitalists to "bleed so freely" to supply this corruption fund. They consider it a profitable investment, and expect to get their money back again, with such additions as will satisfy their proliferate trafficking cupidity.

The country's single-minded focus on the Whigs' costly and colorful campaign was damaging the nation's economy, the *Philadelphia Ledger* maintained. Because of the uncertainty, business people were afraid to start new enterprises, while existing businesses held back on expansion.

"Millions of dollars will now change hands on election bets; millions of days have been taken from useful labor to listen to stump orators, and millions more to build log cabins, erect hickory poles, and march in ridiculous, degrading, mob-creating processions," the newspaper said. "However high the hopes inspired by the election of General Harrison, they will prove to be delusive."

The most explosive money scandal was an alleged conspiracy between the Whigs and British banks to elect Harrison. Supposedly, Whig senator Daniel Webster was at the center of a British scheme to funnel money into the US election. New York merchants, the Democrats charged, had paid Webster $60,000 to go to England in late 1839 to conspire with British bankers.

British moneymen were major investors in both the Bank of the United States and in bonds sold by the various states. Since the Panic of 1837, both investments had dropped sharply in value. Under this conspiracy theory, the victorious Whigs would restore the Bank of the United States as the main holder of federal funds and the federal government would pay off the debts of the states. This would boost the value of the bank stock and the state bonds by as much as $150 million, the Democrats alleged. To achieve this goal, England supposedly was supplying US banks with British funds to help Harrison win the presidency.

Democratic newspapers printed a cartoon of a propped-up log cabin like a mousetrap with hard cider as bait. The headline read, Invented in England by Money-Mongers, to Catch American Voters.

Webster dismissed the conspiracy theory, saying he had gone to England simply to attend his daughter's wedding. Horace Greeley called the charges about British intervention the silliest lies yet.

Actually, the Whigs were getting more help from the US government than any benefit they might get from the British. At the direction of Thurlow Weed, the party and its members of Congress set up a Whig Executive Committee in two rooms of the District of Columbia's City Hall. The action had the approval of DC mayor William Seaton, the publisher of the pro-Whig *National Intelligencer* newspaper.

From this command post and a nearby rented stable, the Whigs worked to mail tens of thousands of pro-Harrison campaign documents free of postage, using the franking privileges of Whig lawmakers. It was a clear violation of the law's intent to allow lawmakers to send public documents to constituents without paying postal charges. The Whigs flooded the country with copies of Congressman Charles Ogle's "Gold Spoons" speech, Harrison biographies, and a pamphlet called "The Contrast," describing the choice between "Harrison and Prosperity, or Van Buren and Ruin."

The Whig surge was obvious in tallies of documents typically mailed by Congress. "The quantity of trash which has passed through the post office here, under the frank of members of Congress, is truly incredible," the *Extra Globe* said. On average, documents mailed out by both parties totaled fifty bushels a day, the paper said. By the summer of 1840, the total had risen to 204 bushels a day. "And eight-tenths of this mass of trash, with which the mails have groaned during nearly eight months, has proceeded from the Whig members of Congress."

The Whigs also used government-paid employees to handle much of the mailing workload. Political pamphlets were printed at Whig printing offices and sent by the government's official horse-drawn wagons to the US Capitol. There congressional workers put the documents in official envelopes and stamped them with congressional franks. The items were shipped by horse-drawn wagons back to the Whig center at City Hall and then over to the post office.

The Whigs supplemented their Washington outreach by organizing the party right down to the lowest state levels. The national Whig Committee sent out a confidential circular to state officials. "Our intention is to organize the whole state, so that every Whig can be brought to the polls in the coming Presidential contest," the circular said.

State officials were instructed to divide each county into small districts and then appoint subcommittees to make a list of all voters in the districts. Not only were they ordered to list the voters, but to find out for whom they planned to vote. The subcommittees were to keep an eye on doubtful voters and to have friends try to sway them to the Whig side.

Local officials were also tasked with making sure Harrison voters got to the polls, even if they had to provide them with horses. The circular concluded, "Our plan of operations will, of course, be concealed from everyone except our good friends."

Democratic newspapers soon got wind of the Whigs' detailed plan, however. One Democratic congressman warned that the Whigs had organized "to bring to the polls every man they can induce, by argument or money, blandishments or threats, liquor or lies, to vote the Whig ticket." By minute organization, said the congressman, the Whigs are out to determine which voters can be bribed, which ones need rides to the polls, and which ones will be away from home and must be brought back to vote. He added, "If persuasion, furnishing conveyances and bribery cannot muster a sufficient force to conquer the Democracy, their final resort is to frauds."

With the political cat out of the bag, Whig newspapers also published details of the party's plan and doubled down on the strategy. "We call upon the Whigs in every county throughout the state to organize on the plan recommended in the circular" and rid the country of the "corrupt horde of hireling office holders, which are now like hungry blood suckers, eating and stealing our substance," said one newspaper.

The Whigs claimed that by using federal resources and focusing on local organizing they were just following the lead of the Democrats. There was some truth to that. The Democratic Party had become a disciplined political machine under Jackson and Van Buren. As a result, the 1840 election became the first presidential election between two organized political parties.

The Van Buren campaign also had plenty of federal help. The administration's mouthpiece newspaper, the *Washington Globe*, had a government contract of $60,000 a year to publish the *Congressional Globe*, a summary of debates and actions in Congress. That amount would be equivalent to about $1.4 million a year today.

After Amos Kendall left as postmaster general to be the coeditor of the *Extra Globe*, he pressured postmasters to distribute the newspaper free of charge. At the same time, the administration allegedly threatened to prosecute steamboat and railroad lines if they carried the *Log Cabin* newspaper for delivery.

Whigs charged that federal employees had to contribute part of their salaries to support the Van Buren campaign, and that the Democrats, too, abused the congressional franking privilege; one Georgia Democrat mailed documents specifically to people in slave-holding states accusing Harrison of being opposed to slavery. The Whigs also charged that during the US census of 1840, census takers distributed pro–Van Buren documents and improperly asked citizens about their voting intentions.

As the election neared, both parties turned their attention to another matter: Keeping the other side from pilfering votes.

22

STEALING VOTES

If Mr. Van Buren's re-election shall be defeated,
IT WILL BE DONE BY FRAUD!

—*Extra Globe*

Voting fraud was a real problem in the election of 1840.

There were no secret ballots. The political parties distributed their own ballots, sometimes in bright colors so that illiterate voters would know which party they were voting for. Both the Whigs and the Democrats warned about such tactics as ballot-box stuffing, removing valid votes from ballot boxes, and importing illegal voters from other states. It was not uncommon for the number of tallied votes in a community to exceed the number of eligible voters. Bribing voters was commonplace.

Both parties hired bullies to scare away likely voters for the opposition party. When the early 1840 voting began in Springfield, Illinois, Harrison elector Abraham Lincoln rushed to a polling place where a man reportedly was harassing Whig voters. Lincoln persuaded the bully to leave. Later he told a friend he wished the man had put up a fight so he could "knock him down and leave him kicking."

In early voting in Pennsylvania, thugs attacked the pro-Whig editor of the *Lancaster Examiner* when he came to vote. The attackers, according to the *Harrisburg Chronicle*, "knocked him down, jumped upon him, and cut his face in the most horrible manner; the flesh was cut nearly off on both sides of his face, and left his cheek and jaw bones nearly bare!"

Political parties also engaged in a practice known as "cooping." A few days before an election, wealthy politicians would invite a number of poor voters into their homes to stay. The voters would be supplied plenty of food, whiskey, and playing cards until Election Day arrived. Then the cooped-up men would be sent out happily to vote the way that their benefactors instructed.

Sometimes cooping took a violent turn. Men were kidnapped off the streets, beaten, and drugged. They were provided changes of clothing and forced to vote multiple times under different names. This tactic might have been a factor in the 1849 death of author Edgar Allan Poe, who was found beaten and semiconscious in the streets near a polling place in Baltimore. He died a few days later at the age of forty.

Democrats charged Whigs with intimidating voters before the election. "We understand that a Whig committee has been sent prowling around our city, enquiring the politics of every working man with the intention of throwing every Democrat out of employment," said the *Rough-Hewer* in Albany, New York.

Some Whig business owners threatened to fire employees if they didn't vote for Harrison, the Democrats charged. One factory owner in Proctorville, Ohio, allegedly ordered his workers, "You *shall* support the Whig ticket, or go to the devil!"

In Kentucky, Whig buyers of hemp allegedly were promising farmers six dollars a bushel for the current year's crop if Harrison won the election. But they would pay only four dollars if Van Buren were reelected. In Virginia, where voting still was restricted to property owners, Harrison backers were selling nearly worthless plots of land to Whig voters for almost nothing—five cents an acre—so that the buyers would then be eligible to vote.

The voting frauds on behalf of Old Tippecanoe, ironically, extended to Tippecanoe County in Indiana. According to the *Extra Globe*, investigators there turned up numerous Whig voting frauds, such as placing on the books "large masses of names not known as citizens of the county." In one town in Maine, Democrats searched a presumably fresh ballot box and found six Whig ballots already placed inside.

The *Extra Globe* urged local Democrats to appoint special inspectors to make sure ballot box votes were legitimate and counted correctly. "Wherever the Whig officers have control of the ballot boxes, let them be watched day and night with unceasing vigilance," the Van Buren administration paper instructed.

Whigs, of course, contended that it was the Democrats who were trying to steal the election. In New York City, men from the Democrats' notorious Tammany Hall would intercept incoming immigrants right at the docks and arrange for them to vote illegally for the Democrats. As for immigrants who became naturalized citizens and thus could vote legally, Horace Greeley charged that the five hundred Democratic employees at the New York Custom House worked day and night to persuade immigrants that the Whigs were hostile to foreign-born voters. They said Whigs wanted to deny immigrants their rights and even deport them.

Democrats began whispering campaigns in an attempt to scare off some foreign-born voters from backing Harrison. In Ohio, they warned that if Harrison was elected, all the Germans and Irish would be sent out of the country immediately. In Illinois, they claimed that Harrison's first act in office would be to sell off all the Irishmen to pay off the state debt.

Both local Democratic and Whig election officials were accused of adding foreign-born voters who had not yet become naturalized citizens. In Hagerstown, Maryland, Whig election officials allegedly signed hundreds of false naturalization certificates for potential Whig voters and sent them around the country. Under the law, anyone holding the certificate would be entitled to vote. "By such means, any number of the worst subjects of foreign monarchies, and the greatest haters of human liberty, might, at any time be brought to the United States, and by going where they are not known, be given a power sufficient to overrule the voters of the nation and naturalized citizens," warned the *Hagerstown Democrat*.

Each side accused the other of hauling in illegal voters from other states. Writing in his *New Yorker* newspaper, Horace Greeley reported that a Democratic officeholder in Baltimore had written an acquaintance in Philadelphia asking him to send five hundred men who could pose as Baltimore voters. The Democrats in turn contended that men being brought into New York State to work on the Erie Railroad planned to smuggle thousands of fraudulent votes for Harrison into ballot boxes. The Democrats also discovered that some theological students at Princeton University in New Jersey were going to vote for Harrison there, even though they were residents of other states. "It is thus that followers of cider barrels and coon skins degrade themselves," said the *Ohio Statesman*.

The *Extra Globe* excitedly disclosed "the most deliberate and astounding fraud that has ever come to light in this country." The news: hired gangs of bullies who could whip their weight in wildcats had been transported to Philadelphia and New York City to go from one polling site to another to vote multiple times. And who would have courage to stop them?

Such charges played into President Van Buren's reelection strategy. Late in the campaign the Little Magician assured friends that he had "a card to play yet that neither party dreamed of." The president had been informed privately that Democratic federal prosecutors in New York City were planning in mid-October to charge several top New York Whig politicians with a "most stupendous and atrocious fraud." It would be the first October surprise in a presidential election.

The prosecutors delayed announcing the charges until the end of October, just before presidential voting would begin. The indictment charged leading New York Whigs with fraud in the 1838 election of Thurlow Weed's protégé, William Henry Seward, as governor of New York. Many of the indicted Whigs were active in the Harrison campaign, so Democrats were hoping for a backlash against the Whig ticket.

To make the biggest possible impact, Democratic newspapers across the country published the news simultaneously. A GIGANTIC PLOT TO ELECT HARRISON PRESIDENT BY FRAUD, blared the headline in the *Globe*. The *Albany Rough-Hewer* declared, SOUND THE ALARM. YOUR LIBERTIES ARE IN DANGER.

The charge was that Whig politicians in New York City had paid a contractor named James B. Glentworth $4,000 to recruit dozens of men from Philadelphia, ostensibly to lay water pipes for construction of the Croton Aqueduct in New York City. In reality, the workers had been sent around the city to illegally vote the Whig ticket in the New York State election. After Seward won, Glentworth was rewarded with a $2,000-a-year post as New York City tobacco inspector.

At first, the Whigs responded with indignation and denials. Glentworth himself filed counter-charges that it was the Democrats who had tried to bribe him to import voters. Van Buren's final card was a joker, the Whig papers said. The Whigs painted the charges as a desperate, last-minute ploy.

Soon, though, incriminating letters were found at Glentworth's home. He later admitted a Whig scheme in testimony before a Grand Jury. At the instruction of New York Whig leaders, he had gone to Philadelphia in late 1838 to recruit fake voters with the help of Philadelphia's mayor. At the city's United States Hotel, Glentworth met with two top police officials and agreed to pay them thirty dollars for every man they could recruit. After obtaining the money from Whigs in New York, Glentworth returned to the hotel to pay the two men a total of about $1,400.

The recruits were provided training for their assignment, though Glentworth noted that some of them seemed to be veterans of such schemes. They were drilled with questions that a voting inspector might ask until they could answer without looking guilty. They were each given slips of papers with the fake names and addresses they were to use when voting. Glentworth said he also gave each man $194 to defray travel expenses.

Clearly, it seemed, a case could be made. To cover himself, Governor Seward fired Glentworth from his job. Eventually, however, the prosecutor could only show that the Philadelphia men had been brought into New York, but he couldn't prove that they had actually voted.

They had, of course. They typically voted twice at each polling place, they later admitted, changing their names and their dress as they went. In some cases, the illegal voters took Democratic voting ballots but then erased the name of the Democratic candidate and wrote in the name of the Whig candidate. Democratic challeng-ers stationed at the polls wrongly assumed the color-coded ballots were used to cast votes for Democrats. The phony voters tipped off cooperative Whig challengers with signals such as putting a pin on the edge of their shirt collar or cuff.

Some of the men boasted about voting several times in different precincts; one man claimed he voted seventeen times. It was esti-mated that sixteen hundred votes were cast illegally in the scheme.

Contrary to Van Buren's hopes, however, the indictments had no noticeable impact on the presidential election. Indeed, one of the New York politicians implicated in the plot won office in the 1840 election. Voters simply shrugged their shoulders. They fig-ured the Democrats were probably doing the same thing. The term *pipe-layers*, however, lived on as a common name for fraudulent voters.

As the election neared, both sides sent their backers to vote as if they were marching off to war. Be "ready for violence" at the polls. "Be firm! Be vigilant! Be fearless!" the *Log Cabin* urged Whigs. The *Albany Argus* told Democratic voters, "Look to your Rights—to your electoral privileges—to your liberties. They are all in danger—imminent danger!"

The time for bickering was over. Finally, it was time to start counting the votes.

23

ELECTION RETURNS

We have been sung down, lied down and drunk down.

—Wheeling Times

The first sign of things to come in the 1840 election arrived in September in an early vote for governor in Maine.

The Whig candidate Edward Kent was a decided underdog. But when the final tally was counted, he won by sixty-seven votes. Whigs across the country promptly celebrated with yet another version of "The Great Commotion":

> *And have you heard the news from Maine, Maine, Maine*
> *And what old Maine can do?*
> *She went hell-bent for Governor Kent*
> *And Tippecanoe and Tyler Too*
> *And Tippecanoe and Tyler Too.*

The victory, and the song, solidified the term *hell-bent* in the American lexicon. All because the winning candidate happened to be named Kent. (One could only imagine what word would have been created if the new governor had another name, like Schwarzenegger.)

Whigs hoped that as Maine went so would the rest of the nation.

There was no single Election Day in 1840. State elections started as early as August. The Whigs scored gains in Indiana, Kentucky, North Carolina, and Vermont, as well as in Maine. In Ohio voters elected "Wagon Boy" Tom Corwin as governor. When Corwin's victory was reported in Cincinnati, Whigs mounted a midnight parade to the home of Harrison's daughter and her husband, where the general was known to be staying overnight. Outside the house the marchers cheered that Old Tip, too, was sure to win the presidential election. A sleepy Harrison came to the door and gave a short speech. This was a more pleasant awakening than at the Battle of Tippecanoe, he said, but he urged the celebrants to wait to see the final returns of the coming presidential vote before assuming he would win.

The federal elections took place from October 29 in Ohio and Pennsylvania to December 2 in South Carolina, which was the only state where the legislature still selected presidential electors. John Bear, the Buckeye Blacksmith who had been stumping the county since March, was in Cleveland the day before the Ohio election. Whigs there arranged for the Ohio Stage Company to rush him home in time to vote. "I arrived just one hour before the polls closed, amid the shouts of the Whigs of our little town," he said.

The nation waited anxiously for signs of an early voting trend. News didn't travel fast in those days. And when it did travel, you never knew if it was correct.

Alexander McClure recalled that as a young boy in Pennsylvania, he was sent to pick up the newspapers for his father's friends, who had gathered at their home several days after the voting in that state. The Whig paper declared that Harrison had won the state by one thousand votes, and put a picture of a raccoon over the printed vote results. The Democratic newspaper claimed that Van Buren had won by a thousand votes. The actual final vote wouldn't be known for several more days.

The biggest voting day was November 2, a Super Monday, when twelve states held elections. The biggest prize was New York, where voting took place in different communities over a three-day period. Since this was President Van Buren's home state, emotions ran high.

"The greatest excitement prevails; men's minds are wrought up to a pitch of frenzy, and, like tinder, a spark of opposition sets them on fire," former New York City mayor Philip Hone wrote in his diary on November 3. There were riots, he wrote, and a gang of several thousand Democratic ruffians wielding clubs paraded in the streets, driving away Whig campaign processions.

The final New York State vote would not be reported until November 9. By that time, Ohio, Indiana, and Georgia had already given big wins to Harrison, and Harrison had carried or was leading in ten of the eleven states reporting thus far.

For the first time in a presidential election, the media projected a winner based on a sampling of early votes. THE GREAT QUESTION SETTLED, read the headline in the Saturday, November 6, edition of Horace Greeley's *New Yorker*: "The agony is over. The most excited and vehement political contest which this country has ever known is substantially terminated, and terminated, we believe, in the election of WILLIAM HENRY HARRISON of Ohio as President and JOHN TYLER of Virginia as Vice President of these United States."

But Democrats still held out hope. From Tennessee Andrew Jackson wrote Van Buren about the early reports, "Do not believe a word of it. Nor will I believe that you are not elected until I see all the official returns."

Van Buren kept informed through voting results sent to him by horse-riding messengers. The news of the loss of New York was the death knell for the president's hopes. He got the word while having his portrait painted. "It is a singular coincidence that I should be taking my last sitting for my portrait on the reception of the news of my defeat," he later wrote a friend.

Harrison did indeed win New York, by a generous margin of 13,000 votes. He squeaked by in Pennsylvania, winning by only 351 votes. He captured nineteen of the twenty-six states, rolling up big victories in Massachusetts, Vermont, Kentucky, North Carolina, and Andrew Jackson's home state of Tennessee. The Harrison-Tyler ticket lost in Illinois, despite Abraham Lincoln's efforts there. Van Buren narrowly won Virginia, even though it was the birth state of both Harrison and Tyler.

In the Electoral College, Harrison won the mudslinging campaign in a mudslide. Old Tippecanoe took 234 electoral votes to only 60 for Van Buren. The popular vote was much closer. Perhaps there was a last-minute backlash to the Whigs' circus campaigning. In any case, Harrison got a total of 1,275,390 votes, while Van Buren received 1,128,854 votes—nearly 47 percent of the total. (Liberty Party candidate James Birney got only 7,453 votes, or less than 1 percent of the total.)

There was no doubt that the Whig show boosted total voter turnout. It was up 60 percent from 1836 to more than 2.4 million voters, the biggest increase ever. A whopping 81 percent of eligible voters cast ballots, making it the third-highest percentage turnout for a presidential contest in history, surpassed only in the elections of 1860 and 1876. The Whigs also won both houses of Congress, three-fourths of the governorships, and control of two-thirds of the state legislatures. In Massachusetts Honest John Davis—whose wife, Eliza, had fed two hundred marching band members after the Whig convention in Worcester—won the governor's race.

States competed for the title of "Banner State"—the one that gave Harrison the biggest victory. Vermont claimed the honor after giving Old Tip the largest proportional victory, with 64 percent of the vote. But Kentucky insisted that it was the Banner State because Harrison won there by the most total votes in any state. They were both wrong, said Delaware, which said it deserved the designation because not a single Democratic candidate was elected in the entire state. The competition led to the term *banner district* in election campaigns.

The Whig press waxed ecstatic over the Harrison win. THE CONFLICT AND THE TRIUMPH! GLORIOUS NEWS, WHIG TRIUMPH, trumpeted Thurlow Weed's *Albany Evening Journal*. Inside the paper, Weed printed a personal proclamation declaring, "To all those with whom we have bet, please call one at a time, approaching our office from Washington Street and departing through Congress Street, keeping in line, so as not to block up the highway."

1840 Presidential Election Results

State	Harrison	Electoral Votes	Van Buren	Electoral Votes
Alabama	28,515		33,996	7
Arkansas	5,160		6,679	3
Connecticut	31,598	8	25,281	
Delaware	5,967	3	4,872	
Georgia	40,339	11	31,983	
Illinois	45,574		47,441	5
Indiana	65,280	9	51,696	
Kentucky	58,488	15	32,616	
Louisiana	11,296	5	7,616	
Maine	46,612	10	46,190	
Maryland	33,528	10	28,752	
Massachusetts	72,852	14	52,355	
Michigan	22,933	3	21,096	
Mississippi	19,515	4	17,010	
Missouri	22,954		29,969	4
New Hampshire	26,310		32,774	7
New Jersey	33,351	8	31,034	
New York	226,001	42	212,733	
North Carolina	46,567	15	34,168	
Ohio	148,043	21	123,944	
Pennsylvania	144,023	30	143,672	
Rhode Island	5,213	4	3,263	
South Carolina	*			11
Tennessee	60,194	15	47,951	
Vermont	32,440	7	18,006	
Virginia	42,637		43,757	23
Totals	1,275,390	234	1,128,854	60

* *no popular vote*

Source: The American Presidency Project

THE GREAT RESULT, declared the headline in the *Log Cabin*. "The verdict of the people has been rendered and its thunder-tones are now pealing through the land. It is the knell of Loco-Focoism, and it is the funeral dirge of Van Burenism."

The *National Intelligencer* in Washington, DC, exulted, "It has pleased the Almighty to give to the oppressed people of this misgoverned and suffering country a victory over their weak and wicked rulers."

"A nation redeemed," said the *Bangor Whig*. "The most important event in the political history of a great nation has just transpired. The sun has set upon Martin Van Buren, and risen in all its moral splendor upon William Henry Harrison. . . . The election of General Harrison is a moral triumph—a brilliant victory of men—high-minded men—over corruption and power."

The pro-Harrison *Cleveland Daily Herald* printed a toast: "To President Martin Van Buren, conquered by a coward, outrun by a man in an iron cage, vanquished by a petticoat general and soundly beaten by an old granny." Several Whig newspapers rubbed it in by printing the election results with the slogan "O.K.," but now, instead of Old Kinderhook, they said, it stood for "out kounted."

Naturally, there were new songs of victory. Observers on both sides said Harrison was sung into the presidency. One song went:

> Hurrah for the father of all the great West;
> For the Buckeye who follows the plow.
> How are the mighty fallen
> And by the PEOPLE'S HAND; Low lie they
> And smitten by the weapons of the POOR!
> The blacksmith's hammer and the woodman's axe;
> THEIR TALE IS TOLD and for that they were rich
> And robb'd the poor and for that they were strong
> And scourged the weak and for that they made laws
> That turned the course of LABOR'S brow to blood—
> FOR THESE THEIR SINS THE NATION CARTS THEM OUT.

A Whig newspaper in New York took up half the front page with verses that began:

Who killed small Matty?
We, says Tippecanoe
I and Tyler, too!
We killed small Matty.

Democrats were in shock. "That the American people should have preferred an incapacitated old man, who has refused boldly to avow his sentiments on great public questions . . . is indeed a phenomenon that occasions no little regret," said the *Richmond Enquirer*. The siren call of "'change, change,' has been rung in their ears," the paper continued, and was "aided by the most shameless humbugs, by Tippecanoe clubs spread over the country and other devices." But the *Enquirer* was confident that "people will ultimately recover from the delusion into which they have fallen."

Democratic newspapers blamed the loss on Whig deceptions and frauds. The *Globe* attributed the vast increase in votes cast to a new species of voters: "mercenaries—hired, bribed and purchased." The paper alleged, "Money has been the chief agent in producing these abominable frauds and enormities. It is the first instance in our Republic of the triumph of the power of money over the intelligence of the country."

Van Buren would later attribute the loss to the "debaucheries" in which "reason and justice had been derided." Democratic senator Silas Wright of New York suggested taking down the US Capitol and replacing it with a log cabin complete with coonskins.

Yet the Whig win went far beyond bamboozling the public. It was true that lots of people really did think Old Tip lived in a log cabin. But many voters knew full well that he didn't. The log cabin was simply a symbol of the plight of average people. Times were hard, and the government was indifferent. Workers couldn't get jobs and farmers couldn't get decent prices for their crops. Voters were angry. "A change in government was what they desired and were determined to have," said journalist Nathan Sargent. The poet Ralph Waldo Emerson called Harrison the "Indignation President."

Even the *Democratic Review* agreed in part. The Whig campaign was indeed a national insult to the intelligence of the American people, the *Review* said. But the Whig victory was "a political phenomenon, so unexpected, so astonishing" that Democrats would be wrong to blame the loss simply on the ignorance of the "vulgar herd." The *Review* concluded, "In the clamor for change which the Whigs raised, there was undoubtedly a very powerful influence."

The Whigs made many honest people believe that since the economic difficulties had arisen under Van Buren, then "Van Buren was the cause of the hard times and the low prices," said the Democratic *New York Evening Post*.

Horace Greeley in the *Log Cabin* summed up the Democrats' response:

Blarney before the election: Dear People! Nobody but us can imagine how pure, patriotic, shrewd and sagacious you are. You can't be humbugged! You can't be misled! You always see right straight through a millstone, whether there's a hole in it or not. You are always right as a book, and nobody can gum you. In short, you are O.K.

Raving after Election: You miserable, despicable, no-nothing good-for-nothing rascals! Bought up by the British Gold! Led away by Log-Cabin fooleries! Gummed by coonskins! Blinded by skunk skins! Dead drunk on hard cider! Senseless, beastly, contemptible, wretched. Go to the devil!

The Whigs had been carried into office on a storm of discontent but with little agreement on how to govern. The Whig Party was a kaleidoscope of differing factions and views. The new president would have his hands full in pulling together support not only from the opposition but from within his own party.

"Harrison comes in upon a hurricane," former president Adams wrote in his diary. "God grant he may not go out upon a wreck!"

24

MR. HARRISON GOES TO WASHINGTON

General Harrison is now the personification of the national harmony. All general discord is to be hushed in his inauguration.

—*New York Express*

Swarms of people flocked to William Henry Harrison's home in North Bend, Ohio, as soon as it was clear that he would be the next president. Unfortunately for Old Tip, most of them came seeking jobs in his new administration. "I understand they have come down on General Harrison like a pack of famished wolves," said New York congressman Millard Fillmore.

The job seekers greatly annoyed the president-elect, reported the editor of the *Troy (OH) Times* after a visit with Harrison. "Some have traveled from the extreme parts of the Union seeking places, whilst others tax his time and patience by enormously long epistles setting forth their vast claims, fine qualifications and great accomplishments, without even paying the postage on the same. This neglect to pay postage is highly culpable and most vexatious to the General, imposing upon him an unjust expense of nearly, if not quite, a hundred dollars per month."

Harrison wouldn't be inaugurated until March 4, nearly four months after the election. To get away from the madding crowd, in late December the president-in-waiting took a trip to Kentucky by steamboat to rest at a farm owned by a close friend. In Ashland, he met with Senator Henry Clay, who stressed that he was not interested in a cabinet post. Why would he be? Clay was clearly planning to control the new government from the US Senate.

189

By late January 1841, Harrison was preparing for the long trip to Washington, DC. He left North Bend on Monday, January 25, as friends escorted him from his home in a two-mile-long procession. His wife, Anna, who was ill, stayed at North Bend until she could join her husband when the weather warmed in May. Harrison took his widowed daughter-in-law, thirty-six-year-old Jane Irwin Harrison, to act as interim White House hostess. She was accompanied by her two young sons and an elderly aunt, Jane Irwin Findley. Harrison's twenty-seven-year-old daughter Anna Tuthill Taylor also made the journey. The president-elect's best friend, Colonel Charles Todd, went along as well.

The long campaign had obviously taken a toll on the old general. Reporter Lawrence Gobright, who had seen Harrison in a Cincinnati marketplace a couple months earlier, said, "he appeared very feeble, as he held his cloak tightly around him."

The travelers stayed overnight in Cincinnati at the Henrie House Hotel. The next day they left for Washington aboard the side-wheeled steamboat called the *Ben Franklin*. More than twelve thousand people jammed the wharf to see them off amid the roar of cannons and the marching music of a military band. Harrison gave a short speech from the boat's deck. His words would turn out to be prophetic. "Fellow citizens," he said, "perhaps this may be the last time I may have the pleasure of speaking to you on Earth or seeing you. I bid you farewell, if forever, fare thee well."

As the boat steamed away, the old hero waved his beaver hat to say good-bye.

All along the way, hordes of well-wishers crowded the shores to shout "Huzzah for Harrison." The *Ben Franklin* went twenty-five miles down the Ohio River to Moscow, Ohio, where Old Tip switched to a boat named *Swift Shure*. At Wheeling, the crowd was so immense that the boat was delayed for six hours. After the celebration, Harrison discovered that somebody had cut the buttons from his coat as souvenirs.

At a stop in Steubenville, Ohio, local Democratic lawyer Edwin M. Stanton mixed with the Whig throngs following Harrison.

Stanton, a future secretary of war, claimed that even some of Harrison's supporters considered the president-elect to be "an old imbecile."

When the boat reached its destination at Pittsburgh, ten thousand people were waiting. Harrison stayed at the Pittsburgh House as admirers stood outside singing and shouting. When the president-elect met with a group of three thousand Whig women, he revealed that as a young man he had exchanged locks of hair with a young woman from Pittsburgh. The woman, as it turned out, was in the audience and "forthwith advanced to the general and tendered him her congratulations," the *Baltimore Patriot* reported.

The next morning Harrison and his party went by boat up the Monongahela River to Brownsville, Pennsylvania, for another overnight hotel stay. Then the president-elect began a road trip to Baltimore along the bumpy Cumberland Trail. He rode in the first stagecoach in a line of six coaches, followed by more carriages and horseback riders. There was no getting away from the crowds as he made stops in Union Town, Pennsylvania, Cumberland, Maryland, and Frederick, Maryland. "He is very much fatigued," wrote a reporter accompanying him.

Twelve days after leaving Cincinnati, Harrison finally arrived in Baltimore on February 6, a Saturday evening. The next Monday he addressed a large crowd there. Then at 9:00 AM Tuesday, he boarded a Baltimore and Ohio train for the sixty-mile trip to Washington, DC. He would be the first president-elect to enter the capital by rail.

On the snowy morning of February 9, 1841, Harrison's train arrived at eleven o'clock at the old train station on Pennsylvania Avenue near the US Capitol. It was Harrison's sixty-eighth birthday.

Perhaps to show his vigor, Harrison declined a carriage ride and walked through the mud to City Hall while crowds cheered along the way. As reporter James Brooks of the *New York Express* dramatically described, the president-elect "walks in the storm along Pennsylvania Avenue to the City Hall amid double columns of human beings, the bells ringing merrily, the flakes of snow mingling with his grey locks, his eyes flashing fire and his step as firm as that of youth or lusty manhood."

The assessment was shared by reporter Gobright, who had fretted that Harrison seemed feeble in Cincinnati. "He was different-looking now from what he was, when, during the November before, I had seen him in the Cincinnati market-place. Instead of being bowed with age, and shivering with cold, he walked with an elastic step. His face was slightly tinged with red, caused by the excitement of the hour, or the keen winter's wind, perhaps from these causes combined."

At City Hall, Mayor William Seaton greeted Harrison. After brief ceremonies, the general moved into Gadsby's Hotel, where a posted sign cautioned, "Travelers are recommended not to leave money in their trunks." So many people had come to town that the hotel converted its dining room into a dormitory with cots.

Washington at that time was a city of thirty-three thousand people. There was only one paved street, Pennsylvania Avenue, which ran between the White House and the Capitol. The avenue was lined with bars, lottery shops, and gambling houses. The rest of the city's streets were muddy dirt roads. The White House stood near the mosquito-infested swamps along the Potomac River.

Washington "is neither a city, nor a village, nor the country: it is a building-yard placed in a desolate spot, wherein living is unbearable," said French diplomat Chevalier de Bacourt. Neighboring the White House were boardinghouses, some private homes, and farms with cows and pigs. The farmers had no stables, and the animals roamed the streets at night. "The nocturnal wanderings of these beasts create an infernal racket, in which they are joined by dogs and cats," Bacourt complained.

The diplomat also griped about the habits of many of Washington's political leaders. "What shocked me most was the sound of continual spitting" of chewing tobacco, he said, a filthy habit common in both houses of Congress. Only President Van Buren seemed exempt from this vice.

On entering the US House of Representatives, added Alexis de Tocqueville, "one is struck by the vulgar demeanor of that great assembly." The Senate, he allowed, was composed of more presentable members.

Washington left much to be desired, many agreed. "Morally and physically, this place has little to recommend it," said Englishman Archibald Maxwell. "It impressed me with the idea of a deserted village in an unwholesome country; and the low, broad, slowly-moving Potomac, with its marshy banks, must make it unhealthy," particularly in the hot summer months.

The day after he arrived in Washington, Harrison went to the White House to see President Van Buren. In contrast to the mocking campaign cartoons that portrayed the president angrily departing the mansion, Van Buren greeted his successor warmly. He even offered to vacate the White House two weeks before the inauguration date so Harrison could move in to get some peace and quiet. The president-elect declined.

It was a generous gesture by Van Buren. On the other hand, he may have wanted to get away from the Whigs who gathered outside the White House every night to shout, "Van, Van. Van is a used-up man."

The next day, Van Buren took the unprecedented action of taking his cabinet members to meet the president-elect at Gadsby's. It was a cold day, and Harrison jokingly asked if the president could arrange to warm things up. Van Buren smiled and promised to try.

That night Harrison dined with the president at the White House. The general was in a jovial mood. Harrison, said Van Buren, "is as tickled with the presidency as is a young woman with a new bonnet."

The incoming president still had plenty of time to kill until the inauguration. He went down to Richmond for a celebration of George Washington's birthday on February 22, exactly one year after the big Columbus parade that had launched Old Tip's campaign. He met up with his incoming vice president, John Tyler, and both were celebrated with parades and dinners. "The general bears up finely under the excitement and consequent fatigue of the incessant collision with company, and the constant exercise of his colloquial powers," one newspaper reported.

From Richmond, Harrison went by steamboat to his boyhood home on the James River at Berkeley Plantation, which was now owned by a nephew, for a welcome feast with relatives and longtime friends. He stayed in his mother's old room on the second floor. There he finished writing his inaugural address, which he had begun at North Bend on yellow, lined, legal-sized paper. (Later that year Berkeley Plantation fell into bankruptcy. The nephew failed to rotate the crops, rendering the land useless for growing tobacco. The plantation and its slaves were sold to pay off the debts.)

After his return to Washington, Harrison practiced giving his speech during daily horseback rides along the banks of Rock Creek. Old Tip had moved into the home of Mayor Seaton. Harrison asked Senator Daniel Webster, who also was a guest at the house, to look over his inaugural speech, which reflected the general's long interest in Roman history. Upon arriving late for dinner one night, Webster apologized but said he had been editing Harrison's speech and was busy killing off Roman leaders.

Tens of thousands of people poured into Washington for the inauguration. Many of them flocked to Washington's first restaurant, which was run by a French chef named Bolanger. The eatery had opened on G Street during the Jackson administration. The chef specialized in oysters, quail, and terrapin. The streets were as crowded as Broadway on a Sunday morning, said former New York mayor Philip Hone. And everybody was so good looking and well behaved, he noted, unlike those roughnecks who had torn up the White House at Andrew Jackson's first inauguration.

Long before there was such a thing as Secret Service protection, Harrison walked around Washington alone in plain black clothes, shaking hands and cracking jokes with passersby. To give his overworked hand a break, he began saluting well-wishers instead. Hone marveled at the sight of the president-elect of the United States mingling easily with average citizens. "There he was, unattended, and unconscious of the dignity of his position," Hone said. "People may say what they will about the naked simplicity of Republican institutions; it was a sublime moral spectacle."

Finally, inauguration day arrived. At dawn on March 4, 1841, an artillery unit dressed in Revolutionary War uniforms fired a twenty-six-gun salute on the Washington Mall—one shot for each state. Early that morning, a farmer from Delaware County, Pennsylvania, presented Harrison with the meat of a fatted calf, which he had carved up and carried to Washington preserved in ice.

It was a cold, cloudy day with a stiff wind blowing from the northeast. At 10:00 AM, the procession escorting president-elect Harrison to the Capitol set off, traveling up Pennsylvania Avenue led by the uniformed militia of the District of Columbia. It was the first inaugural parade in history. Four white horses pulled a new carriage that Baltimore Whigs had just presented to Harrison. The general declined to ride in it. Instead, Old Tip chose to ride his horse Old Whitey to the Capitol. Despite the chilly weather, he wore no coat and regularly doffed his hat to the cheering crowd.

Watching from the front window of his home on Pennsylvania Avenue, the dour John Quincy Adams thought Harrison's white steed to be "a mean looking horse." But the son of the second president of the United States conceded that Harrison's inauguration "was celebrated with demonstrations of popular feeling unexampled since that of Washington in 1789, and at the same time with so much tranquility that not the slightest symptom of conflicting passions occurred to mar the tranquility of the day." Harrison and many in the crowd were dressed in plain clothes—what Adams described as "showy shabby."

Behind Harrison came an inauguration version of the Tippecanoe political rallies, complete with rolling log cabins, cider barrels, and raccoons. The Prince George's County Club from Maryland rode on a working power-loom on wheels drawn by six white horses.

Thousands of people lined Pennsylvania Avenue, cheering and waving as Harrison rode by. In the crowd was a little boy with chubby cheeks "rosy with joy," a reporter for the *National*

Intelligencer wrote. The boy was proudly waving over his head a little banner, "purchased probably by the savings of his pocket money." The banner showed a picture of a log cabin and the words THE HERO OF TIPPECANOE.

A number of black laborers were in the crowd, the reporter went on, dressed in their "Sunday best" and "staring at the bright figures which passed them. . . . The ladies, too (God bless them)! the ladies shared, fully, in the excitement of the hour: their eyes glancing, their cheeks glowing, and their tongues [for ladies have such things], were in rapid and harmonious motion."

After the procession arrived at the Capitol just before noon, John Tyler went directly to the Senate chamber, accompanied by outgoing vice president Richard Mentor Johnson. The Senate president pro tem swore in Tyler, who gave a five-minute speech. Then the newly elected Senate was sworn in.

Harrison arrived in the Senate chamber at about 12:20 PM and took a seat. "He looked cheerful but composed," the *National Intelligencer* reported. "His bodily health was manifestly perfect; there was an alertness in his movement which is quite astonishing, considering his advanced age, the multiple hardships through which his frame has passed, and the fatigues he has lately undergone."

At about 12:30 PM, Senate leaders led Harrison to the steps on the eastern front of the Capitol, where a fifteen-foot-high speaking platform had been erected. More than fifty thousand people jammed into the grounds in front of the Capitol steps. Some found viewing spots in trees. Carriages carrying women lined up around the edges of the crowd. It was the largest turnout for a presidential inauguration seen to date.

The crowd erupted in loud cheers at the first sight of Harrison. The president-elect moved to a seat at the front of the platform next to black-robed Chief Justice of the Supreme Court Roger Taney. To their right sat members of the diplomatic corps. Behind were members of Congress, military officers, and other invited guests. A number of women were present. President Van Buren did not attend.

William Henry Harrison's presidential inauguration, March 4, 1841. *Library of Congress*

As Harrison rose to speak, ear-splitting cheers rang out. Others on the speaker's platform were bundled up in overcoats and thick cloaks to protect against the chilling wind. Harrison wore no coat or hat, even though he must have felt the piercing cold swirling around him. "Of this I can speak feelingly, as I sat within a few feet of him," said journalist Nathan Sargent.

The great crowd fell silent. Harrison, who had yet to be sworn in as president, began speaking in a strong and commanding voice. "Called from a retirement which I had supposed was to continue for the residue of my life, to fill the Chief Executive office of this great and free nation, I appear before you, fellow citizens, to take the oath which the Constitution prescribes as a necessary qualification for the performance of its duties."

Then Harrison dove into his speech. It quickly became clear that Webster hadn't killed enough Roman leaders as Old Tip evoked repeated references to old Romans. As in his campaign, Harrison offered few specifics about his presidential plans in what arguably was the dullest presidential inaugural address in history. It definitely was the longest. He rambled on for one hour and forty-five minutes. His speech totaled 8,845 words, compared with just 135 words in George Washington's second inaugural speech, the shortest in history.

About the only remark that might remotely apply to future generations was a warning about excessively divided political parties. "To me it appears perfectly clear," said Harrison, "that the interest of the country requires that the violence of the spirit by which those parties are at this time governed must be greatly mitigated, if not entirely extinguished, or consequences will ensue which are appalling to be thought of."

Just before his final words, Harrison paused, and Chief Justice Taney approached. It was at this point that Harrison, placing his hand on a Bible, finally was sworn in as the ninth president of the United States. People in the crowd stood and removed their hats.

Then Harrison—at last—concluded: "Fellow citizens, being fully invested with that high office to which the partiality of my countrymen has called me, I now take an affectionate leave of you. You will bear with you to your homes the remembrance of the pledge I have this day given to discharge all the high duties of my exalted station according to the best of my ability, and I shall enter upon their performance with entire confidence in the support of a just and generous people."

Cannons fired to announce that the republic had a new president. (Or maybe just to announce that he had finally stopped talking.) At age sixty-eight, Harrison was the oldest president until Ronald Reagan took office in 1981 at age sixty-nine.

At the conclusion of the event, the railroad ran extra trains to get a copy of Harrison's speech to Horace Greeley in New York City for publication in the *New Yorker*. It arrived at eleven o'clock that night. Just in case the train broke down, relays of fast horses were ready to pick it up. Greeley published the entire speech in the March 6 edition, stating, "It is of unusual length; but its views are expressed with remarkable clearness and force, and we believe it will meet with general favor."

The speech failed to meet favor with one reader in Albany, New York. "It is not what was needed," said Whig party boss Thurlow Weed. "It gives the administration no strength. We can lean on it a few weeks, but there must be action then, or we sink. There must be something accomplished on which the people can fasten their hopes."

Right after his speech, Harrison had paused inside the Capitol when two amateur photographers from Philadelphia, Justus Moore and Captain Ward, asked to take his picture with the new daguerreotype system. He agreed. The resulting picture is considered by many historians to be the first presidential photograph. It was used as the model for many subsequent paintings and engravings of Harrison as president.

The newly minted president then remounted his white horse to lead a joyful inaugural parade back down Pennsylvania Avenue to the White House for a reception. He went directly to the upstairs of the presidential mansion, where he laid down for a half an hour while his head and temple were rubbed with alcohol. Then he went downstairs to greet an overflow crowd of visitors—but he still refrained from shaking hands.

That night the president attended three inaugural balls. First, he stopped in at the Tippecanoe Ball, which was aimed at Old Tip's less fancy supporters. Next came a formal affair in Carusi's Assembly Rooms, where guests filled two large areas. The main party was at the National Theatre, which was arranged into large ballrooms. Musicians played from the second tier of box seats. The walls were adorned with flags and pictures of General Harrison on horseback.

Tickets for this party quickly sold out. More than three thousand people crowded into the theater, including many women in fine dresses. President Harrison came in after 10:00 PM "looking very happy and not fatigued," the *New York Herald* reported. He wore a black suit and gloves and "stepped about with the activity of a much younger man." The president stayed a little over an hour, chatting with guests, including Daniel Webster and his former rivals for the Whig presidential nomination, Henry Clay and General Winfield "Old Fuss and Feathers" Scott. The imperious General Scott was attired in a full dress military uniform with medals and yellow plumes.

President Harrison appeared to be none the worse for wear after his grueling campaign, a long speech in the cold, and the festivities of his inauguration day. That would soon change.

25

DEATH OF A PRESIDENT

Death! Death in the White House. Ah, never before
Trod his skeleton foot, on the President's floor.

—N. P. Willis

President Harrison moved into the White House without his wife, who was still back in Ohio. Tending to his needs were the family members who had accompanied him to Washington and a long-time African American servant. Harrison also had a pet, a goat named His Whiskers.

The new president retained the services of Martin Renehan, a witty and warm-hearted Irish American White House servant who had served under Presidents Jackson and Van Buren. Renehan told Harrison that he had fully expected to be replaced, since he had supported the opposing political party. Harrison laughed and replied, "John Quincy Adams told me all about you, and as long as I remain in the White House, the cabinet even can't remove you."

The president invited friends in for social events, with his daughter-in-law Jane Harrison as White House hostess. Jane, with a "singular fine form and a face of uncommon sweetness," performed her duties admirably, according to a writer for the *Raleigh Register*.

Merely visiting the White House didn't require a presidential invitation. In those days, people could just walk right in. Old Tip was a down-to-earth man who treated the humblest caller with the same hospitality he'd shown unexpected guests back home in Ohio. One cold day the president chastised a servant for showing a plainly dressed visitor to a room without a lit fireplace.

The servant said he feared the man would tramp mud from his boots on the carpet. Never mind the carpet, the president said; the man was one of the people, and the carpet—and the house too—belonged to the people.

Harrison also tried to maintain the same schedule that he had kept on his Ohio farm. He rose at dawn and walked the grounds before breakfast, and then he often went out to shop for food at local markets. On one of his first shopping trips, he walked to a bookstore, where he bought a Bible and prayer book. He had been surprised to discover that there wasn't a Bible at the White House. The deeply religious Harrison went to church twice on Sundays—to an Episcopal church in the morning and a Presbyterian church in the evening.

Soon, however, he had to cut back on going out to the market, because he would be swarmed by job seekers. For that matter, he couldn't avoid them inside the White House either. The mansion's open-door policy meant that he would often walk into a room to find more job hopefuls sitting there waiting for him. "I am so much harassed by the multitude that call upon me that I can give no proper attention to business of my own," Harrison remarked.

One day at the White House the president had to push his way through a crowd of job seekers as he prepared for a meeting with his cabinet. He told them he was too busy at the moment to look at their individual requests. The intruders stuffed the president's pockets and filled his arms with their résumés, which he carried upstairs to his meeting.

Back home in North Bend, Harrison had gone to bed early. As president he rarely retired before 1:00 AM. He told friends that he was so busy that he hardly had time to perform "the necessary functions of nature." Fortunately, President John Quincy Adams had installed a bathroom inside the White House, complete with presidential chamber pots.

On Harrison's first day in office, a special session of Congress had confirmed his cabinet. He had named Daniel Webster as his secretary of state. But there was no cabinet post for his early supporter, testy Thaddeus Stevens of Pennsylvania, who thought that he had been promised the job of postmaster general. The truth was that Harrison simply didn't like the guy.

In the Senate, the Whigs quickly sought to terminate the contract by which the Democratic newspaper the *Washington Globe* published Congress's daily activities in its *Congressional Globe*. The move got Senator Henry Clay in a heap of trouble. Clay lambasted the *Globe's* publisher, Francis P. Blair, as an "infamous man." When Democratic senator William King of Alabama retorted that Blair's character would compare gloriously to Clay's, Clay leaped to his feet to decry King's characterizations as "false, untrue, and cowardly."

Calling a fellow senator a coward was an unpardonable insult. To defend his honor, King soon challenged Clay to a duel. Realizing that he had gone dangerously overboard, Clay apologized three days later on the Senate floor. Then to defuse the tensions, he sauntered over to King's desk and asked, "King, give us a pinch of your snuff?" The two men smilingly shook hands. (Despite the Whig efforts to terminate it, the *Congressional Globe* would remain Congress's official record until being replaced in 1873 by the *Congressional Record*.)

After campaigning against appointed "office holders," Harrison named some of his own. His old friend Colonel Todd was tapped to become the minister to Russia. The president named another old military colleague as governor of the Missouri territory. John Bear, the Buckeye Blacksmith, was rewarded with an appointment to the Wyandotte Indian Agency.

Many Democratic jobholders were sent packing. One of them was a thirty-six-year-old writer named Nathaniel Hawthorne, who lost his $1,500-a-year post as a weigher at the federal customhouse in Boston. Hawthorne would go on to publish his famous novel *The Scarlett Letter* in 1850.

The demands of the spoils system continued to weigh on the president's mind. One evening Richard Smith Elliott, the young Harrisburg editor who had helped create the log cabin image, dined at the White House along with about a half-dozen guests whom Harrison knew wouldn't pester him for government jobs.

"The President led the conversation in a manner so genial and pleasant that everybody was charmed," Elliott said. "But not a word about offices or appointments." (Another key supporter, *Log Cabin* editor Horace Greeley, never even went to Washington to see the president he helped put in office. Greeley said he had never met Harrison and doubted that the president even knew his name.)

Harrison soon clashed on appointments with some of his top backers, especially Henry Clay. Since Harrison had promised not to interfere with Congress, Senator Clay assumed he would be the power in the new government. But once in office, Harrison began to assert himself. When Clay persisted in pushing his friends for jobs, an irritated Harrison fired back, "Mr. Clay, you forget that I am President." Finally, Harrison wrote a note to Clay ordering him to stay away from the White House and to contact him only in writing.

Back at his room in a Washington boardinghouse, Clay angrily crumpled the note in his hand. "And it has come to this!" he said angrily. "Here is my table loaded with letters from my friends in every part of the Union, applying to me to obtain offices for them, when I have not one to give, nor influence enough to procure the appointment of a friend to the most humble position." With the new Congress not scheduled to meet again until the fall, Clay stormed out of town. He would never see Harrison again.

Perhaps to answer concerns that he might move too slowly, Harrison ordered a special session of Congress to convene at the end of May. In issuing the order, Harrison cited "the condition of the revenue and finance of the country." In other words, the government was running short of money.

With Congress out of session, Vice President John Tyler went home to his plantation on the James River in Williamsburg. Tyler was perturbed that he didn't get any patronage to award jobs to his friends. There wasn't much for a vice president to do anyway. He also needed to care for his wife, Letitia Christian Tyler, who in 1839 had suffered a stroke that left her partially paralyzed.

President Harrison had been in office for less than week when the US Supreme Court handed down its decision in the case of the slaves from the Spanish schooner *Amistad*. The new administration hadn't taken a position on the case, but the court ruled against returning the slaves to Spain as the Van Buren administration had sought. Instead, the justices ruled that the Africans should be freed because they had been unlawfully kidnapped in Cuba and carried on board the schooner. Former president John Quincy Adams had spoken for four hours before the court in favor of freeing the slaves. Adams went to see the new secretary of state, Daniel Webster, to ask for a ship to send the former slaves back to Africa. Webster seemed startled by the request but agreed to look into it.

President Harrison meantime continued his daily routine of an early-morning walk, and despite the threat of job seekers would still make trips to the Marsh Market more than six blocks away. Though the weather was cold, he refused to wear an overcoat. After getting a haircut in the White House on Wednesday, March 24, he headed to market and got caught in some rain showers. He rushed back to the White House but didn't change his wet clothes.

The next day, the president came down with a cold. It didn't seem to slow him down. The following morning, a Friday, he took his usual walk and ran into an old friend who was down on his luck. He brought the friend to the White House for breakfast. That day, the president wrote his son John Scott Harrison back in North Bend, Ohio, asking him to send some bacon and beef from the family farm.

After dinner, Harrison felt ill and called a doctor. The physician, Dr. Thomas Miller, reported that the president was "slightly ailing," but not enough to be confined to bed. Harrison complained about fatigue.

In the early afternoon of Saturday, March 27, Harrison did go to bed, complaining of violent chills and pain over his right eye. The doctor was called again. Dr. Miller applied mustard to the president's stomach and gave him a mild laxative. The president, presumably drawing on his long-ago days as a medical student, suggested some of his own treatments.

By Sunday, March 28, Harrison's condition had worsened. After being summoned at 4:00 AM, Dr. Miller diagnosed the president as having pneumonia in the right lung complicated by congestion of the liver with "derangement" of the stomach and bowels. At this point the doctor ignored the physician's maxim of "Do No Harm." First he tried bleeding Harrison, but stopped when the president's pulse began dropping. He decided Harrison was too old and frail for this traditional treatment.

Then things got even worse. Miller "cupped" the president. This meant heating the inside of an inverted cup with a lit candle and then applying the hot cups over small incisions to suction up Harrison's skin and cause blisters. This supposedly improved the blood flow. It also was painful as hell. As if this wasn't enough, the doctor gave the president harsh laxatives to purge the bowels and other powerful medicines to force vomiting.

The next day, Monday, March 29, Dr. Miller called in more physicians. They treated Harrison with everything from opium and enemas to a brandy toddy. They even tried a Seneca Indian remedy, a mixture of petroleum and Virginia snakeweed as a type of liniment. Nothing seemed to be working.

On Thursday, April 1, the doctors continued to assault the president's weakened body. They blistered him again and rubbed the blisters with mercurial ointment. They gave him stimulants and more brandy. At about four o'clock, news spread around the capital that the president was fading fast. Cabinet members were summoned to his bedside. The public wasn't informed.

Hopes rose the next day when the president seemed to rally. But on Saturday, April 3, Harrison developed severe diarrhea and became delirious. He uttered his final words, which presumably were meant for the absent Vice President Tyler: "Sir, I wish you to understand the true principles of the government. I wish them carried out. I ask nothing more."

President Harrison died just past midnight in the early morning of April 4, Palm Sunday. His death came exactly thirty-one days after he was inaugurated. He was the first US president to die in office.

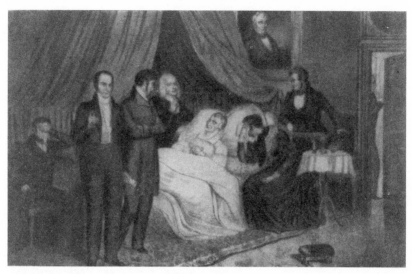

Death of President Harrison. *Library of Congress*

The doctors reported the official cause of death as pneumonia. "The age and debility of the patient, with the immediate prostration, forbade a resort to general blood letting," the physicians said. "Topical depletion, blistering and appropriate internal remedies subdued in great measure the disease of the lungs and liver, but the stomach and intestines did not regain a healthy condition. Finally, on the 3rd of April at 3 o'clock p.m., profuse diarrhea came on, under which he sank at thirty minutes to 1 o'clock on the morning of the 4th."

Critics soon questioned the handling of the president's ills. Within a week of Harrison's death, one newspaper said the doctors probably "quacked him out of existence." In August 1841, an article in the *Boston Medical and Surgical Journal* stated that the president's physicians seemed to have yielded to Harrison's own medical observations to the point of "being somewhat influenced" by him. While Harrison's doctors diagnosed his illness as a form of pneumonia, the article continued, they treated it as if it were an ordinary winter cold. The article suggested that Harrison might have survived "had timely and active measures been used, instead of cups, mustard plasters," and powders. A modern theory is that

Harrison died from a "deadly bacteria" contracted through the White House water supply, which may have been contaminated by raw sewage that flowed into the ground nearby.

Whatever the cause, America suddenly was without a president, and Vice President John Tyler was nowhere around. Tyler had been informed that Harrison was gravely ill, but he felt it would be unseemly to rush to Washington to hover over the ailing president. He was still back at his plantation in Williamsburg, more than 150 miles away. Secretary of State Daniel Webster immediately called on his son Fletcher Webster, who was the chief clerk at the State Department, and Robert Beale, doorkeeper of the Senate, to go bring Tyler to the capital.

The day of Harrison's death, the two men took a train to Richmond, chartered a steamboat down the James River, and then rode to Tyler's home on horseback. They arrived at five o'clock Monday morning. Contrary to myth, they did not find Tyler playing marbles with some boys. Tyler was in his bedclothes when he answered the frantic knock on his door. The two visitors handed him as message from the cabinet: "To John Tyler, Vice President of the United States. Sir: It becomes our painful duty to inform you that William Henry Harrison, late President of the United States, has departed this world."

Within two hours, the vice president left with Webster and Beale, making the trip to Washington by steamboat and train in the near record time of twenty-one hours. He arrived in the capital at 4:00 AM on Tuesday, April 6. He took up interim residence at Brown's Indian Queen Hotel. Tyler's swearing in as president took place at noon at the hotel with the cabinet and other officials in attendance. Chief Justice Taney of the US Supreme Court was unavailable, so Chief Justice William Cranch of the Circuit Court of the District of Columbia administered the oath.

The nation was in shock. "A nation mourns its chief!" said the *Baltimore Republican*. "We have never seen such a universal gloom thrown over the people." The *New York Herald* lamented, "This awful and sudden event, so unexpected to the people of the United States, is fraught with political consequences that no one can conceive." An elderly black man in Baltimore was quoted as saying about the dead president, "May he have as many angels to attend him in heaven as he had persons to witness his inauguration."

Newspapers announced the death with thick black lines called "mourning rules" surrounding the columns containing the articles. All except the anti-Harrison *Evening Post*. Its publisher, William Cullen Bryant, refused to use the black-lined columns, calling it "typographical foppery." Philip Hone complained that the hard-hearted Bryant regretted the death of Harrison "only because he did not live long enough to prove his incapacity as President."

"Few better men than Gen. Harrison ever lived. He had no thought but for his country," said newspaperman and recent White House guest Richard Smith Elliott. "He was sadly out of place as President" because "his genuine kindness of heart bade him listen to all comers, and he wished to satisfy everybody."

"General Harrison was never a great man," Horace Greeley said later, "but he had good sense, was moderate in his views, and tolerant of adverse convictions; he truly loved and aspired to serve his country, and was at the summit of a broadly based and substantial popularity which, had he lived out his term, would have averted many impending evils." (A notice tucked into one corner of the *Log Cabin* newspaper's final edition reported that on April 10, 1841, Greeley would begin publishing "A New Morning Journal of Politics, Literature and General Intelligence." It would be called the *New York Tribune*.)

Back in Ohio, Harrison's wife and family still hadn't received word of the president's death. They were already dealing with another crisis there: a fire had broken out at Harrison's North Bend house, destroying the west wing of the home. Anna Harrison was still preparing to leave the damaged Big House and join her husband in Washington when a courier finally arrived with the news that her husband had died. By this point it was too late for her to make it to Washington in time for the funeral, so she canceled the trip.

It fell to the State Department and the military to arrange the first funeral for a US president. The department later reported the details right down to "dressing and shaving the deceased."

Harrison's body lay in state in the East Room of the White House for two days so citizens could pay their final respects. Mourners could see the dead president's face through a glass under the lid of the mahogany casket. "The expression was calm and natural; his white hair lying close to his head, and his features regular and peaceful, as if they had been quietly composed to their last long sleep," wrote journalist Henry Montgomery.

A black velvet cloth with gold fringe covered the casket. Two swords were placed on top. Next to the casket were the Bible and prayer book that he had purchased for the White House.

Services were set for Wednesday, April 7. At sunrise that day, cannons fired. The sky was overcast, but the clouds cleared for a dry, cool day. During the morning, more people filed through the East Room. At noon, the Rev. William Hawley of St. John's Episcopal Church in Lafayette Square began the private religious ceremony. On one side of the casket sat President Tyler and members of Congress. Former president Adams sat next to them. Members of Harrison's family and close friends sat on the other side of the casket.

After the ceremony, officials gathered for the somber funeral parade up Pennsylvania Avenue. The streets were lined with more than ten thousand people who watched in silence. Many buildings were draped with black crepe. The event was in sharp contrast to the cheering crowds and the log cabins on wheels of Harrison's inauguration parade just a month earlier. The Adjutant General had issued a program for the procession. Military escorts would lead the way. Bringing up the rear would be "citizens and strangers."

The funeral procession began its slow march. Marshals on horseback, carrying white batons with black tassels, rode alongside the cortege. First came General Winfield Scott on horseback with more than two dozen military units—the District of Columbia's Artillery, the Dragoons from Georgetown, the Maryland Cadets, the York Riflemen from Pennsylvania, a battalion of the US Marines, and others. Next came the late president's physicians and local officials, including the mayors of the

District of Columbia, Georgetown, and Alexandria, Virginia. Bands marched with muffled drums.

This time the focus was not Harrison on horseback but the president's huge funeral car carrying the casket, which had been placed in a sealed lead coffin. The car was draped in black velvet that flowed over the sides, nearly to the ground. It was pulled by six white horses covered with black crepe and wearing white plumes. Guiding each horse was an African American groomsman dressed in a white turban and sash. Next to them were pallbearers dressed in black and wearing white scarves. There were twenty-six pallbearers, one for each state in the union. Prancing behind was Harrison's riderless horse, Old Whitey, as a symbol of the fallen hero.

Members of Harrison's family rode behind the funeral car. Behind them came the president's successor, John Tyler, former president Adams, members of Congress, Supreme Court justices, and other officials. Next came soldiers who had served under Harrison, and then representatives from dozens of civic societies. In all, it took ninety-seven carriages to transport the entire entourage.

The two-mile-long procession moved up Pennsylvania Avenue, past the Capitol on to the nearby congressional burying ground. At the gate, the sealed coffin was taken down and carried by the pallbearers to a vault, where the body would remain until it could be moved to Ohio later in the year. Military troops fired three volleys in one final salute to the old hero.

In early July, some of Harrison's family and friends escorted the coffin to North Bend, Ohio, where the president was reunited with his wife and given his final burial on July 7. Anna Harrison is the only First Lady aside from Martha Washington never to have lived in the White House. "I wish that my husband's friends had left him where he is happy and content in retirement," she had said during her husband's campaign.

The Harrison funeral arrangements would set the model for future services of presidents who died in office. But the firsts from the 1840 campaign of Tippecanoe and Tyler were not yet over.

26

AND TYLER TOO

There was rhyme but no reason to it.

—Whig politician Philip Hone on the
slogan Tippecanoe and Tyler Too

At first, nobody was sure what to call John Tyler after the death of President William Henry Harrison. The cabinet secretaries continued to address him as "vice president." Others suggested "vice president acting as president." One senator even proposed legislation to call him "the Vice-President, on whom, by the death of the late President, the powers and duties of the office of President have devolved." Tyler himself insisted that nothing but "president" would do.

Tyler was the first vice president to succeed a president who died in office. The US Constitution was vague on succession. It said only that in the event of a president's death, the vice president would assume the president's duties. It didn't specifically say he also would assume the office. Tyler's insistence on being called "president" was an important precedent in establishing the presidential succession.

Eventually, the public gave Tyler another title: His Accidency.

Tyler, who had just turned fifty-one, was the youngest president to date, succeeding the oldest one. He had long government experience as governor and US senator from Virginia. He was a tall, thin man, with a long Roman nose. When two US tourists traveling in Italy saw the face of a sculptured bust of Cicero, they exclaimed, "President Tyler!"

Tyler was a dignified and courtly man who was fond of poetry and told humorous stories with a twinkle in his light blue eyes.

Articulate and refined, he read Shakespeare and played the violin. He also was strong-minded and vain. He drank wine and loved champagne. Some friends called him Captain Tyler, because he had been a captain in the War of 1812. He also believed strongly in states' rights and slavery.

Former president John Quincy Adams was unhappy with Tyler's elevation. Nobody ever thought the Virginian would be president, Adams wrote in his diary. Tyler, he said, was a Southerner with all the "passions and vices of slavery rooted in his moral and political constitution, with talents not above mediocrity, and a spirit incapable of expansion to the dimensions of the station on which he has been cast by the hand of Providence."

The abolitionist newspaper the *Emancipator*, which after Clay's defeat at Harrisburg had declared that no slaveholder would ever be president, was distraught. Now a man who owned more than forty slaves had risen to the highest post in the land. Tyler, the newspaper said, "is a slave breeder, is devoted to the slave interest, even to bigotry."

Tyler had no vice president. Samuel L. Southard of New Jersey, president pro tem of the Senate, became next in the line of presidential succession. After he resigned in 1842, William Person Mangum of North Carolina, a Clay ally, became Senate president pro tem.

Upon taking office, Tyler declared a national day of mourning. He retained Harrison's cabinet—but on his own terms. At the first meeting, Secretary of State Webster told Tyler that Harrison's policy was to put decisions to the cabinet and go with the majority. I assume, he said, you will do the same. Tyler replied that he would be the decider, thank you very much, and he politely suggested that if any cabinet members didn't like that arrangement they could resign. None did.

Tyler settled in at the White House. His son John Tyler Jr. was his private secretary. The new president brought slaves from his Williamsburg estate to handle household duties. His ailing wife, Letitia, was unable to take on the work of White House hostess, so he gave the assignment to his daughter-in-law Priscilla Cooper Tyler, the former actress.

Tyler made use of his new position to appoint friends to office, a power that had been denied him as vice president. He named author Washington Irving to be minister to Spain. He appointed the writer of the song "Home Sweet Home," John Howard Payne, to the consulship in Tunis. He later personally found a job for Richard Smith Elliott, the Harrisburg editor who helped create the log cabin image. Elliott, who had obtained a law degree, took a post as a $750-a-year subagent for the federal Indian Service in Council Bluffs, Missouri. He later gained fame as a correspondent during the Mexican-American War.

The special session of Congress that Harrison had ordered began on May 31, 1841, and Senator Clay quickly moved ahead on the Whig agenda. The first move was to terminate the independent treasury and sub-treasuries that Van Buren had obtained a year before. Congress passed the bill in early June, and President Tyler signed it into law. Jubilant Whigs marched up Pennsylvania Avenue behind a hearse with a coffin labeled THE SUB-TREASURY PLAN. So far, so good.

Next came Clay's main goal: the establishment of a new Bank of the United States. The legislation passed Congress in early August. But when the measure was sent to President Tyler, the wheels began to wobble on the Whig legislative bandwagon. The president vetoed the bill. He asserted that the measure was unconstitutional, because it took power from the states.

This time it was the opposition Democrats who celebrated. Shortly after the veto, an angry Henry Clay was walking past the Treasury Building when he saw a procession of men heading toward him in rows of two. It was a group of Congressional Democrats led by Pennsylvania senator James Buchanan. The lawmakers were on their way to the White House to congratulate the president. Tyler invited them in, and the popping of champagne corks echoed through the White House until midnight.

The Whigs were not so pleased. That night a mob of about thirty drunken people gathered outside the White House at about

2:00 AM. They loudly called Tyler names, blew bugles, and burned an effigy of the president.

Whig leaders looked for a compromise. Tyler indicated that he would sign a bill that barred the national bank from opening branches without the consent of the affected state. That put the Whigs in a better mood. On the evening of August 28, Clay and others went to the home of Attorney General John Crittenden (who, like the rest of Tyler's cabinet, had been appointed by President Harrison), to map out plans. They invited President Tyler, who politely declined.

After much drinking, the mood of the gathering turned festive. Several of the men went over to the White House to invite Tyler to join the party, and this time he reluctantly agreed. When Tyler arrived, Clay greeted the president, shouting, "Well, Mr. President, what are you for, Kentucky whiskey or champagne?" Tyler was a champagne man, of course.

After the merrymaking, the Whigs passed a second bill to establish a new National Bank and sent it to Tyler. A cartoon of the day showed President Tyler seated at a table, holding a pen in his hand raised over a large paper before him. The president was saying, "To sign, or not to sign—that is the question."

Despite the socializing, on September 9 President Tyler vetoed the second bill, saying the members of his party were moving too quickly. The Whigs were livid. On September 11, the entire cabinet resigned, except for Secretary of State Webster. When Webster informed Tyler of his decision to stay, Tyler rose from his chair, shook Webster's hand and said, "Henry Clay is a doomed man from this hour."

Politically, it was Tyler who was a doomed man. More than seventy Whig congressmen caucused in Capitol Square to denounce the president. More effigies were burned. There were even assassination threats, and Tyler was expelled from the Whigs. It was the first time that a president was officially booted from his own party.

One of Tyler's old friends, Virginia congressman John Botts, even began impeachment proceedings. Botts said he was close friends with Tyler—he'd even slept on a cot in Tyler's room at the Brown Hotel the night before Harrison's inauguration—but vowed to "head him, or die." The impeachment move, however, went nowhere.

Democrats were jubilant at the turn of events. Still, they considered the president, a former Democrat, to be a turncoat. Tyler had become a man without a party. The Democratic press mocked the Whigs with its own version of the Tippecanoe and Tyler Too song:

> *What has caused this great commotion, motion,*
> *The country through?*
> *Tis the veto, that's just come on from Washington and*
> *Tyler, too.*
> *From Tyler too—how the feds look blue*
> *Oh he's broke the heart of poor Clay-Clay, Poor Henry*
> *Clay.*

Tyler's clashes with Congress continued, even after Henry Clay resigned his Senate seat in 1842, citing poor health. In contrast to Harrison's promise to rarely veto anything Congress did, Tyler vetoed bills left and right. He cheered when the Democrats won control of the House in the fall of 1842. He began to hope that he could still win enough Democratic support to seek election in 1844 as a Democrat.

Tyler sought to build bridges with lawmakers by holding two or three White House parties a week while Congress was in session. One party in March 1842 was held in honor of Charles Dickens, the famous British author of such books as *Oliver Twist*. The thirty-year-old Dickens was making his first trip to America.

Dickens and his wife, Catherine Hogarth Dickens, arrived at the White House at about 10:00 PM. They were escorted past the main party of about three thousand people to a small drawing room where President Tyler was holding court. Tyler "looked somewhat worn and anxious, and well he might, being at war with everybody—but the expression of his face was mild and pleasant, and his manner was remarkably unaffected, gentlemanly, and agreeable," Dickens wrote later. "I thought that, in his whole carriage and demeanor, he became his nation singularly well."

Amid the political turmoil, Tyler suffered an even more painful loss. His wife, Letitia, suffered another stroke, and on September 10, 1842, at the age of fifty-one, she died. She was the first First Lady of a sitting president to pass away. The couple had eight children. Most were grown, but the youngest were a fifteen-year-old daughter and a ten-year-old son.

Tyler soldiered on, a president without a party and a man without a wife.

His prospects began to change on the evening of February 7, 1843—just five months after his wife's death—at a small party in the White House. Among the guests were a wealthy couple from Long Island, New York—David Gardiner and his wife, Juliana. With them were their two attractive daughters, twenty-two-year-old Julia and twenty-year-old Margaret.

Julia had briefly met Tyler about a year before when the family attended a party in the White House Green Room. She had been impressed with the tall, dignified president. She later recalled especially "the silvery sweetness of his voice, that seemed in just attune with the incomparable grace of his bearing and the elegant ease of his conversation."

This time it was Tyler who was impressed with Julia. The president arrived at about 9:30 PM and soon was flirting with both of the young Gardiner sisters. He invited the family up to his private chambers. As they left later in the evening, the fifty-three-year-old president kissed Margaret on the cheek and playfully chased Julia around the room.

Tyler invited the sisters to stop at the White House on February 13 on their way to a ball for Secretary of State Webster. They did, and Margaret said later that the president admired the dresses the sisters wore and kissed both of them several times.

Soon it became clear that the president had his eye on Julia. She was a black-haired beauty who was smart and charming. She stood just five foot three inches tall and was, according to the

Scioto Gazette, "rather above the middling size" and "beautiful in both form and face."

The high-spirited Julia had gained some notoriety in 1839 by posing for a lithograph in a magazine advertisement for a New York City clothing store, Bogert and Mecamly on lower Ninth Avenue. The ad showed Julia strolling in front of the store carrying a small handbag with the words, "I'll purchase at Bogert and Mecamly's . . . Their Goods are Beautiful and Astonishingly Cheap." Julia was also wearing a sunbonnet with big ostrich feathers sticking up, and a winter coat. At her side was a well-dressed older man carrying an expensive cane. The caption on the ad read, "Rose of Long Island."

Tyler invited the Gardiner girls to a White House Ball on George Washington's birthday, February 22. While Julia was dancing with a young naval officer, the president cut in. Julia was radiant that night in a white tartan and crimson Greek cap with a dangling tassel. Tyler asked Julia to marry him. Surprised, she laughingly shook her head no, swinging the tassels to and fro.

Tyler may have been partly joking at the time, but his love for Julia grew ever more serious. In November, the Gardiners moved into a house on Lafayette Square across the street from the White House. In February 1844, while Mrs. Gardiner was back in Long Island, President Tyler invited Julia, Margaret, and their father to a special event: a boat excursion down the Potomac River on the new steam frigate, the *Princeton*. The guest list of 250 men and 150 women included cabinet members, congressmen, naval officers, and much of Washington's social elite. Dolley Madison was one of them.

On the day of February 28 the group took a boat to nearby Alexandria, Virginia, where the 164-foot-long *Princeton* was docked. From there the *Princeton* carried the guests down the Potomac River. The major attraction was a demonstration of the world's biggest naval gun, the "Peacemaker." As the boat approached George Washington's home at Mount Vernon, the guests gathered on deck for a firing of the gun in honor of the first president. Then they headed below deck for food and music.

Sometime during the drinking and toasting, Thomas Gilmer, the secretary of the navy, suggested firing the gun again. The captain agreed, and many of the guests, including David Gardiner, headed back up on deck. President Tyler and most of the women, including Julia, stayed below to hear the end of a song. Just as the singer was finishing, a loud blast shook the boat. Black smoke began blowing through the salon.

President Tyler and others scrambled on deck. They discovered a horrendous scene. The breech of the great gun had exploded, sending red-hot metal in all directions. Six people lay dead on the deck. Among them were Navy Secretary Gilmer and Secretary of State Abel P. Upshur, who had replaced Daniel Webster several months earlier. Tyler's African American body servant was another of the victims. Many more were injured. Tyler broke into tears at the gruesome sight.

Then the president spotted another dead body. It was Julia's father, David Gardiner. His watch had stopped at 4:06 PM. Julia finally arrived on deck. At the news that her father had died, she fainted.

The dead were being covered as a boat arrived to take away the wounded and the surviving guests. The president picked up Julia and carried her across the gangplank to the rescue boat. At that moment, she regained consciousness. Not realizing at first who was carrying her, she tried to shake loose. "I almost knocked us both off the gang-plank," she said later. "I did not know at the time . . . that it was the President whose life I almost consigned to the water."

The dead bodies were brought to the White House and placed in coffins in the East Room. Julia and Margaret Gardiner spent the night at the presidential mansion. Then they returned to New York to be with their mother.

Soon afterward, during a carriage ride with Virginia senator Henry Wise, President Tyler revealed his intent to marry Julia. Wise gently cautioned that some people might think that he was a tad too old for such a young wife. "Pooh," the president replied with a chuckle. "Why, my dear sir, I am just full in my prime." Tyler proposed to Julia, and he wrote her mother to tell her the news.

Mrs. Gardiner was pleased but wondered if the president had the means to support Julia in the way that she was accustomed.

One morning in late June, President Tyler secretly slipped away from Washington by train to go to New York. The next day, June 26, 1844, Tyler became the first president to marry while in office. He and Julia tied the knot at 2:00 PM at a small family wedding at the Church of the Ascension on Fifth Avenue at Tenth Street. Tyler was fifty-four years old and Julia was twenty-four. The bride wore white with a gauze veil and white flowers in her hair.

One of the Gardiner family's high-society rivals in New York City was less than gracious about the nuptials. George Templeton Strong sniffed, "I've just heard a rumor that infatuated old John Tyler was married today to one of these large, fleshy Miss Gardiners of Gardiner's Island. Poor, unfortunate, deluded old jackass."

Julia Gardiner Tyler. *Library of Congress*

The marriage wasn't kept secret for long. Two days later the newlyweds held a well-attended wedding reception in the Blue Room of the White House. The couple stayed in Washington through the July Fourth celebration, then left for a month-long honeymoon at Hampton, Virginia, just south of Williamsburg. They stayed at Tyler's summer residence, a four-room, one-story cottage.

The marriage raised eyebrows among the old guard in Washington. President Tyler and his bride "are the laughing stock in this city," John Quincy Adams wrote in his diary. The president is "performing with a young girl from New York, the old fable of January and May."

The Tylers ignored the critics. They threw parties, with the new First Lady openly inviting publicity from the local newspapers. She sometimes drew more scorn than admiration. One newspaper reported that at one party "the lovely lady Presidentess" was attended by twelve maids of honor, six on either side of her and all dressed alike. The paper added that "her serene loveliness" received guests while sitting in a large armchair placed on a raised platform above the crowd while wearing a headdress resembling a crown.

Since crowds were often large at the parties, Mrs. Tyler wanted to be sure that her husband was noticed. So she ordered the Marine Band to play "Hail to the Chief" whenever the president entered a room. The idea would catch on. She also adopted the etiquette of England's Windsor Castle by having the names of each guest announced as they entered the door. She livened up the White House parties by introducing a scandalous new dance from Europe, the polka.

Meanwhile, President Tyler managed to win a few accomplishments. During Secretary of State Webster's tenure, he had obtained a treaty with Great Britain officially setting the border between the United States and Canada. They obtained the first US trade treaty with China. The president also helped inventor Samuel Morse to get Congress to approve $30,000 for his new telegraph system from Washington to Baltimore. In the system's first test, Morse sent a message from the US Supreme Court to an assistant in Baltimore on May 24, 1844. The message: "What hath God wrought?"

President Tyler had one last goal: the annexation of the Republic of Texas, which had split away from Mexico. "Texas shall crown off my public life," he declared. It didn't bother him that Texas would be a state where slavery was legal, but it had bothered Secretary of State Daniel Webster, who opposed adding a slave state. It was this issue that had led Tyler to replace Webster with Abel Upshur as secretary of state in mid-1843.

After Upshur's tragic death, Tyler had tapped former vice president John C. Calhoun to head the State Department, but the president had a more important new ally where Texas was concerned. Julia Tyler shared her husband's views on the subject and helped him lobby for Texas statehood. She was amused one day to see her name connected to the cause in a newspaper rhyme:

> Texas was the captain's bride
> Till a lovelier one he took;
> With Miss Gardiner by his side,
> He, with scorn, on kings may look.

Julia used the first large dinner party at the White House after her marriage to push the Texas cause. On the other side of her table sat Justice John McLean, the most political justice on the Supreme Court and an old beau. Julia urged him to show his support for Texas statehood as a matter of honor.

Secretary of State Calhoun snapped, "There is no honor in politics." Julia replied, "We'll see," and she slipped a note to McLean. On it she had written "Texas and John Tyler." The judge gallantly raised his glass, bowed, and said, "For your sake." (Julia later came to agree with Calhoun: "Experience has taught me that politics is not the best school for the propagation of the purest code of morals!")

Tyler briefly ran as an independent candidate for president, hoping public support on the Texas issue would propel him to a second term. It didn't; he dropped out in August before the election at the urging of Andrew Jackson. But in early 1845, Congress narrowly passed a joint resolution approving the annexation of Texas. Tyler signed the measure just three days before leaving office. Texas became the 28th state in December 1845, and a new town was named Tyler, Texas, in honor of President John Tyler.

Finally, the time came for the president and Julia to leave the White House. They threw one last party on February 19, 1845. Horse-drawn carriages lined up and down Pennsylvania Avenue as more than two thousand guests poured into the Blue Room. A staffer announced the name of each arriving guest, who then was greeted by a smiling President Tyler and the First Lady. Around her neck, Julia Tyler wore a necklace with a golden pen that the president had used to sign the Texas treaty.

When a guest congratulated Tyler on the festive gathering, he replied, "Yes, they cannot say now that I am a president without a party."

The Whig Party—after its triumph of Tippecanoe and Tyler Too in the great campaign of 1840—would struggle for its very existence in the years to come.

EPILOGUE

I have only a vague memory of my grandfather, as I was only a child when he died. But I will show all my family's famous name is safe in my keeping.

—President Benjamin Harrison

After the setbacks of the Tyler administration, the key figures in the Whig party fought to regain influence in American politics.

Charles Ogle, the Pennsylvania congressman who had helped seal President Martin Van Buren's fate in the 1840 election with his Golden Spoons speech, had little time to enjoy his notoriety. Ogle died of tuberculosis in May 1841 at the age of forty-three. Even in death, his Democratic critics couldn't forgive his attacks on Van Buren. "He has gone no doubt to pay the forfeit of his perfidy," said the *Raleigh (NC) Register*.

In 1844, Henry Clay captured the Whig presidential nomination he thought he had deserved in 1840. The Democrats were so badly split at their convention in Baltimore in May that they couldn't agree on a nominee after eight ballots. Finally, on the ninth ballot, they nominated the first "dark horse" presidential candidate, James K. Polk, who hadn't even been in the running.

The Whigs were overjoyed. "Who is James Polk?" they mocked. They soon found out. Polk, a former Tennessee congressman and governor, had the strong backing of former president Andrew "Old Hickory" Jackson. Indeed, the forty-eight-year-old Polk was referred to as "Young Hickory." Polk, who like Clay was a slaveholder, also ran on a compelling campaign issue. He vowed to expand the United States not only to Texas but also to Oregon, a territory coveted by the British. His slogan was "Oregon, Texas and Democracy."

Both campaigns tried to revive the lively excitement of the 1840 Tippecanoe and Tyler Too campaign. The Whigs marched, sang songs, put up Clay posters, and sold Clay snuffboxes. The Democrats also organized rallies, this time including women. But the spirit never caught on. For one reason, Clay never bought into the carnival atmosphere of the 1840 contest. Believing that campaigning as Harrison did was below his dignity, he conducted his effort from home in Lexington, Kentucky. Polk also stayed home in Tennessee.

Clay waffled on the Texas question, badly damaging his campaign. Meanwhile, the Democrats launched personal attacks that went beyond even the assaults on Harrison's reputation in 1840. As a longtime politician, Clay carried more baggage than the four o'clock train from Richmond. One popular Democratic pamphlet declared, "Mr. Clay's Gambling, Mr. Clay's Profanity. Mr. Clay—A Sabbath Breaker. Henry Clay Duels." The Democrats also accused Clay of adultery and mistreating his slaves.

Clay lost the election in a close vote. He tried one more time for the Whig nomination in 1848, but fell short.

Polk served one term in office. Following a bloody two-year war with Mexico, America expanded under his presidency to include not only Texas and Oregon but also California.

John Tyler and his family moved back to Charles City County, Virginia, to Walnut Grove, a sixteen-hundred-acre plantation that the president had purchased a few years before for $12,000 (more than $300,000 in twenty-first-century dollars). Tyler soon expanded the main house to the length of one football field and one foot, making it the longest frame house in America. The plantation was four miles from Tyler's boyhood home at Greenway and right down the Old Indian Trail (later the John Tyler Memorial Highway) from William Henry Harrison's childhood home at Berkeley Plantation. In fact, Harrison had once owned the land; he had it in 1793.

The Tylers lived quietly at Walnut Grove. But after some critics declared the former president an outlaw like Robin Hood, Tyler embraced the comparison and changed the name of the plantation to Sherwood Forest Plantation. The Tylers would sometimes go to parties a mile down the road at the North Bend Plantation, named after the Harrison farm in Ohio and now owned by family of William Henry Harrison's late sister, Sarah Harrison Minge.

In 1860, as the Civil War loomed, Tyler went to Washington to take part in an attempted peace conference between the North and the South. When war broke out in 1861, Tyler backed the South and won election to the Confederate Congress. In the North, the Accidental President was given a new nickname: the Traitor President.

In early 1862, the former president went to Richmond to join the Confederate Congress, but he never took his seat. Tyler fell ill at the city's Exchange Hotel. He died there on January 17, 1862, with Julia at his side, at the age of seventy-one. In his obituary, the *New York Times* labeled Tyler as "the most unpopular public man that had ever held any office in the United States."

When the Civil War fighting drew near Sherwood Forest, Julia moved with her children to Staten Island, New York. She remained an outspoken supporter of the South. After the war ended, Julia moved into a Georgetown residence in Washington, DC, for a while, billing herself as "Mrs. Ex-President John Tyler."

Julia returned to Sherwood Forest in 1874, but in the late 1880s, she moved into Richmond, where in 1889 she suffered a stroke and died at age sixty-nine. She passed away in the very same Exchange Hotel where John Tyler had died twenty-seven years earlier. She was buried at her husband's side in Richmond's Hollywood Cemetery.

President John Tyler left one record that is unlikely ever to be matched: most children by a US president. He was the father of fifteen children, eight with Letitia and seven with Julia. Two of Tyler's grandsons—yes, grandsons, not great-grandsons—were still alive in the early twenty-first century. One of them, Harrison Ruffin Tyler, and his wife, Payne Bouknight Tyler, own Sherwood Forest Plantation. Paynie Tyler bought the plantation in 1974 and restored it to its former glory.

Martin Van Buren made a bid for the Democratic presidential nomination in 1844. In fact, he led on the first several ballots. But the former president had a problem in the eyes of many Democrats: he opposed annexing Texas as a slave state. Proslavery Southern delegates moved to block Van Buren and nominated Polk instead.

Van Buren wasn't done. In 1848 he came back as the nominee of a new independent party, the Free Soil Party. The party's stated goal was to prohibit any new slave states or slave territories. Its slogan: "Free Soil, Free Speech, Free Labor and Free Men." It was a quixotic candidacy. Van Buren finished far behind the two major party candidates, receiving no electoral votes.

The Little Magician had played his last card. After a two-year trip to Europe, he returned to his hometown of Kinderhook, New York. In contrast to his humble beginnings there, Van Buren had purchased the Lindenwald mansion that had been owned by the wealthy Van Ness family when he was a boy. In his later years, Van Buren wrote his autobiography. The most remarkable fact about the book was that in more than eight hundred pages he never once mentioned his late wife, Hannah. Van Buren died at Lindenwald at the age of seventy-nine in July 1862, just six months after Tyler had passed away.

The Whigs made a comeback in 1848. The party adopted the tried and true strategy that had won the election of 1840. They nominated a popular general for president.

This time the general was sixty-four-year-old Zachary "Rough and Ready" Taylor, a hero of the Mexican-American War. Like Harrison, Taylor didn't attend the presidential nominating convention. In fact, he almost didn't find out he had been nominated because the Whigs sent the official notification letter to his Louisiana plantation postage due. Taylor had been receiving so much postage-due mail that he told his postmaster to deliver only the postage-paid letters. So the Whig letter sat in the Baton Rouge dead letter department for six weeks. The Whigs finally mailed another letter with the postage paid, and Taylor accepted the nomination.

As the owner of more than one hundred slaves, Taylor appealed to Southerners. To balance the ticket, the Whigs picked as Taylor's running mate New York's Millard Fillmore, the former Harrison supporter, who was a moderate on slavery. At that point, Taylor had never met Fillmore. The folksy general hardly bothered to campaign, but he won the presidency anyway.

The general kept up his informal ways in the White House. Taylor didn't drink, but the tobacco-chewing president kept the spittoons overflowing. His horse Whitey grazed on the White House lawn.

Taylor ended up emulating Harrison in a way that shook the nation. On July 4, 1850, he strolled over to a celebration beside the unfinished Washington Monument. It was a hot, humid day. Taylor ate some cherries and iced milk, which may have been contaminated with bacteria. By that evening he began suffering stomach pains, which became more severe over the next few days. Doctors diagnosed his condition as cholera. Taylor passed away on July 9 at the age of sixty-five. So far, the Whigs had elected two presidents, and both of them had died in office.

Vice President Millard Fillmore became President Fillmore. The Whigs weren't sure he could win reelection in 1852, so they went back to basics. They nominated another general, this time Old Fuss and Feathers himself, General Winfield Scott, who was now sixty-six years old. The old military magic was gone. Scott lost in a landslide to Democrat Franklin Pierce.

As the country headed toward civil war, the Whig Party split apart and faded away. Proslavery Whigs moved into the Democratic Party. Antislavery Whigs went with the new Republican Party.

Abraham Lincoln, the former Harrison elector, emerged as the Republican presidential nominee in 1860, running on a platform opposing the expansion of slavery. The Democrats split into two parties, one from the South and one from the North. The Northern party's candidate was Lincoln's old Illinois rival, Stephen Douglas.

Lincoln adopted many of the strategies from the Log Cabin campaign. He ran an image campaign that styled him as "Honest Abe," who was born in a log cabin and had been a common rail-splitter. The difference was that Lincoln's claims were true. His supporters held rallies, torchlight parades, and barbecues patterned after the great Tippecanoe and Tyler Too campaign of 1840.

Despite his reputation as a political speaker, though, Lincoln followed tradition and refrained from going on the campaign trail. Douglas, like Harrison before him, took to the stump. He became the first presidential candidate to give speeches in every state (thirty-three at the time). Nevertheless, when the votes were counted, Lincoln had won, becoming the first Republican president.

Like Harrison, president-elect Lincoln rode into Washington on a train. Unlike Harrison's grand entrance, Lincoln stole into town on an overnight, one-car private train from Philadelphia. The train skipped stopping in Baltimore, where security adviser Allan Pinkerton had warned of a threatened assassination attempt. According to some fanciful press reports, Lincoln dressed up like a Scotsman in a plaid cap and kilt, wore dark glasses, and carried brass knuckles. Actually, on his early-morning arrival in Washington he wore a hat low over his eyes and an overcoat as he was hustled to the Willard Hotel.

The secretive arrival drew contempt from some of the press. The *Baltimore Sun* harrumphed, "Had we any respect for Mr. Lincoln, official or personal, as a man, or as President elect of the United States . . . the final escapade by which he reached the capital would have utterly demolished it."

President Lincoln surrounded himself with numerous people from the old Harrison campaign. Unofficial advisers included Thurlow Weed and Francis P. Blair, the former editor of the anti-Harrison *Washington Globe*, who had come to oppose slavery. Blair's son Montgomery Blair was Lincoln's postmaster general. The secretary of war was former Pennsylvania senator Simon Cameron, who now owned the Harrisburg mansion where the log cabin image had been created. Cameron's most famous quote was "An honest politician is one who, when he is bought, will stay bought."

Just over a month after Lincoln was inaugurated the Civil War broke out when Confederates fired on Fort Sumter in South Carolina on April 12, 1861. The president picked General George McClellan to lead the Union army against the rebels, but "Little Mac" was hesitant to engage the enemy. Lincoln objected that his general "has the slows." So he eventually replaced McClellan with General Ulysses S. Grant.

Now Lincoln turned to another old Harrison backer for support. Thaddeus Stevens, the man who had largely gotten Harrison nominated at Harrisburg in 1839, was now a "Radical Republican" congressman from Pennsylvania. As chairman of the powerful House Ways and Means Committee, Stevens saw the war as the opportunity to end slavery once and for all. At first, he complained that President Lincoln was moving much too slowly on the matter.

Lincoln bided his time. Then, after Union forces scored a major victory at the bloody battle of Antietam in Sharpsburg, Maryland, in September 1862, he decided on a plan of action. On January 1, 1863, Lincoln issued the Emancipation Proclamation, freeing the slaves. Stevens cheered the move and supported Lincoln's reelection in 1864. "Well may every honest man, well may any man who loves God and loves liberty," Stevens said, "exclaim 'Thank God for Abraham Lincoln.'"

Both Lincoln and Stevens knew that the president's executive order could be overturned later by a new president, or by Congress or the courts. What was needed was a Thirteenth Amendment to the Constitution to abolish slavery. Previous efforts in Congress had fallen short, but after his reelection, Lincoln tried again with Stevens's help. Passage would require hardball politics; Stevens was up to the challenge.

Congress passed the amendment in January 1865. Said Stevens, "The greatest measure of the nineteenth century was passed by corruption, aided and abetted by the purest man in America." The amendment was ratified by the states by December 1865.

Stevens had personal reasons for his feelings against slavery. The worst-kept secret in Washington was that the bachelor had lived for nearly twenty years with his African American house-keeper, Lydia Smith. The intelligent Lydia was the daughter of a black woman and an Irish father.

The Civil War ended when the South surrendered at Appomattox Court House in Virginia on April 9, 1865. But the deep wounds did not heal. Less than a week later, on April 14, Lincoln and his wife, Mary Todd Lincoln, decided to go to Ford's Theatre to see a popular comedy called *Our American Cousin*. The Lincolns arrived late and took their seats in the presidential box overlooking the right side of the stage.

At that time, US presidents weren't under the protection of the Secret Service. So a District of Columbia policeman, John F. Parker, was assigned to guard Lincoln. Initially, he sat right outside the door to the presidential box. But at intermission, he left to go to a bar next door and never came back. During the second act, the actor John Wilkes Booth, a radical Southern sympathizer, walked into the box with a pistol and shot Lincoln in the back of the head. Then Booth jumped off the balcony onto the stage and temporarily escaped.

Lincoln was carried to the Petersen house across the street, where he died the next morning. It was then that War Secretary William Stanton—the former Democrat and Steubenville, Ohio, lawyer—famously said, "Now he belongs to the ages." Lincoln thus became the third president to die in office—all of them Whigs or former Whigs.

The Lincoln assassination was part of a conspiracy. Another man was assigned to kill Vice President Andrew Johnson at his boardinghouse, but he backed out. Lincoln's secretary of state, William Seward, wasn't so lucky.

Seward, a key strategist in the Log Cabin campaign, was resting at his house on Lafayette Square at the same time that Lincoln was murdered at Ford's Theatre just a few blocks away. Seward was in his upstairs bedroom, recovering from a carriage accident. A cohort of Booth, who got into the house by pretending to be delivering medicine, repeatedly stabbed Seward in the face and neck. The secretary barely survived.

Seward continued as secretary of state under President Andrew Johnson. In 1867 he made headlines by arranging for the United States to purchase more than 586,000 square miles of mostly snow- and ice-covered land in the Northwest from Russia for $7.2 million. Ninety-nine hundredths of the land "are absolutely useless," said the *Holt County Sentinel*, and the rest "is certainly not worth seven million of dollars to a nation already possessed of more territory than it can decently govern, and burdened with debt." People called the big land buy Seward's Folly. Today it is called the state of Alaska.

After serving in the Johnson administration, Seward, a widower, returned to his home in Auburn, New York, as his star faded. Meanwhile, the aspirations of an old ally from the Harrison campaign were on the rise.

Horace Greeley, the gangly editor of the *Log Cabin* newspaper, had become America's most influential journalist as publisher of his *New York Tribune*. Greeley supported Lincoln's 1860 election, but—like Thaddeus Stevens—chastised the president for not moving fast enough against slavery.

After the Civil War, Greeley decided to leave the sidelines and enter the arena. In 1872, he ran for the White House against Republican president Ulysses S. Grant as the nominee of the new Liberal Republican Party, a group of Republicans who had split from the main party. The new party was for equal rights and civil service reform, and against the rampant corruption in the Grant administration. The Democratic Party chose to nominate the sixty-one-year-old Greeley as its candidate as well.

Several minor parties also nominated candidates. Victoria Woodhull of Ohio became the first woman to run for president as the candidate for the new Equal Rights Party. The thirty-four-year-old Woodhull and her sister had started their own successful Wall Street brokerage firm and also a newspaper. Woodhull ran on a then-controversial platform: "Women are the equals of men before the law, and are equal in all their rights."

Even more controversial was Woodhull's complaint about the double standard that sexual affairs by men were condoned while the women were condemned. After a prominent New York minister accused her of advocating free love, Woodhull published a story about the married minister's affair with a parishioner. The day before the election, police jailed Woodhull for sending an obscene article through the mails. (On Election Day, another women's rights advocate, Susan B. Anthony, also was arrested in Rochester, New York, after she unlawfully became the first woman to vote, casting a ballot for Grant.)

In the race between the two major candidates, both sides adopted many of the techniques of Tippecanoe and Tyler Too. One was campaign songs. A pro-Greeley song satirized Grant's reputation for giving jobs to family members; it was called "Horace and No Relations." Greeley even tried to take advantage of his early days working on a farm. A poster reminiscent of Harrison's farmer image promoted Greeley as "Our Farmer President."

The mudslinging descended to new lows. Following the war, Greeley had supported amnesty for Southerners along with equal rights for blacks. The famous cartoonist Thomas Nast drew a picture of Greeley giving bail money to Confederate president Jefferson Davis, throwing mud on Grant, and shaking hands with John Wilkes Booth across Lincoln's grave. After such assaults, Greeley said, "I have been assailed so bitterly that I hardly knew whether I was running for the presidency or the penitentiary."

Taking a leaf from Harrison's playbook, Greeley went on a nationwide speaking tour. Instead of horseback, Greeley made whistle-stop appearances from the back platforms of trains. Sometimes his speeches lasted only a minute or so as the train stopped just long enough to take on water for the engine.

The newspaper publisher ran a strong race, but it wasn't enough. Though the popular vote was relatively close—3,598,468 for Grant and 2,835,315 for Greeley—Grant won handily in the Electoral College, with Greeley taking only six southern states. Ironically, Grant's vice president was Henry Wilson, the famed Natick Cobbler from the Log Cabin campaign of 1840.

As with Harrison, the strenuous campaign had taken a toll on Greeley, and even if he had won, he might never have served.

He passed away in Pleasantville, New York, on November 29, 1872—the same day the electoral votes were being tallied.

Now one of the final pillars of the Tippecanoe and Tyler Too campaign was gone. Yet Old Tip's links to presidential politics still endured.

Anna Harrison had continued to live in Ohio. After President Harrison's death, Congress voted her one year of presidential pay, or $25,000. But not without a fight. Some senators objected to setting a precedent, while others said the widow didn't need the money. The Senate narrowly approved the payments, by a vote of twenty for and sixteen against.

Anna stayed at the house in North Bend, surrounded by the families of her children and the servants. In 1858, the house caught fire again during the night, a fire allegedly set by a "she devil" of an Irish housekeeper. This time the house burned to the ground. Anna moved in with the nearby family of her son, John Scott Harrison. She died in 1864 at age eighty-eight and was buried next to her husband at North Bend.

The Harrison political name lived on through one of the late president's grandsons. Benjamin Harrison, John Scott's son, grew up at North Bend; he was seven years old when his grandfather died. The younger Harrison became a Union general in the Civil War and then a US senator from Indiana. In 1888 the Republicans nominated Harrison as their presidential candidate, with New York governor Levi Morton as his running mate. The fifty-four-year-old Benjamin Harrison, in contrast to his genial grandfather, was so cold that his nickname was the Human Iceberg.

In a variation of his grandfather's campaign, Harrison spoke for himself, but instead of traveling, he gave more than ninety speeches from the front porch of his house in Indianapolis. Thousands of people poured into the neighborhood for Tippecanoe-style parades. A Harrison ball was even rolled in from Maryland to keep the ball rolling for the candidate. The campaign also sent surrogate orators around the country, including African American abolitionist Frederick Douglass, who gave two speeches for Harrison.

References to Old Tippecanoe were everywhere in the campaign. Like his grandfather, Harrison often wore a beaver hat. One opposition slogan about Harrison was "His Grandfather's Hat—It's Too big for Ben." The Republicans replied, "The Same Old Hat—It Fits Ben Just Right." Other Harrison slogans were "Tippecanoe and Morton too" and "Tippecanoe and Tariff, Too." Tariffs were the big issue of the campaign.

In the election, Harrison got a hundred thousand fewer votes than incumbent Grover Cleveland, but he won the electoral vote 233 to 168. Benjamin Harrison became the twenty-third US president, and the only one who was the grandson of a former commander in chief.

Harrison and his wife, Caroline Lavinia Scott Harrison, moved into the White House as the first electric lights were being installed in the mansion. The Harrisons were afraid of the new invention and they always asked White House servants to turn the lights on and off for them. Benjamin Harrison ran for reelection in 1892, but campaigned only half-heartedly after his wife became ill and died. This time he lost to Grover Cleveland, who became the only president to serve two nonconsecutive terms.

The loss finally ended the Harrison family's direct involvement in presidential politics, but the tactics pioneered by the Tippecanoe and Tyler Too campaign of 1840 live on to this day. Every four years, presidential candidates put up their tents and become ringmasters of a three-ring circus of hoopla, high-wire hijinks, and political promises.

Perhaps the most positive effect of the 1840 campaign is that subsequent presidential campaigns have had to appeal to grassroots Americans. Today's candidates go among the people to make speeches and, unlike Harrison, to spell out their positions. Women have become increasingly involved in presidential politics—as activists, voters, and candidates. Even mixing some entertainment with politics has added a touch of fun to the grinding and increasingly lengthy campaigns.

Unfortunately, the carnival-like atmosphere can sometimes overshadow the substance. The 1840 campaign also paved the way for demagoguery and for the influx of big money. It created a strategy of image advertising, some of it designed to bamboozle voters about the true background or character of a candidate. The campaign also laid the groundwork for vicious personal attacks on a candidate's opponent.

Some might argue that today's voters are less gullible than their 1840 counterparts. Besides, modern voters can research political claims, thanks to the Internet. But the Internet is a double-edged disseminator of data that also spreads malicious misinformation. Based on recent history, it isn't all that far-fetched to think that a sizable number of people would believe twisted tales, such as the claim that a candidate for president wasn't born in the United States and instead came from Mars.

Though deception and personal political assaults sometimes backfire, as they did in 1840 when the Democrats tried to paint Harrison as a log cabin granny, it's unlikely that they'll ever go away. Give today's presidential candidates a choice between a new type of positive campaign based mainly on issues and their own ideas or the traditional slash-and-burn attacks on their opponents, and, realistically, what is the likely response?

Keep the ball rolling. Huzzah. Huzzah.

ACKNOWLEDGMENTS

Many people helped make this book possible. I especially thank my wife, Mary Rogers, for her loving support and red editing pencil. My longtime friend Judith Windeler, a London-based novelist under the pen name of Minerva Taylor and writer of the novels *The Blood Stiller* and *The Blood Archive*, provided welcome suggestions.

Research for the book was made easier by access to two world-class libraries at the College of William and Mary in Williamsburg, Virginia: the college's Earl Gregg Swem Library and the law school's Wolf Law Library.

My hope is that this book will encourage a wider interest in American history.

A TIPPECANOE
AND TYLER TOO TOUR

(Along John Tyler Memorial Highway, Route 5, between Richmond and Williamsburg, Virginia)

Berkeley Plantation
Boyhood home of President William Henry Harrison.
12602 Harrison Landing Road
Charles City County, VA 23030

Sherwood Forest Plantation
Home of President John Tyler and his wife Julia Gardiner Tyler.
14501 John Tyler Memorial Highway (Route 5)
Charles City County, VA 23030

North Bend Plantation B&B and tours by appointment
Original home of William Henry Harrison's sister Sarah Harrison and her husband John Minge.
12220 Weyanoke Road
Charles City County, VA 23030

Shirley Plantation
Circa 1738 mansion of John Carter and his wife, Elizabeth Hill Carter. John Carter's sister was Anne Carter Harrison, the grand-mother of President William Henry Harrison and great-great-grandmother of President Benjamin Harrison.
501 Shirley Plantation Road
Charles City County, VA 23030

Hollywood Cemetery
Burial site of President John Tyler and his wife Julia Gardiner Tyler.
412 South Cherry Street
Richmond, VA 23220

William Henry Harrison Tomb
Tomb of William Henry and Anna Symmes Harrison.
Brower and Cliff Roads
North Bend, OH 45052

Fort Meigs
Defended by General William Henry Harrison in the War of 1812.
29100 River Road West
Perrysburg, OH 43551

Ohio History Center
800 East 17th Avenue
Columbus, OH 43211

Indiana Historical Society
450 West Ohio Street
Indianapolis, IN 46202

Tippecanoe Battlefield Museum
Site of Tippecanoe Battle of 1811.
National Park Service
200 Battleground Avenue
Battle Ground, IN 47920

Harrison Mansion
Governor William Henry Harrison's "Grouseland" estate.
3 West Scott Street
Vincennes, IN 47951

Martin Van Buren National Historic Park
Lindenwald mansion, the retirement home of President Van Buren.
National Park Service
1013 Old Post Road
Kinderhook, NY 12106

The John Harris–Simon Cameron Mansion
Birthplace of the Log Cabin campaign theme.
219 South Front Street
Harrisburg, PA 17104

NOTES

INTRODUCTION

"The most remarkable political contest ever": Norton, *Great Revolution*, 7.

1. A COMPROMISE CANDIDATE

"[The Whig nominee's] imbecility": *Ohio Statesman*, January 8, 1840.

"I had rather be right": Clay, quoted in *Congressional Globe*, 25th Congress, 3rd session, 167.

"all the energy": *New York Herald*, December 2, 1839.

"a lively and active": Adams, *Memoirs*, 7:530.

"Praise God!": *Emancipator*, December 13, 1839.

"to throw a ray of light": Burnet, quoted in Whig Party, *Proceedings of the Democratic Whig Convention*, 40.

a "penetrating mind": Ibid., 35.

"Let me assure you": Ibid., 41.

"Union for the sake of Union!": Ibid., 42.

"I envy Kentucky": Sargent, *Life and Public Services*, 71.

"My friends are not worth": Wise, *Seven Decades*, 171–172.

"We are now in the field": Gunderson, *Log-Cabin Campaign*, 72.

2. THE FIRST IMAGE CAMPAIGN

"Passion and prejudice": Elliott, *Notes Taken*, 121.

"but I am sure": Ibid., 56.

"Give him a barrel": *Baltimore Republican*, December 11, 1839.

"Mrs. Harrison of Ohio": *New York Herald*, December 9, 1839.

the "war-worn hero": *New York Evening Post*, quoted in *Vermont Phoenix*, February 14, 1840.

"the direct and infallible path": Adams, *Life*, 320.

"As soon as a pioneer arrives": Tocqueville, *Democracy in America*, 1:316.

"Why ye graceless": *Catskill Reader*, June 25, 1840.

"The log cabin is a symbol": Weed, *Memoir*, 2:81.

"who sneer at the idea": *New York Daily Whig*, quoted in *National Intelligencer*, January 14, 1840.

"Listen to the fawning minions": *North Carolina Star*, quoted in *National Intelligencer*, January 14, 1840.

"Do they not know": Parton, *Life of Horace Greeley*, 150.

"a shrewd old gentleman": Elliott, *Notes Taken*, 121.

DEMOCRACY, REFORM: *Harrisburg Daily Telegraph*, quoted in *Jeffersonian Republican*, January 31, 1840.

"the air became vocal": Ibid.

"They say that he lived": Norton, *Great Revolution*, 52.

"By whom, tell me whom": Norton, *Tippecanoe Songs*, 58.

"The people are of the opinion": *Jeffersonian Republican*, January 31, 1840.

3. HELLO, COLUMBUS

"We marched through the streets": Elliott, *Notes Taken*, 125.

HARRISON AND TYLER—THE PILLARS: Miller, *Great Convention*, 6.

"It was Harrison that fought": Elliott, *Notes Taken*, 122.

"On they came": *Dayton Journal*, quoted in *Niles' Register*, March 14, 1840.

"Yes, they are bank men": *Ohio State Journal*, February 22, 1840.

"Whoo-oo-oo-o-ra-aa-ah": Ibid.

"I am this evening half crazed": Ibid.

"but we cannot describe it": Ibid.

"songs and drinking and carousing": *Ohio Statesman*, February 22, 1840.

"touched a cord": Miller, *Great Convention*, 6.

"What has caused the great commotion": Galbreath, *Alexander Coffman Ross*, 21.

4. OLD TIP: HERO OR COWARD?

"[General Harrison is] the hero of defeat": *Washington Globe*, quoted in *Vermont Watchman and State Journal*, March 9, 1840.

"By my sword": Goebel, *William Henry Harrison*, 36.

"The system is to live": Jefferson to Harrison, February 28, 1803, in Harrison, *Messages and Letters*, 1:70.

"These lands are ours": *Fraser's Magazine* 29 (1844).

DON'T GIVE UP THE SHIP: Perry, *Mere Matter of Marching*, 154.

"We have met the enemy": Hickey, *War of 1812*, 44.

"But I was fully": Perry, *Mere Matter of Marching*, 163.

"The people were then hurrahing": *Niles' Register*, November 1813.

"not as he is in his old age": Crary, quoted in *Congressional Globe*, 26th Congress, vol. 8, appendix, 238–243.

"Anyone who will put himself": Ibid.

"very nearly terminating": Todd and Drake, *Civil and Military Services*, 37.

"I know, sir": Norton, *Great Revolution*, 86.

"I can safely say": *Pittsburgh Gazette*, April 2, 1840.

"deadly implements of war": Corwin, quoted in *Congressional Globe*, February 15, 1840.

"the late General Crary": Poore, *Perley's Reminiscences*, 1–2:237.

5. HOME SWEET LOG CABIN HOME

"He is a rich man": Duncan, quoted in *Congressional Globe*, April 10, 1840.

"a beautifully kept velvety lawn": Harrison granddaughter Fanny Hendryx in Harrison, *Messages and Letters*, 1:9.

"There is a degree of gravity": *Boston Atlas*, August 22, 1840.

"the simplicity of his manners": *New York Express*, May 23, 1840.

"which is so destructive": Burr, *Life and Times*, 295.

"absolutely rabid": Adams, *Memoirs*, 7:530.

"the greatest beggar": *Democrat's Almanac and People's Register for 1841* (Boston: E. Littlefield, 1840), 10.

"is poor with a numerous family": Stoddard, *Lives of Presidents*, 112.

"does not live in a log cabin": Duncan, quoted in *Congressional Globe*, April 10, 1840.

"in splendor and luxury": Quoted in *Extra Globe*, May 16, 1840.

6. LITTLE MATTY

"As a rule we simply assailed": Elliott, *Notes Taken*, 126.

"mountain in labor has brought forth": *Ohio Statesman*, January 8, 1840.

"like a cat": Muller, *William Cullen Bryant*, 163.

"It was said that at a year old": Crockett, *Life of Martin Van Buren*, 9.

"get him without violence": Library of Congress, *Calendar of the Papers of Martin Van Buren* (Washington, DC: Government Printing Office, 1910), 72.

"a woman of sweet nature": Harris, *First Ladies*, 136.

"There never was a woman": Holland, *Life and Political Opinions*, 72.

"Van Buren is as opposite": Crockett, *Life of Martin Van Buren*, 13.

"The political history of the last 30 years": Parton, *Life of Andrew Jackson*, 3:287.

"I have my bread and butter": Safire, *Safire's Political Dictionary*, 80.

"prone to expect too much": Richardson, ed., *Compilation of Messages and Papers*, 2:344.

"Damn the panic": Shephard, *American Statesmen*, 386.

"Our sufferings is intolerable": Gunderson, *Log-Cabin Campaign*, 12.

"to give him and all his office-holders": *Campaign*, April 23, 1840.

"Matty's policy, fifty cents a day": Shephard, *American Statesmen*, 324.

"heartless, hypocritical, selfish": MacKenzie, *Life and Times*, 26.

"heartlessness in friendship": Burstein, *Original Knickerbocker*, 298.

"Why the deuce is it": Boller, *Presidential Anecdotes*, 88.

7. PALACE OF SPLENDOR

"[Why should the American people] support": Seale, ed., *White House History*, 228.

"is laced up in corsets": Crockett, *Life of Martin Van Buren*, 80.

"The Nero of the White House": "A Workingman," *More Than One Hundred Reasons Why William Henry Harrison Should and Will Have the Support of the Democracy* (Boston: Tuttle, Dennett & Chisholm, 1840), 13.

"We want you out": Gobright, *Recollections*, 38.

"a watery compound": Poore, *Perley's Reminiscences*, 1–2:221.

"It seems that it is not": Bacourt, *Souvenirs of a Diplomat*, 79.

$3,665 for "alteration and repairs": Seale, ed., *White House History*, 240.

"the sum of $3,805.55": Ibid., 242.

"I protest against spending": Ibid., 253.

"Oh, how delightful": Ibid., 259.

"to wash his pretty": Ibid., 261.

"every pair of which": Ibid., 236.

"with the little Kinderhook": Ibid., 233.

"that he actually burst his corset": *Daily Political Tornado*, November 5, 1840.

"omnibus of lies": *Washington Globe*, April 17, 1840.

"not the least foundation": *Extra Globe*, August 19, 1840.

"The man who walks upon": *Log Cabin*, May 23, 1840.

8. SHOWDOWN IN BALTIMORE

"In no country": *Baltimore Patriot*, quoted in *Niles' Register*, May 9, 1840.

THE HERO OF TIPPECANOE: *Log Cabin*, May 9, 1840.

THE COWARD OF TIPPECANOE: Ibid.

"The steam must be kept up": Fillmore, *Papers*, 2:209.

"*The people are coming*": *Baltimore American*, May 5, 1840.

"With heart and soul": *Baltimore Patriot*, quoted in *Niles' Register*, May 9, 1840.

"really a great and inspiring sight": Parsons, *Tour Through Indiana*, 5.

"We have fallen upon hard times": *National Intelligencer*, May 5, 1840.

"fell dead in the street": *Ohio Statesman*, May 8, 1840.

"the heartless throng": *Washington Globe*, quoted in *Niles' Register*, May 16, 1840.

9. A DEMOCRATIC SPLINTER

"I have not solicited a re-nomination": *Niles' Register*, May 10, 1840.

"We wish no deceptive parade": Democratic Party, *Proceedings*, 4.

"have a candidate whom they want": Ibid., 5–6.

"young dandies in hunting shirts": *Ohio Statesman*, May 8, 1840.

the Whig "animal show": *Niles' Register*, May 9, 1840.

a nine-point platform: Democratic Party, *Proceedings*, 8.

"The firmness of Mr. Van Buren": Democratic Party, *Proceedings*, 12.

"openly and shamefully lives": Kendall to Van Buren, August 22, 1839, in Van Buren MSS, Library of Congress.

"a dead wait": Jackson to Van Buren, in Jackson, *Correspondence*, 49.

"ache to drop 'Old Dick'": Granger to Weed, April 22, 1840, in Granger MSS, Library of Congress.

"made no inflammatory appeals": McMaster, *History of the People*, 6:573.

"*Pretty little Martin*": *Harrison Medal Minstrel*, 74.

10. TIPPECANOE AND RALLIES TOO

"The prairies are on fire": Hurst, *Whig Activities*, 58.

"the wildest freaks of fun": Sargent, *Public Men*, 108.

"song singing, huzzahing": *Bay State Democrat*, September 10, 1840.

"Martin Van Buren, you won't do": Norton, *Great Revolution*, 161.

"I battled with right good will": Poe, *Complete Works of Edgar Allan Poe*, 17:91.

"monster meeting": Julian, *Political Recollections*, 21.

"Nothing attracts a crowd": Seward and Seward, *Autobiography of William H. Seward*, 498.

"*Come, all you Log Cabin Boys*": *Jeffersonian Republican*, August 14, 1840.

WE WANT WORK: Norton, *Great Revolution*, 144.

"Tip-tip! Tip-tip! Tyler": McMaster, *History of the People*, 6:565.

OUT WITH THE SPOILERS: Sutor, *Past and Present*, 114.

"abandoned their ordinary business": Buchanan to Van Buren, September 5, 1840, in Van Buren MSS, Library of Congress.

"These popular movements": *Detroit Free Press*, June 15, 1840.

"It seems as though men": *Extra Globe*, July 22, 1840.

"Our village has been in turmoil": *Ohio Statesman*, February 24, 1840.

"Where will it end?": Adams, *Memoirs*, 10:352.

"You are no doubt certain": Morrow, *Life and Speeches*, 37.

"Take care of the laborer": Norton, *Great Revolution*, 346.

"We have taught them": *Democratic Review*, June 1840, 486.

"This must be called the Log Cabin": Ibid.

"*And we'll vote for Tyler*": Norton, *Great Revolution*, 374.

"grandeur surpasses the power": *Niles' Register*, September 26, 1840.

"The prairies are on fire": Safire, *Safire's Political Dictionary*, 804–805.

11. THE FIRST GENDER GAP

"This way of making politicians": Georgia Democrat, quoted in Cole, *The Whig Party in the South*, 60–61.

"with delight upon the scene": *Baltimore American*, May 5, 1840.

"The balconies and windows were filled": Hone, *Diary*, 42.

WHIG HUSBANDS OR NONE: Gunderson, *Log-Cabin Campaign*, 139.

"a warm Harrison woman": *Richmond Yeoman*, September 10, 1840.

"like all other pretty girls": *Supplement to the Courant* 6: 207.

"in the worst way": Helm, *True Story of Mary*, 74.

"No," Lincoln replied: Ibid., 72.

"*Young men and Bachelors*": Casper, *Constructing American Lives*, 99–100.

"I never thought of all this": Norton, *Great Revolution*, 348–351.

"*The beautiful girls*": *Cleveland Axe*, May 28, 1840.

"When you fair daughters": Norton, *Great Revolution*, 243.

"I know you hardly expect": *Richmond Whig*, October 9, 1840.

"vast influence" of women: Varon, *We Mean to Be Counted*, 79.

"Are the ladies of Virginia": *Richmond Enquirer*, October 15, 1840.

"They ride around in log cabins": *Spirit of the Age*, September 18, 1840.

the words HARRISON and TYLER: *Niles' Register*, April 18, 1840.

through the "coarser sex": Ibid.

"every Whig house": Varon, *We Mean to Be Counted*, 78.

"My heart sank": Zboray and Zboray, *Voices Without Votes*, 87.

"Boo-hoo-hoo": *Ohio Statesman*, September 23, 1840.

"married women are never invited": Bacourt, *Souvenirs of a Diplomat*, 215.

GEN. WM. H. HARRISON, THE GLORY: Varon, *We Mean to Be Counted*, 76.

"Women are the very life": *Cincinnati Gazette*, quoted in *National Intelligencer*, September 21, 1840.

12. PETTICOAT POWER

"We have been pained": *North Carolina Standard*, October 28, 1840.

"with gay bonnet": Buckingham, *Eastern and Western States*, 2:134–136.

"peace, plenty and prosperity": Kenney, *Strongest of All Government*.

"hurl you from the place": Kenney, *Letter Addressed to Martin Van Buren*.

"flaming Whig partisan": Pugh, *Memorial*, 37.

"When the sound of war whoops": *Sangamo Journal*, June 10, 1840.

"lady toasts": Cole, *Fragile Capital*, 64.

"*Down with the Locos*": *Richmond Yeoman*, October 15, 1840.

"If there's to be any killed": *Log Cabin*, July 25, 1840.

women of "doubtful reputation": *National Intelligencer*, August 28, 1840.

"Indeed, to see him actually called": *Burlington Free Press*, April 10, 1840.

"to show how wide-awake": Robinson, *Loom and Spindle*, 87.

"This is all wrong": *Indiana Democrat*, quoted in *Spirit of the Age*, October 2, 1840.

"Ladies are better mending": *New York Herald*, quoted in *Ohio Statesman*, March 9, 1840.

"They now claim the right": *Tennessee Whig*, January 13, 1840.

"I go for all sharing": Herndon and Weik, *Herndon's Lincoln*, 1:166.

13. READ ALL ABOUT US!

"[The *Log Cabin* newspaper] was the best": Maverick, *Henry J. Raymond and the New York Press*, 362.

"As for the country press": Greeley to Weed, quoted in Weed, *Memoir*, 2:92.

"If they do not lie": Hone, *Diary*, 400.

Log Cabin "will be a zealous": Parton, *Life of Horace Greeley*, 183.

"devoted to the dissemination": *Log Cabin*, May 2, 1840.

"Is not this paper": Ibid.

"On many accounts, I think him": Ibid.

"All persons who have obtained credit": Ibid., September 26, 1840.

"Oats and chop for the horse": Ibid., May 16, 1840.

"their miseries are outraged": Ibid., June 6, 1840.

"cavalier reception": Ibid., June 13, 1840.

"*Yes, social friend*": Ibid., May 9, 1840.

"Stammering cured": Ibid., August 15, 1840.

"Whenever you find a bitter": Ibid., August 29, 1840.

"Mr. Van Buren's coach": Ibid., August 15, 1840.

"Oh, I don't know much": Ibid., June 17, 1840.

"Every Whig in the state": Lincoln, *Writings*, 1:39.

"Strangers reading our Whig journals": Elliott, *Notes Taken*, 90.

WHAT WE INTEND: *Extra Globe*, May 16, 1840.

"THE LOW PRICES HUMBUG": Ibid., September 11, 1840.

"The son of a farmer": Ibid., June 16, 1840.

"Fellow citizens": *Log Cabin*, October 10, 1840.

14. SING US A SONG

"I shall never forget": Norton, *Great Revolution*, 374.

"*Old Tip's the boy*": Norton, *Tippecanoe Songs*, 53.

"They did laugh and sing": Fox, *History of Political Parties*, 116.

"*Old Tip he wears*": *Niles' Register*, November 7, 1840.

"*Things ain't now*": *Log Cabin*, August 22, 1840.

"*They call him a granny*": Ibid., May 16, 1840.

"Our songs are doing more": Zabriskie, *Horace Greeley*, 73.

"His dress, his figure": Eddy, *Life of Thomas J. Sawyer*, 434.

"In short, it is the genuine article": *Log Cabin*, May 23, 1840.

"*Van Buren cannot be*": *Harrison Medal Minstrel*, 20.

"*Oh say have you heard*": Norton, *Tippecanoe Songs*, 30.

"*Should good old cider*": Ibid., 21.

"*Can grateful freemen*": Ibid., 29.

"*The Day is all over*": Ward, *Life and Letters*, 442.

"Let me hear the line": Galbreath, *Alexander Coffman Ross*, 20.

"*What has caused the great commotion*": Ibid., 21.

"We know of daughters": Norton, *Great Revolution*, 375.

SINGING FOR THE PRESIDENCY: *Extra Globe*, July 8, 1840.

"*What has caused this great commotion*": *Ohio Democrat*, October 30, 1840.

"We could meet the Whigs": *New York Evening Post*, quoted in *Washington Globe*, June 12, 1840.

"The plain language": Elliott, *Notes Taken*, 125.

15. THE MARKETING OF A CANDIDATE

"ALL you Tips": *Log Cabin*, May 16, 1840.

"Log cabins were everywhere": Elliott, *Notes Taken*, 126.

"Perhaps the '1840' indicated": Van Rensselaer, *Early American Bottles*, 119.

"While our great manufacturing": *Extra Globe*, August 19, 1840.

"superior razors": *Extra Globe*, August 26, 1840.

"Harrison's Kindness": *Harrison Almanac for 1841* (New York: J. P. Giffing, 1840); published in several different editions.

"Log Cabin Anecdotes": Library of Congress.

"Matty's Dream": Ibid.

"Our sufferings is intolerable": Ibid.

"HARRISON GOODS": *Burlington Free Press*, August 28, 1840.

"efficiently removing all pimples": *Log Cabin*, August 15, 1840.

"a compound of the finest essences": Ibid.

"We took it to our barber": *New York Morning Herald*, August 25, 1840.

"We expect before the farce": *Illinois Free Trader*, quoted in *Burlington Free Press*, April 10, 1840.

"If General Harrison had been murdered": *New York Evening Signal*, December 7, 1840.

16. GOING NEGATIVE: THE DEMOCRATS FIGHT BACK

"I am the most persecuted": Friedenberg, *Notable Speeches*, 22.

"DEMOCRATS, now is the moment": *Extra Globe*, June 16, 1840.

"In my judgment": Ibid., August 27, 1840.

"vivacity and almost youthfulness": Cleaves, *Old Tippecanoe*, 323.

"*Hush-a-bye baby*": *Washington Globe*, March 21, 1840.

"SHOCKING PROFANITY": Ibid., July 31, 1840.

"Now it happens that I": Harrison to J. G. Williams, January 29, 1840, Harrison MSS, Indiana Historical Society.

HARRISON THE SEDUCER: *Ohio Statesman*, July 11, 1840.

"bastard slave children": Janken, *Walter White*, 3.

"a man who believes in ghosts": *40 Reasons Why the People in the Northwestern Part of Ohio Cannot Support General Harrison for the Presidency*, pamphlet, 1840.

"exposed the bare backs": *Washington Globe*, August 25, 1840.

"place the BLACKS on an EQUALITY": *Delaware Gazette*, quoted in *Ohio Statesman*, October 6, 1840.

"There goes the President": Pancake, *Thomas Jefferson & Alexander Hamilton*, 252.

"a quick voyage, take care": Library of Congress.

"No Sirrah": *Ohio Statesman*, July 11, 1840.

"Down with the Whigs": *Saturday Review of Literature*, July 19, 1942, 3–10.

"*He never was seen*": Lincoln/Net, University of Northern Illinois, http://lincoln .lib.niu.edu/islandora/object/niu-lincoln%3A34613.

"We are credibly informed": *Washington Globe*, April 17, 1840.

17. GENERAL MUM SPEAKS

"When was there ever before": *Cleveland Advertiser*, quoted in *Cleveland Axe*, June 25, 1840.

"Let him say not one": Biddle, *Correspondence*, 256.

"The story goes that I": *Niles' Register*, June 27, 1840.

"It seems almost incredible": Ibid.

"We were charged": *Ohio Statesman*, June 9, 1840.

"the General himself has not": Green, *William Henry Harrison*, 362.

"There he stood": Ibid., 363.

"You have stood by my side": Norton, *Great Revolution*, 179.

"you could plainly see": *Extra Globe*, July 8, 1840.

"and on one occasion especially": *Dayton Journal*, June 23, 1840.

"What a prodigy": *Washington Globe*, quoted in *Niles' Register*, September 5, 1840.

"The precedent thus set": *Cleveland Advertiser*, quoted in *Cleveland Axe*, June 25, 1840.

18. OLD TIP ON THE CAMPAIGN TRAIL

"General Harrison is going": *Ohio Statesman*, September 20, 1840.

"I would be gratified": Clay, *Papers*, 9:424.

"Nobody expected to see": Green, *William Henry Harrison*, 366.

"Fellow citizens, you have undoubtedly": Norton, *Great Revolution*, 246.

"there is nothing old granny": *Log Cabin*, September 5, 1840.

"In vain we look": *Extra Globe*, August 19, 1840.

"then the battle will no longer": Norton, *Great Revolution*, 183.

"It is true that a part": *Niles' Register*, June 27, 1840.

"He was the first 'great man'": Julian, *Political Recollections*, 17.

"I rise, fellow citizens": Norton, *Great Revolution*, 288–289.

"Methinks I hear": Ibid., 295.

"General Harrison was a forcible speaker": Howe, *Historical Collections of Ohio*, 2:289.

"I have detained you": Norton, *Great Revolution*, 298.

"The multitude swayed": Ibid., 301.

"fair daughters of Ohio": *Niles' Register*, September 20, 1840.

"sang most sweetly": Green, *William Henry Harrison*, 38.

"If General Harrison's friends": *Ohio Statesman*, September 20, 1840.

"Indeed, sometimes I fear": Friedenberg, *Notable Speeches*, 22.

19. STUMP SPEAKERS

"This practice of itinerant speech": Adams, *Life*, 352.

"gentle scents of his mellow voice": Poore, *Perley's Reminiscences*, 1–2:35.

"We are all Whigs": *Baltimore Patriot*, quoted in *Niles' Register*, May 9, 1840.

"and, that, of course, could not": Remini, *Henry Clay*, 564.

"'Ah,' I said": Colton, *Life and Times of Henry Clay*, 113.

"coons, log cabins, and big balls": Remini, *Andrew Jackson*, 466.

"Every breeze says change": *Baltimore Patriot*, quoted in *Niles' Register*, May 9, 1840.

"The man that says": Webster, *Writings and Speeches*, 118.

"I was not myself born": Webster, *Speeches and Orations*, 477.

"the small-beer statesmen": Braden, ed., *Oratory in the Old South*, 113.

"a very large mouth": *Ohio Statesman*, October 9, 1840.

"They came in carriages": Tarbell, *Life of Abraham Lincoln*, 1:166.

"I know that the great volcano": Baskerville, *People's Voice*, 73.

"When an individual's hairs": Wilson, ed., *Uncollected Works of Abraham Lincoln*, 1:340.

"Damn such a book": Browne, *Every-Day Life of Abraham Lincoln*, 175.

"only one pair of breeches": Sandburg, *Lincoln: The Prairie Years*, 236.

"I have made more than": Corwin to John J. Crittenden, November 20, 1840, in Crittenden MSS, Library of Congress.

"the most famous stump speaker": Ohio Historical Society, *Governors of Ohio*, 47.

"the right way": Parton, *Life of Andrew Jackson*, 640.

20. THE BUCKEYE BLACKSMITH

"With horny hands": McClure, *Recollections of a Half a Century*, xii.

"Bear, a speech": Bear, *Life and Travels*, 43.

"the name Buckeye became": Howe, *Historical Collection of Ohio*, 1:204–205.

"*Oh where, tell me where*": Norton, *Tippecanoe Songs*, 57.

"*Come arouse ye*": Ibid., 68.

"*Hurrah for the father*": Ibid., 11.

"I am a Buckeye": Galbreath, *Alexander Coffman Ross*, 21.

"Make us a horseshoe": Bear, *Life and Travels*, 70.

"to take such a stand": Ibid., 64.

"If low and vulgar ribaldry": *Washington Globe*, quoted in *Niles' Register*, June 16, 1840.

"In your dirty, lying paper": *Extra Globe*, July 22, 1840.

"Ladies and gentlemen": Bear, *Life and Travels*, 96.

"none did better work": Elliott, *Notes Taken*, 128.

"striking while the iron": *Galena Advertiser*, May 29, 1840.

"Bear and Kellogg make": *Log Cabin*, May 7, 1840.

"The first thing next": *Boston Olive Branch*, December 5, 1840.

"and your Constitutional liberties": *Niles' Register*, November 7, 1840.

"How are politicks": Miller, ed., *Selected Letters of Whitman*, 10.

"*Rumpsey, Dumpsey. Johnson killed*": Gunderson, *Log-Cabin Campaign*, 245.

"You might as well ask": Norton, *Great Revolution*, 365.

"Of the character": *Burlington Free Press*, March 6, 1840.

"There is nothing forcible": Mark O. Hatfield, *Vice Presidents of the United States* (Washington, DC: US Government Printing Office, 1997), 141.

"Did you ever see": Guild, *Old Times in Tennessee*, 159.

21. MONEY TALKS

"A diabolical scheme": *Extra Globe*, September 11, 1840.

WHERE DOES THE MONEY: Ibid.

"merchant princes": Weed, *Autobiography*, 515.

"a weak and wicked executive": Norton, *Great Revolution*, 319.

"as compactly wedged together": Maxwell, *Run Through the United States*, 1:145.

"What we need is some": *Niles' Register*, October 10, 1840.

THE GOVERNMENT FOR SALE: *Extra Globe*, October 26, 1840.

"Millions of dollars will now": McMaster, *History of the People*, 6:592.

INVENTED IN ENGLAND: Library of Congress.

"Harrison and Prosperity": Green, *William Henry Harrison*, 511.

"The quantity of trash": *Extra Globe*, August 5, 1840.

"Our intention is to organize": Lincoln, *Writings*, 1:229–231.

"to bring to the polls every man": *Extra Whig*, September 11, 1840.

"We call upon the Whigs": Thompson, *Illinois Whigs Before 1846*, 69.

22. STEALING VOTES

"If Mr. Van Buren's re-election": *Extra Globe*, October 13, 1840.

"knock him down and leave": Sandburg, *Lincoln: The Prairie Years*, 146.

"knocked him down, jumped": *Harrisburg Chronicle*, quoted in *Jeffersonian Republican*, November 6, 1840.

"We understand that a Whig": *Rough-Hewer*, September 24, 1840.

"You *shall* support": *Extra Globe*, July 18, 1840.

"large masses of names": *Extra Globe*, October 26, 1840.

"Wherever the Whig officers": Ibid., October 6, 1840.

"By such means, any number": *Hagerstown Democrat*, quoted in *Extra Globe*, July 15, 1840.

"It is thus that followers": *Ohio Statesman*, quoted in *Extra Globe*, September 18, 1840.

"the most deliberate and astounding": *Extra Globe*, October 26, 1840.

"a card to play": Poore, *Perley's Reminiscences*, 1–2:241.

A GIGANTIC PLOT: Gunderson, *Log-Cabin Campaign*, 249.

SOUND THE ALARM: Ibid.

"ready for violence": *Log Cabin*, October 31, 1840.

"Look to your Rights": *Albany Argus*, quoted in *Extra Globe*, September 18, 1840.

23. ELECTION RETURNS

"We have been sung down": McMaster, *History of the People*, 6:590.

"*And have you heard*": Julian, *Political Recollections*, 21.

"I arrived just one hour": Bear, *Life and Travels*, 90.

"The greatest excitement prevails": Hone, *Diary*, 47.

"The agony is over": *New Yorker*, November 4, 1840.

"Do not believe": Parton, *Life of Andrew Jackson*, 742.

"It is a singular coincidence": Gobright, *Recollections*, 38.

THE CONFLICT AND THE TRIUMPH!: *Albany Evening Journal*, November 6, 1840.

THE GREAT RESULT: *Log Cabin*, November 9, 1840.

"It has pleased the Almighty": *National Intelligencer*, quoted in *Niles' Register*, November 14, 1840.

"A nation redeemed": *Bangor Whig*, quoted in *Niles' Register*, November 28, 1840.

"To President Martin Van Buren": *Cleveland Daily News*, quoted in *Leavenworth (IN) Arena*, January 21, 1841.

"*Hurrah for the father*": *Albany Evening Journal*, November 6, 1840.

"*Who killed small Matty*": Mansfield, *Personal Memories*, 326.

"That the American people": *Richmond Enquirer*, quoted in *Niles' Register*, November 28, 1840.

"mercenaries—hired": *Washington Globe*, quoted in *Niles' Register*, November 14, 1840.

the "debaucheries" in which: Van Buren, *Autobiography*, 772.

"A change in government": Sargent, *Public Men*, 110.

the "Indignation President": Emerson, *Journals*, 5:549.

"a political phenomenon": *Democratic Review* 8: 390.

"Van Buren was the cause": *New York Evening Post*, quoted in *Niles' Register*.

"Blarney before the election": *Log Cabin*, December 5, 1840.

"Harrison comes in upon": Adams, *Memoirs*, 10:366.

24. MR. HARRISON GOES TO WASHINGTON

"General Harrison is now": *New York Express*, quoted in *Niles' Register*, November 28, 1840.

"I understand they have come": Fillmore, *Papers*, 2:215.

"Some have traveled": Green, *William Henry Harrison*, 377.

"he appeared very feeble": Gobright, *Recollections*, 39.

"Fellow citizens," he said: Green, *William Henry Harrison*, 382–383.

"an old imbecile": Stanton letter to Sen. Tappan, March 7, 1841, in Stanton MSS, Library of Congress.

"forthwith advanced": *Baltimore Patriot*, quoted in *Niles' Register*, February 13, 1841.

"He is very much fatigued": Ibid.

"walks in the storm": Green, *William Henry Harrison*, 389.

"He was different-looking now": Gobright, *Recollections*, 40.

"Travelers are recommended": Maxwell, *Run Through the United States*, 2:237.

Washington "is neither a city": Bacourt, *Souvenirs of a Diplomat*, 72.

"one is struck by the vulgar": Tocqueville, *Democracy in America*, 1:196.

"Morally and physically, this place": Maxwell, *Run Through the United States*, 2:12.

"is as tickled with the presidency": Boller, *Presidential Anecdotes*, 92.

"The general bears up finely": *Niles' Register*, February 27, 1841.

"There he was, unattended": Hone, *Diary*, 66.

"a mean looking horse": Adams, *Memoirs*, 10:438.

"rosy with joy": *National Intelligencer*, March 5, 1841.

"He looked cheerful": Ibid.

"Of this I can speak": Sargent, *Public Men*, 114.

"Called from a retirement": *New Yorker*, March 6, 1841.

"It is of unusual length": Ibid.

"It is not what was needed": Weed, *Memoir*, 2:91.

The resulting picture: O'Neill, *Virginia's Presidential Homes*, 88.

"looking very happy": *New York Herald*, March 10, 1841.

25. DEATH OF A PRESIDENT

"Death! Death in the White House": Willis, *Poetical Works*, 136.

"John Quincy Adams told me": Gobright, *Recollections*, 51.

"singular fine form": *Raleigh Register*, April 6, 1841.

"I am so much harassed": Cavinder, *Indiana Book of Records*, 156.

"the necessary functions of nature": Hone, *Diary*, 72.

"infamous man": Gobright, *Recollections*, 45.

"King, give us a pinch": Ibid., 49.

"The President led the conversation": Elliott, *Notes Taken*, 137.

"Mr. Clay, you forget": Wilson, *Washington*, 1:361.

"And it has come to this!": Sargent, *Public Men*, 116.

"the condition of the revenue": Brinkley and Dwyer, eds., *American Presidency*, 120.

"slightly ailing": Green, *William Henry Harrison*, 398.

"Sir, I wish you to understand": *Niles' Register*, April 10, 1841.

"The age and debility of the patient": Ibid.

"quacked him out of existence": *New York Commercial*, quoted in *Pennsylvania Inquirer*, April 19, 1841.

"being somewhat influenced": *Boston Medical and Surgical Journal* 25–26 (August 18, 1841): 28.

"had timely and active measures": Ibid., 30.

"deadly bacteria": *New York Times*, March 31, 2014.

"To John Tyler": *Niles' Register*, April 10, 1841.

"A nation mourns": Ibid.

"This awful and sudden event": Ibid.

"May he have as many angels": *Baltimore Clipper*, quoted in *Cleveland Daily Herald*, April 15, 1841.

"typographical foppery": Muller, *William Cullen Bryant*, 164.

"only because he didn't live": Hone, *Diary*, 73.

"Few better men than Gen. Harrison": Elliott, *Notes Taken*, 186.

"General Harrison was never": Greeley, *Autobiography*, 135.

"dressing and shaving the deceased": Green, *William Henry Harrison*, 405.

"The expression was calm": Montgomery, *Life of William Henry Harrison*, 488.

"citizens and strangers": "Order of the Procession," government pamphlet, April 6, 1841, American Presidency Project, www.presidency.ucsb.edu /ws/?pid=67340.

"I wish that my husband's": *Niles' Register*, April 24, 1841.

26. AND TYLER TOO

"There was rhyme": Hone, *Diary*, 553.

"President Tyler!": Remini, *Henry Clay*, 582.

"passions and vices": Adams, *Memoirs*, 10:457.

"is a slave breeder": *Emancipator*, April 8, 1841.

THE SUB-TREASURY PLAN: Chitwood, *John Tyler*, 216.

"Well, Mr. President": Adams, *Memoirs*, 10:544.

"To sign, or not": Bacourt, *Souvenirs of a Diplomat*, 285.

"Henry Clay is a doomed man": Byrd, *Senate 1789–1989*, 1:168.

"head him, or die": Botts, *Speech of Mr. Botts*, 13.

"*What has caused this great commotion*": *Ohio Statesman*, September 22, 1841.

"looked somewhat worn": Singleton, *Story of the White House*, 279.

"the silvery sweetness": Tyler, *Letters and Times of the Tylers*, 2:383.

"rather above the middling": *Scioto Gazette*, July 18, 1841.

"I'll purchase at Bogert": Seager, *And Tyler Too*, 34.

"I almost knocked us both off": Tyler, *Letters and Times of the Tylers*, 3:247.

"Pooh," the president replied: Wise, *Seven Decades*, 233.

"I've just heard a rumor": Strong, *Diary*, 238.

"are the laughing stock": Adams, *Memoirs*, 7:67.

"the lovely lady Presidentess": Singleton, *Story of the White House*, 292.

"Texas shall crown": Armistead C. Gordon, "Monument to John Tyler" (Washington, DC: Government Printing Office, 1916), 23.

"*Texas was the captain's bride*": Tyler, *Letters and Times of the Tylers*, 2:197–199.

"There is no honor in politics": Ibid.

"Yes, they cannot say": Ibid., 200.

EPILOGUE

"I have only a vague memory": "Family Ties," episode of *The American President*, PBS, 2000.

"He has gone no doubt": *Raleigh Register*, May 25, 1841.

"Mr. Clay's Gambling": *North Carolina Standard*, April 10, 1844.

"the most unpopular public man": *New York Times*, January 22, 1862.

"Had we any respect": Sandburg, *Lincoln: The War Years*, 79.

"An honest politician is one": Sherrill, *Governing*, 261.

his general "has the slows": Browne, *Every-Day Life of Abraham Lincoln*, 203.

"Well may every honest man": Woodburn, *Life of Thaddeus Stevens*, 199.

"The greatest measure of the nineteenth century": *Lippincott's Monthly Magazine* 61: 550.

"are absolutely useless": *Holt County Sentinel*, May 3, 1867.

"Women are the equals of men": Weatherford, *Women in American Politics*, 279.

"I have been assailed so bitterly": *New York Times*, June 2, 1872.

"His Grandfather's Hat": Graff, *Grover Cleveland*, 93.

BIBLIOGRAPHY

BOOKS

Abell, Alexander Gurdon. *Life of John Tyler, President of the United States.* New York: Harper & Bros., 1843.

Adams, John Quincy. *Memoir of the Life of John Quincy Adams.* Edited by Josiah Quincy. Boston: Crosby, Nichols, Lee, 1860.

———. *Memoirs of John Quincy Adams.* Vols. 7, 8, 9, 10, 11, 12. Edited by Charles Francis Adams. Philadelphia: J. B. Lippincott, 1876.

Bacourt, Chevalier de. *Souvenirs of a Diplomat.* New York: Henry Holt, 1885.

Bancroft, George. *Martin Van Buren to the End of His Public Career.* New York: Harper & Bros., 1889.

Barber, Edwin Atlee. *Anglo-American Pottery.* Indianapolis: Clay Worker, 1899.

Bartlett, Irving H. *Daniel Webster.* New York: W. W. Norton, 1978.

Baskerville, Barnet. *The People's Voice: The Orator in American Society.* Lexington: University Press of Kentucky, 1979.

Bear, John W. *The Life and Travels of John W. Bear, the Buckeye Blacksmith.* Baltimore: Dinswanger, 1875.

Biddle, Nicholas. *The Correspondence of Nicholas Biddle.* Edited by Reginald C. McGrane. New York: Houghton Mifflin Company, 1919.

Boller, Paul F. *Presidential Anecdotes.* Oxford: Oxford University Press, 1981.

Botts, John. *Speech of Mr. Botts of Virginia.* Washington, DC: National Intelligencer Office, 1841.

Braden, Waldo W., ed. *Oratory in the Old South.* Baton Rouge: Louisiana State University Press, 1970.

Brinkley, Alan, and Davis Dwyer, eds. *The American Presidency.* Boston: Houghton Mifflin, 2004.

Browne, Francis Fisher. *The Every-Day Life of Abraham Lincoln.* New York: N. D. Thompson, 1887.

Buckingham, James Silk. *The Eastern and Western States of America.* Vol. 2. London: Fisher, Son, 1842.

Burr, S. J. *The Life and Times of William Henry Harrison*. New York: L. W. Ransom, 1840.

Burstein, Andrew. *The Original Knickerbocker: The Life of Washington Irving*. New York: Basic Books, 2007.

Byrd, Robert C. *The Senate 1789–1989: Addresses on the History of the United States Senate*. Edited by Mary Sharon Hall. Vol. 1. Washington, DC: US Government Printing Office, 1988.

Casper, Scott E. *Constructing American Lives: Biography and Culture in Nineteenth-Century America*. Chapel Hill: University of North Carolina Press, 1999.

Cavinder, Fred D. *Indiana Book of Records*. Bloomington: Indiana University Press, 1985.

Chitwood, Oliver Perry. *John Tyler: Champion of the Old South*. New York: Appleton Century, 1939.

Clay, Henry. *The Papers of Henry Clay*. Vols. 9–10. Edited by Robert Seager II. Lexington: University Press of Kentucky, 1988.

———. *Works of Henry Clay*. Vol. 1. Edited by Calvin Colton. New York: Henry Clay Publishing, 1896.

Cleaves, Freeman. *Old Tippecanoe*. Newtown, CT: American Political Biography Press, 1939.

Cole, Arthur Charles. *The Whig Party in the South*. Washington: American Historical Association, 1913.

Cole, Charles Chester, Jr. *A Fragile Capital: Identity and the Early Years of Columbus, Ohio*. Columbus: Ohio State University Press, 2001.

Collins, Gail. *William Henry Harrison*. New York: Times Books, 2012.

Colton, Calvin. *The Life and Times of Henry Clay*. New York: A. S. Barnes, 1846.

Congressional Globe. *Volume of Speeches Delivered in Congress in 1840*. Washington, DC: Globe Offices, 1840.

Conover, Charlotte Reed. *Concerning the Forefathers*. Dayton, OH: National Cash Register, 1902.

Cornell, William M. *Life and Public Career of Hon. Horace Greeley*. Boston: Lee and Shepard, 1872.

Crapol, Edward. *John Tyler, The Accidental President*. Chapel Hill: University of North Carolina Press, 2006.

Crockett, David. *The Life of Martin Van Buren*. Philadelphia: Nafis & Cornich, 1835.

Cushing, Caleb. *Outlines of the Life and Public Services of William Henry Harrison*. Boston: Weeks, Jordan, 1840.

Dana, Edmund. *A Voice from Bunker Hill*. Boston: Bunker Hill, 1840.

Democratic Party. *The People's Democratic Guide*. Vol. 1. New York: James Webster Publishing Agent, 1842.

————. *Proceedings of the National Democratic Convention of 1840*. Baltimore: Office of the Republican, 1840.

Eddy, Richard. *Life of Thomas J. Sawyer and Caroline M. Sawyer*. Boston: Universal Printing House, 1900.

Elliott, Richard Smith. *Notes Taken in Sixty Years*. St. Louis: R. P. Studley, 1883.

Emerson, Ralph Waldo. *Journals*. Vol. 5. Cambridge, MA: Riverside Press, 1911.

Emmons, William. *Authentic Biography of Col. Richard M. Johnson of Kentucky*. Boston: Ashel Langworth, 1834.

————. *Biography of Martin Van Buren*. Washington, DC: Jacob Gideon Jr., 1835.

Fillmore, Millard. *Millard Fillmore Papers*. Edited by Frank A. Severance. Vol. 2. Buffalo, NY: Buffalo Historical Society, 1907.

Fischer, Robert A. *Tippecanoe and Trinkets Too*. Urbana: University of Illinois Press, 1988.

Fox, Dixon Ryan. *The Decline of Aristocracy in the Politics of New York*. New York: Dixon Ryan Fox, 1919.

Fox, Dorus Morton. *History of Political Parties: National Reminiscences and the Tippecanoe Movement*. Des Moines: Col. Dorus M. Fox, 1895.

Friedenberg, Robert V. *Notable Speeches in Contemporary Presidential Campaigns*. Westport, CT: Praeger, 2002.

Galbreath, C. B. *Alexander Coffman Ross: Author of "Tippecanoe and Tyler Too."* Columbus, OH: F. J. Heer, 1905.

Garber, Virginia Armistead. *The Armistead Family, 1635–1910*. Richmond, VA: Whittet and Shepperson, 1910.

Garrison, Francis Jackson, and Wendell Phillips. *William Lloyd Garrison: The Story of His Life Told by His Children*. New York: Century, 1885.

Glentworth, James. *A Statement of the Frauds on the Elective Franchise of the City of New York*. New York: Clerk's Office of Southern District of New York, 1841.

Gobright, L. A. *Recollections of Men and Things at Washington*. Philadelphia: Claxton, Remsen & Haffelfinger, 1869.

Goebel, Dorothy. *William Henry Harrison: A Political Biography*. Indianapolis: Historical Bureau of the Indiana Library, 1926.

Graff, Henry F. *Grover Cleveland*. The American President Series. New York: Henry Holt, 2002.

Greeley, Horace. *The Autobiography of Horace Greeley*. New York, E. B. Treat, 1872.

————. *Recollections of a Busy Life*. New York: J. B. Ford, 1868.

Green, James A. *William Henry Harrison: His Life and Times*. Richmond, VA: Garrett & Masie, 1941.

Grinnell, Josiah Bushnell. *Men and Events of Forty Years*. Boston: D. Lothrop, 1891.

Guild, Jo C. *Old Times in Tennessee*. Nashville: Tavel, Eastman & Howell, 1878.

Gunderson, Robert Gray. *The Log-Cabin Campaign*. Lexington: University of Kentucky Press, 1957.

Harris, Bill. *First Ladies Fact Book*. New York: Black Dog & Leventhal, 2005.

Harrison, William Henry. *Messages and Letters of William Henry Harrison*. Vol. 1. Edited by Logan Esaray. Indianapolis: Indiana Historical Society, 1922.

Harrison Medal Minstrel, The. Philadelpha: Grigg & Elliott, 1840.

Haunton, Thomas. *Tippecanoe and E.G. Booz Too!* Medford, MA: Jerseyana Antiques and Collectibles, 2014.

Helm, Katherine. *The True Story of Mary, Wife of Lincoln*. New York: Harper & Bros., 1918.

Herndon, William H., and Jesse William Weik. *Herndon's Lincoln: The True Story of a Great Life*. Vol. 1. Chicago: Belford, Clarke, 1889.

Hickey, Donald. *The War of 1812*. Chicago: University of Illinois Press, 2012.

Hildreth, Richard. *The People's Presidential Candidate*. Boston: Weeks, Jordan, 1839.

Holland, William M. *The Life and Political Opinions of Martin Van Buren*. Hartford, CT: Belknap & Hamersley, 1836.

Hone, Philip. *The Diary of Philip Hone*. Edited by Bayard Tuckerman. New York: Dodd, Mead, 1910.

Hooper, O. C. *The Log Cabin Song Book of 1840*. Columbus, OH: H. A. Smythe, 1888.

Howe, Henry. Historical Collections of Ohio. Vols. 1–3. Columbus, OH: C. J. Kribbiel, 1888.

Hunter, Bob. *A Historical Guide to Old Columbus*. Athens: Ohio University Press, 2012.

Hurst, Lawrence. *Whig Activities from 1837 to 1840*. Madison: University of Wisconsin, 1914.

Irelan, Dr. John Robert. *Life and Times of John Tyler*. Vol. 10, *History of the United States of America in Administrations*. Chicago: Fairbanks and Palmer, 1888.

Jackson, Andrew. *The Correspondence of Andrew Jackson*. Edited by John Spencer Bassett. Vols. 6–7. New York: Krause Reprint Company, 1969.

Jackson, Isaac Rand. *Life of William Henry Harrison*. Philadelphia: Marshall, Williams & Butler, 1840.

James, Marquis. *The Life of Andrew Jackson*. Indianapolis: Bobbs-Merrill, 1938.

Janken, Kenneth Robert. *Walter White: Mr. NAACP*. Chapel Hill: University of North Carolina Press, 2003.

Julian, George W. *Political Recollections, 1840 to 1872*. Chicago: Jansen, McClurg, 1884.

Kendall, Amos. *Autobiography of Amos Kendall.* Edited by William Stickney. Boston: Lee and Shepard, 1872.

Kenney, Lucy. *A Letter Addressed to Martin Van Buren, President of the United States.* 1838.

———. *A Pamphlet Showing How Easily the Wand of a Magician May Be Broken.* 1838.

———. *The Strongest of All Government Is That Which Is Most Free: An Address to the People of the United States.* 1840.

Keys, E. D. *Fifty Years' Observations of Men and Events.* Charles Scribner's Sons, 1884.

Lee, Alfred Emory. *History of the City of Columbus, Ohio.* Vol. 2. New York: W. W. Munsell, 1892.

Leeson, M. A. *Historical and Biographical Record of Wood County, Ohio.* J. M. Beers, 1897.

Lincoln, Abraham. *Life and Works of Abraham Lincoln.* Vol. 2. Edited by Marion Mills Miller. New York: Current Literature, 1907.

———. *The Wisdom of Abraham Lincoln.* New York: Brentano's Fifth Avenue, 1908.

———. *The Writings of Abraham Lincoln.* Vol. 1. Edited by Arthur Lapsey. New York: G. P. Putnam's Sons, 1923.

Lockwood, Mary Smith. *Yesterdays in Washington.* Vol. 1. Rosslyn, VA: Commonwealth Company, 1915.

Lynch, Denis Tilden. *An Epoch and a Man: Martin Van Buren and His Times.* New York: Horace Liveright Inc., 1929.

MacKenzie, William L. *The Life and Times of Martin Van Buren.* Boston: Cooke, 1846.

Mansfield, Edward D. *Memories of the Life and Times of Daniel Drake, M.D.* Cincinnati: Applegate, 1855.

———. *Personal Memories, Social, Political and Literary.* Cincinnati: Robert Clarke, 1879.

Marshall, Henrietta Elizabeth. *This Country of Ours: The Story of the United States.* New York: George H. Doran, 1917.

Marx, Rudolph. *The Health of Presidents.* New York: G. P. Putnam's Sons, 1960.

Maverick, Augustus. *Henry J. Raymond and the New York Press.* Hartford, CT: A. S. Hale, 1870.

Maxwell, Archibald Montgomery. *A Run Through the United States During the Autumn of 1840.* Vols. 1–2. London: Noyes and Barkley, 1841.

McCall, Laura, and Donald Yacovone. *A Shared Experience: Men, Women and the History of Gender.* New York: New York University Press, 1998.

McCaskey, John Piersol. *Treasury of Favorite Songs*. Vol. 2. Lancaster, PA: J. P. McCaskey, 1916.

McClure, Alexander. *Men of War Times*. Philadelphia: Times Publishing, 1892.

———. *Our Presidents: And How We Make Them*. New York: Harper & Bros. 1900.

———. *Recollections of Half a Century*. Salem, MA: Salem Press Company, 1902.

McElliney, Thomas M. *Life of Martin Van Buren*. Pittsburgh: J. T. Shryock, 1853.

McMaster, John Bach. *A History of the People of the United States from the Revolution to the Civil War*. Vol. 6. New York: D. Appleton, 1914.

Merry, Robert W. *A Country of Vast Designs: James K. Polk, the Mexican War and Conquest*. New York: Simon & Schuster, 2009.

Miller, Captain. *Hero of Tippecanoe*. New York: J. P. Giffing, 1840.

Miller, Edwin Haviland, ed. *Selected Letters of Whitman*. Iowa City: University of Iowa Press, 1990.

Miller, John G. *The Great Convention of the People of Ohio*. Columbus, OH: Cutler & Wright, 1840.

Montgomery, Henry. *The Life of Major-General William Henry Harrison*. Philadelphia: Porter & Coates, 1852.

Morrow, Josiah. *Life and Speeches of Thomas Corwin*. Cincinnati: W. H. Anderson, 1896.

Muller, Gilbert H. *William Cullen Bryant: Author of America*. Albany: SUNY Press, 2010.

Niles, William Ogden. *The Tippecanoe Text-Book*. Philadelphia: P. G. Collins, 1840.

Norton, A. B. *The Great Revolution of 1840: Reminiscences of the Log Cabin and Hard Cider Campaign*. Mt. Vernon, OH: A. B. Norton, 1888.

———. *Tippecanoe Songs of the Log Cabin Boys and Girls of 1840*. Dallas: A. B. Norton, 1888.

Ohio Historical Society. *The Governors of Ohio*. Columbus: Ohio Historical Society, 1954.

O'Neill, Patrick. *Virginia's Presidential Homes*. Charleston, SC: Arcadia, 2010.

Orth, Samuel P. *A History of Cleveland, Ohio*. Vol. 1. Chicago: S. J. Clarke, 1910.

Owens, Robert W. *Mr. Jefferson's Hammer*. Norman: University of Oklahoma Press, 2007.

Pancake, John. *Thomas Jefferson & Alexander Hamilton*. Woodbury, NY: Barron's Educational Series, 1974.

Parsons, John. *A Tour through Indiana in 1840*. New York: Robert M. McBride, 1920.

Parton, James. *Life of Andrew Jackson*. New York: Mason Brothers, 1861.

———. *The Life of Horace Greeley*. Boston: Houghton, Mifflin, 1889.

Perry, James M. *A Mere Matter of Marching*. Washington, DC: James M. Perry, 2011.

Poe, Edgar Allan. *The Complete Works of Edgar Allan Poe.* Vol. 17. Edited by James A. Harrison. New York: John D. Morris, 1902.

Poore, Benjamin Perley. *Perley's Reminiscences.* Vols. 1–2. Philadelphia: Hubbard Bros., 1886.

Prentice, George. *Prenticeana, or Wit and Humor in Paragraphs.* Philadelphia: Claxton, Remsen and Haffelfinger, 1871.

Pugh, Sarah. *Memorial of Sarah Pugh: A Tribute of Respect from Her Cousins.* Philadelphia: J. B. Lippincott, 1888.

Remini, Robert V. *Andrew Jackson.* Vol 3, *The Course of American Democracy, 1833–1845.* Baltimore: Johns Hopkins University Press, 1984.

———. *Henry Clay: Statesman for the Union.* New York: W. W. Norton, 1991.

Richardson, James D., ed. *A Compilation of Messages and Papers of Presidents 1780–1902.* Vol. 2. Washington, DC: Bureau of Literature and Art, 1907.

Robinson, Harriet Jane Hanson. *Loom and Spindle.* New York: Thomas W. Crowell, 1898.

Safire, William. *Safire's Political Dictionary.* Oxford: Oxford University Press, 1978.

Sandburg, Carl. *Abraham Lincoln: The Prairie Years.* New York: Harcourt, World and Brace, 1926.

———. *Abraham Lincoln: The War Years.* New York: Harcourt, World and Brace, 1939.

Sargent, Epes. *The Life and Public Services of Henry Clay.* New York: Greeley & McElrath, 1848.

Sargent, Nathan. *Public Men and Events.* Philadelphia: J. B. Lippincott, 1875.

Schlesinger, Arthur Jr., ed. *The Election of 1840.* Philadelphia: Mason Crest, 2003.

Schurz, Carl. *Life of Henry Clay.* New York: Houghton, Mifflin, 1887.

Seager, Egbert, II. *And Tyler Too.* New York: McGraw-Hill, 1963.

Seale, William, ed. *White House History.* Washington, DC: White House Historical Society, 2004.

Seward, Henry, and Frederick William Seward. *Autobiography of William H. Seward.* New York: D. Appleton, 1877.

Shephard, Edward M. *American Statesmen: Martin Van Buren.* Boston: Houghton, Mifflin, 1890.

Sherrill, Robert. *Governing America.* New York: Harcourt Brace Jovanovich, 1978.

Singleton, Esther. *The Story of the White House.* New York: McClure Company, 1907.

Stoddard, William Osborn. *The Lives of Presidents.* New York: White, Stokes & Allen, 1886.

Strong, George Templeton. *Diary: Young Man in New York, 1835–1849.* New York: Macmillan, 1952.

Sutor, J. Hope. *Past and Present of the City of Zanesville.* Chicago: S. J. Clarke, 1905.

Tarbell, Ida M. *The Life of Abraham Lincoln*. Vols. 1–2. New York: Doubleday & McClure, 1900.

Thompson, Charles Manfred. *The Illinois Whigs Before 1846*. Urbana: University of Illinois, 1918.

Tindall, William. *Standard History of the City of Washington*. Knoxville, TN: H. W. Crew, 1914.

Tocqueville, Alexis de. *Democracy in America*. Vol. 1. New York: George Adlard, 1839.

Todd, Charles, and Stewart Drake. *Sketches of the Civil and Military Services of William Henry Harrison*. Cincinnati: U. P. James, 1840.

Tyler, Frances Payne Bouknight. *A Time of High Cotton*. Richmond, VA: Dietz Press, 2014.

Tyler, Lyon Gardiner. *The Letters and Times of the Tylers*. Vols. 1–3. Richmond, VA: Whittet & Shepperson, 1884–1896.

Van Buren, Martin. *The Autobiography of Martin Van Buren*. Washington, DC: American Historical Society, 1919.

Van Rensselaer, Stephen. *Early American Bottles and Flasks*. Rev. ed. Stratford, CT: J. Edmund Edwards, 1971; orig. publ. 1926.

Varon, Elizabeth R. *We Mean to Be Counted*. Chapel Hill: University of North Carolina Press, 1998.

Ward, Julius H. *The Life and Letters of James Gates Percival*. Boston: Ticknor and Fields, 1856.

Weatherford, Doris. *Women in American Politics: History and Milestones*. Los Angeles: Sage Publications, 2012.

Webster, Daniel. *The Speeches and Orations of Daniel Webster*. Edited by Edwin P. Whipple. Boston: Little, Brown, 1914.

———. *The Writings and Speeches of Daniel Webster*. Boston: Little, Brown, 1903.

Weed, Thurlow. *Autobiography of Thurlow Weed*. Edited by Harriett Weed. Boston: Houghton, Mifflin, 1884.

———. *Memoir of Thurlow Weed*. Vol. 2. Edited by Thurlow Weed Barnes. Boston: Houghton, Mifflin, 1884.

Whig Party. *Proceedings of the Democratic Whig National Convention*. Harrisburg, PA: R. S. Elliott, 1839.

Whiting, Isaac. *The Harrison Log Cabin Song Book*. Columbus: I. N. Whiting, 1840.

Widmer, Ted. *Martin Van Buren*. New York: Times Books, 2005.

Willis, Nathanial Parker. *The Poetical Works of N. P. Willis*. London: George Routledge and Sons, 1867.

Wilmot, Robert. *A New Work, in Favor of the Whig Cause and the Election of William Henry Harrison to the Presidential Chair*. Cincinnati: J. P. and R. B. Donogh, 1840.

Wilson, James Grant. *The Presidents of the United States, 1789–1914*. Vol. 2. New York: Scribner's Sons, 1914.

Wilson, Rufus Rockwell, ed. *Uncollected Works of Abraham Lincoln*. Vol. 1. Elmira, NY: Primavera Press, 1947.

———. *Washington: The Capital City and Its Part in the History of the Nation*. Vol 1. Philadelphia: J. B. Lippincott, 1902.

Wise, Barton. *The Life of Henry A. Wise*. London: MacMillan, 1899.

Wise, Henry A. *Seven Decades of the Union*. Philadelphia: J. B. Lippincott, 1872.

———. *The Humanities and Materialism Illustrated by a Memoir of John Tyler*, J. B. Lippincott, 1881.

Woodburn, James Albert. *The Life of Thaddeus Stevens*. Indianapolis: Bobbs-Merrill, 1913.

Zabriskie, Francis Nicoll. *Horace Greeley, the Editor*. New York: Funk & Wagnalls, 1890.

Zboray, Ronald J., and Mary Saracino Zboray. *Voices Without Votes: Women and Politics in Antebellum New England*. Lebanon: University of New Hampshire Press, 2010.

NEWSPAPERS AND MAGAZINES

Baltimore Patriot
Baltimore Republican
Burlington Free Press
Campaign (KY)
Cleveland Axe
Congressional Globe
Dayton Journal
Emancipator
Extra Globe
Jeffersonian Republican
Log Cabin
National Intelligencer
New York Express
New York Herald
New York Tribune
New Yorker
Niles' Register
Ohio State Journal
Ohio Statesman
Spirit of the Age
Washington Globe
Washington Intelligencer

INDEX

Italicized page references denote illustrations